500

cheeses

500

cheeses

the only cheese compendium you'll ever need

Roberta Muir

SELLERS
PUBLISHING

A Quintet Book

Published by Sellers Publishing, Inc.
161 John Roberts Road, South Portland, Maine 04106
For ordering information:
(800) 625-3386 Toll Free
(207) 772-6814 Fax
Visit our Web site: www.sellerspublishing.com
E-mail: rsp@rsvp.com

ISBN: 978-1-4162-0786-3
Library of Congress Control Number: 2010921819
QTT.FHC

This book was conceived, designed, and produced by
Quintet Publishing Limited
6 Blundell Street
London N7 9BH
United Kingdom

Series Editor: Robert Davies
Assistant Editor: Carly Beckerman
Designers: Rod Teasdale, Zoe White
Art Director: Michael Charles
Managing Editor: Donna Gregory
Publisher: James Tavendale

10 9 8 7 6 5 4 3 2 1

Printed in China by 1010 Printing International Ltd.

contents

introduction

The first thing we need to understand about cheese is that it's a living food. Not in the sense that vegetables or animals are living, but in the sense that the cheese forms a home for millions of bacteria and often molds. These grow and multiply in the young curds, altering their nature and turning them into the complex food that we enjoy, while simultaneously preserving the nutritious, highly perishable milk that would otherwise be wasted if it wasn't consumed immediately.

The fact that there can even be a book called *500 Cheeses* is testament to the incredible diversity of these fermented milk products, which are now produced virtually all over the world from the milk of almost every domesticated herbivore, including reindeers, camels, and yaks. There are many thousands of cheeses worldwide. This book describes the most commonly known ones, including those recognized under an appellation system (see page 270), as well as a few of the more unusual ones, such as Ragya (see page 209) made from yak's milk.

No one knows who made the first cheese, or where, but it was already a popular food by the time of the Ancient Egyptians, Greeks, and Romans. The most likely scenario is that as early as 10,000 years ago, somewhere in the region of the Middle East or Asia, a goatherd used the dried stomach of a goat as a vessel to carry fresh milk. The enzymes in the stomach (rennet), together with the warmth from the sun, acted on the milk, curdling it and turning it into solid curds and liquid whey. This early cheese would have been eaten out of hunger and found to be OK, even tasty perhaps, and a welcome change from the monotonous diet of fresh milk. Over time it would have been discovered that treating milk in this way also helped to preserve it, so that it became a valuable food source during winter when there was less feed for the livestock and they stopped producing milk. By trial and error, Man learned to prepare his fermented milk in different ways to extend its shelf life and vary its flavor. The methods employed and types of cheeses made were often dictated by the local environment, and different cheesemaking techniques were spread around the world as people migrated from one place to another.

We can catch a glimpse into the history of various cheeses through old documents detailing payments of some kind, as cheese was often used to pay taxes to landlords and

Yak's milk is used to make serkam cheese (see page 63) in the high regions of central Asia.

tithes to the clergy. The names of cheeses also give an insight into history, as some are named for ancient regions that no longer exist. Typically cheeses were named for the place where they were made; some, however, were named for the place where they were sold. That's how the cheese sold in Stilton came to be named for that town, even though it was produced many miles away in a different county of England (see page 176).

In the past 100 years, cheesemaking has moved from the farm to the factory. Like so much of our food production, it has become big business and been sanitized and

There are only six dairies in the world licenced to make Blue Stilton Cheese.

regulated until the end product bears little resemblance to the original, traditional food. In the early 1900s James L. Kraft developed American processed cheese, a long-life product that found a ready market as soldiers' rations during World Wars I and II. It quickly found its way into the kitchens of average Americans because of its long life and "safety" (all the molds and bacteria, which give traditional cheeses their identity and flavor, having been destroyed in the name of hygiene and shelf life; see page 156). As more milk had to be transported from the farm to sometimes distant factories, where it was mixed with milk from many other farms, pasteurization became important.

In the past few decades, however, there's been a resurgence in all sorts of traditional foods, including cheeses. Many dairy farmers have chosen to make cheese from their own herds' milk, removing the need for pasteurization because they know the health of the animals and that the milk is used immediately after being collected. Other artisanal producers have revived traditional cheeses, digging up old recipes and using milk from local farms, as well as creating modern cheeses using traditional methods.

With the renewed interest in artisan and farmhouse cheeses, cheese awards have become popular and many countries hold regular competitions to judge the best cheeses in various categories. Two of the best-known and internationally respected are the World Cheese Awards, organized annually by the Guild of Fine Food in the UK, and the World Championship Cheese Contest, organized by the Wisconsin Cheese Makers Association every two years. Many of the award-winners are included in this book.

how to use this book

Cheeses are grouped according to the style. Broadly speaking, the book is organized so that the styles of cheese get progressively stronger and more firm.

snack cheeses

Italian poet Dante Alighieri coined the phrase *bel paese*, "beautiful country," to describe Italy; 600 years later it became the name of a mild, semi-soft cheese. Such commercially produced, firm yet supple, mild cheeses account for a large percentage of world cheese production and are popular for snacks in many countries. On the beaches of Brazil, queijo coalho, a light, rather salty cheese with an almost "squeaky" texture, is browned on sticks in hand-held charcoal ovens and sold by wandering vendors, often with a sprinkling of oregano and garlic-flavored sauce. Hushållsost, one of Sweden's most popular cheeses, is known throughout Scandinavia.

Serve: with crackers and pickles or fruit paste, such as guava.
Drink: a lager or pilsner beer.

Each cheese type comes with quick food and beverage pairing ideas.

Chanco cheese is sold at the Angelmo market, Puerto Montt, Chile.

Within each cheese style, the author has selected one classic variety to highlight. Includes sizes you can buy, affinage, and tasting notes.

≡ 🐄 Bel Paese

Meaning "beautiful country," this cheese, created in 1906 by Egidio Galbani, is named for a book by geologist Antonio Stoppani (though Dante coined the phrase). It's produced in Italy and under license in the USA, with a map of Italy on the Italian cheese and one of the Americas on the US-produced product.

Size: 4½–6lb wheels; Affinage: From about 4 weeks

Tasting notes: A thin, pale yellow-waxed rind covers a firm, supple, cream-colored interior with small eyes; mild, buttery, slightly tangy flavor; and milky aroma. The range now includes a crescenza-mozzarella blend spread (see pages 76 and 149), and foil-wrapped triangular or circular portions of spreadable cheese.

Pasteurized: Yes; Country: Italy, USA

Symbols next to each cheese tell you the main or traditional types of milk used.

🐄 cow

🐐 goat

🐑 sheep

🐃 buffalo

🐂 yak

🦌 reindeer

🐄 Butterkäse

Buttery in taste and color, this yellow to orange-rinded, supple German and Austrian cheese was introduced to the USA by immigrants; Roth Käse in Wisconsin makes a good version. Also called damenkäse, as the mild flavor appealed to the ladies.

Pasteurized: Yes; Country: Germany, Austria, USA

⬛ 🐄 Chanco Cheese

Originally from Chanco in central Chile, this semi-hard, yellow cheese scattered with eyes is now produced all over south-central Chile and accounts for about half the country's cheese consumption. It has a mild, slightly sour and salty flavor.

Pasteurized: Yes; Country: Chile (traditionally Maule)

◉ 🐄 Queijo Minas

Originally made by farmers in the Brazilian state of Minas Gerais, this cheese is now mainly factory-produced, with production spreading to São Paulo and Rio de Janeiro. Soft-rinded wheels have a white, semi-hard, open-textured interior with a slightly sour taste.

Pasteurized: No; Country: Brazil (Minas Gerais)

▀▄ 🐄 Hushållsost TSG

One of Sweden's most popular cheeses, these pale, smooth, supple cylinders with small scattered eyes have a mild, creamy, lemony flavor. It was originally farm-produced and is sold as "farmer's cheese" in the USA. Oltermanni and Pohjanpoika are popular Finnish brands.

Pasteurized: Yes; Country: Sweden

A concise description of each cheese includes anecdotes from the cheese's history as well as a brief look at its characteristic appearance, texture, and flavor.

Pasteurization information and specific region of origin conclude each entry.

semi-soft cheeses 159

cheesemaking

How plain milk becomes the complex array of cheeses we love is part science, part craft, and, many cheesemakers would say, part luck. Different techniques are used to produce different types of cheese; these are discussed in more detail in the introduction to each chapter.

All cheeses, however, are produced by extracting the proteins and fats (the solid curds) from milk and discarding more or less of the liquid (the watery whey). This is done through a number of basic steps.

curdling the milk

The first step in cheesemaking is breaking fresh milk down into solid curds and liquid whey. This is usually done in two steps, though for very soft, fresh cheeses, sometimes just the first step is used.

lactic coagulation

Typically milk is warmed to about body temperature, then bacteria, called a "starter culture," are stirred into the milk. The bacteria multiply in the warm milk, eating the lactose (milk sugars) and producing lactic acid, which turns the milk sour, curdling it into very soft curds floating in liquid whey. Originally milk left in a warm place would have been attacked by airborne bacteria and soured naturally. In the most basic cheesemaking, sour whey left over from the previous batch of cheesemaking (or even a spoonful of natural yogurt, which contains live bacteria) is used. Some cheeses are set using only lactic coagulation; these are very soft, fresh cheeses with a short shelf life.

adding rennet

Most cheeses then have rennet (or a rennet substitute) added to further the coagulation of the milk solids into firmer curds. Traditionally rennet was extracted from the stomach of young calves, lambs, or kids. It contains enzymes, which help break down the protein in milk, forming it into more solid, rubbery curds. Some substances extracted from plants and molds achieve the same effect; for example, many Portuguese cheeses are traditionally made with an extract of cardoon thistle instead of animal rennet (see page 236). Today a laboratory-produced rennet substitute (often called "vegetarian rennet") is widely used in cheesemaking, because it's less expensive and more reliable than both animal and vegetable rennet.

extracting the whey

Once the curds and whey are formed, most of the whey has to be extracted from the curds, leaving behind a firm mass. How much whey is drained off will depend on the texture required in the final cheese—the firmer the cheese, the more whey is removed. This is done through several steps.

cutting the curds

The curds are cut to encourage more whey to drain out. This is usually done by dragging a device called a cheese harp through the curds, so that the fine strings slice the curds into sections. The more finely the curds are cut, the more liquid will be released. Consequently, curds intended to produce a soft cheese are cut into relatively large pieces to retain moisture, while those destined to become hard cheeses are very finely cut or even minced in a mill.

heating

If the curds are destined to become a firm cheese, they are usually heated to some extent. The higher the temperature, the more the curds contract, the more whey they expel, and the harder the resulting cheese. The curds may also be stirred at this stage to encourage them to expel more whey.

draining

The curds are then put into perforated molds to allow the remaining whey to drain off. These molds will also determine the final size and shape of the cheese; many are round to form wheels or cylinders, but all sorts of shapes are used, from pyramids to hearts.

pressing

If the curds are destined to become a semi-hard or hard cheese, the curds will then be pressed to expel even more whey. The more pressure and the longer it's applied, the more whey will be expelled. Sometimes the only pressure is the weight of several cheeses stacked on top of one another; other cheeses destined to become quite hard are put under strong pressure in a hydraulic press.

salting

When they're firm enough, the freshly formed cheeses are removed from their molds and salted, either in brine or with dry salt, to extract more moisture and preserve the outside of the cheese until a protective rind can form. For some cheeses, salt is added to the curds before they're drained in their molds, while other cheeses, such as Feta (see page 58), are stored in salty brine.

maturation

Some cheeses, such as fresh mozzarella (see page 76), are eaten as soon as they're made, but most are matured for anywhere from a few days to a few years. They may be aged in natural caves, traditional underground cellars, or climate-controlled storerooms. The environment, temperature, and humidity will depend on the types of molds and bacteria that the cheesemaker wants to encourage to produce the individual character of the cheese.

The rinds of some cheeses are washed during maturation to encourage certain bacteria, while others are brushed to remove surface mold. Some are rubbed with oil to create a smooth shiny rind. Many cheesemakers will say that the maturation stage is at least as important as all the stages that come before it. In Europe there is a separate profession—called an *affineur* in French and *stagionatoro* in Italian—that doesn't make cheese but buys young cheeses and ages them.

types of milk

Cheese can be made from the milk of almost any domesticated herbivore; cows, goats, and sheep are most common, but water buffalos, reindeers, yaks, llamas, camels, and even horses are used in some areas.

goats

The first domesticated dairy animal, goats wandered in small herds with early nomads, providing milk, meat, and skin; much later they were even taken aboard ships to provide milk during long sea voyages. Goats are small and nimble, willing to eat a varied diet, and are a useful source of milk in mountainous, rocky areas that are inhospitable to cows. However, being small, they produce less milk (3–4 quarts a day) and, because their milk is lower in fat and solids than cow's milk, it takes more milk to make the same quantity of cheese. The fat and protein particles in their milk are smaller, making the milk and subsequent cheese more easily digestible and often suitable for people who are intolerant of cow's milk. And as goat's milk doesn't contain carotene (the substance that gives cow's milk its creamy color), the cheeses are very white.

Goat's milk is seasonal, typically produced from around the end of winter (when kids are born) until mid-fall, when milking usually stops to allow them to keep their energy for the birth of the next lot of kids. The first couple of months of milk (late winter/early spring) may be given to the kids or they may be fed formula so the milk is available for cheesemaking. Through modern farming practices, some producers do have goat's milk year-round, though many argue that the best cheeses are still made during the traditional season. Goat's milk is traditionally used to produce fresh, young, finely textured, acidic cheeses, especially popular in France where goats were introduced by Arabic invaders many centuries ago (see page 106). French tradition dictates that goat's milk cheese should be on the table from Easter until All Saint's Day (November 1).

sheep

Also popular since nomadic times, sheep were kept mainly for meat and wool, as their lactation (milk-producing) season is the shortest of all dairy animals. The milk they did produce, however, would have been used to make yogurt and simple yogurt-based cheeses (see page 64) when it was available. They often lived in mixed herds with goats, and mixed goat's and sheep's milk cheeses are still popular today, especially in Greece, Portugal, and Spain (see page 234).

Sheep's milk cheese is much higher in fat, protein, and solids than goat's or cow's milk (but lower in cholesterol), so less milk is needed to make the same quantity of cheese (1 gallon makes 2lb 3oz). This is just as well, as being small animals they only give a few quarts of milk per day. Like goat's milk, their milk, and the resulting cheese, is more digestible than cow's milk, as the fat particles are smaller. Their milk also lacks carotene, so cheeses produced from it are much paler than similar cow's milk cheeses. Many classic European cheeses, such as Roquefort (see page 168), Manchego (see page 242), Ossau-Iraty (see page 244), and pecorino (see page 246), are made from sheep's milk.

Sheep's milk is much higher in protein, fat, and solids than goat's or cow's milk.

COWS

Cattle were among the last animals to be domesticated, as their naturally wild temperament (think of bulls, not placid cows) and large size made them difficult to control; their size and grazing nature also meant that they required a lot of feed over large areas of flat land, which was not always available. Gradually, however, they were domesticated and are now the most common dairy animal in regions with good pastures, producing the largest volume of milk per animal (an average 5 gallons per day).

Many European cheeses now made from cow's milk were originally made from sheep's milk; it seems this change began to occur around the 11th century when religious orders began to establish large monasteries in fertile valleys all over Europe. The monks used their lush pastures to keep large herds of dairy cattle and preserved their milk by making cheese. They passed these skills on to local farmers and slowly, over the next thousand years, cows began to replace sheep and goats as the primary dairy animal. Chauris are yak–cow hybrids, common in Nepal, Pakistan, and Mongolia, where female yaks (called dris) are also often milked.

Cows produce more milk per animal than goats or sheep.

buffalo

Happy in hot, humid climates, water buffalos were domesticated in India and southeast Asia more than 4,000 years ago, mainly as draft animals. They were introduced to the marshlands around Naples in southern Italy probably by Arab traders as early as the 6th century.

Their milk is the richest of all, with the highest protein and solid levels and over twice the fat content of cow's and goat's milk, but the lowest cholesterol levels. Buffalos also have the benefit of having the longest natural lactation period of any animal, though they produce only 5 to 7 quarts of milk per day.

Their milk is low in carotene, making their cheeses quite white. The fat particles are small and naturally homogenized; therefore, like sheep's and goat's milk, they are more easily digested.

Dairy herds of buffalo have recently been introduced into the USA, UK, South America, and Australia, and buffalo's milk cheeses have been developed in these countries. Carabao is a breed of water buffalo common in the Philippines.

reindeers, yaks, horses & camels

When early Man abandoned a hunter-gatherer lifestyle, he began to domesticate herds of whatever large wild herbivores were at hand. They helped plough fields or carry loads, and provided milk, meat, and hides. Nothing went to waste and excess milk was preserved as yogurt, butter, and cheese.

Some of the Sami people of the Arctic north still follow a semi-nomadic life, herding reindeer, and making cooked cheeses from their milk (see page 68). In the mountains and high plateaus of Central Asia, yak's milk is used to make cheese (see pages 63 and 209) and butter, which is mixed into tea to make Tibet's national beverage, *po cha*. Mare's milk is occasionally used to make cheese in Turkey as well as a fermented drink, and in the dry desert areas of West, Central, and East Asia, camels are domesticated, and their milk turned into cheese.

Water buffalo's milk is high in fat but low in cholesterol.

selecting, storing & serving

In order to get the most out of your cheese, it helps to follow a few basic tips on what to look for when buying it, and how to store it once you get home.

It also helps to think about tasting cheese, what to expect from a piece of cheese and how best to approach it. Then there's the dilemma of how to serve it: at what stage in the meal? What accompaniments should you use? How is cheese best presented? It can be as complex or as simple as you like, but here are a few guidelines to get you started.

buying

Avoid buying cheese from supermarkets; while they may have a large range, good cheese is a living, breathing food and requires the care of a specialized vendor to be at its best. Buy from a cheese shop or delicatessen with a good display and a busy trade to ensure high turnover.

A good vendor will let you taste before you buy, as he'll want to educate you so that you become as addicted to cheese as he is (if you aren't already); be prepared to ask questions and ask to taste. Buy cheese cut fresh from a whole wheel, not pre-cut and wrapped in plastic as the cheese won't be able to breathe through the plastic wrapping; cheesemongers will generally wrap cheese in waxed paper (or parchment paper).

Buy small quantities frequently, rather than stocking up; this way you can try many different cheeses when they're at their best. If buying for a cheese course, allow roughly 3½–5oz per person.

Remember some cheeses are only available seasonally, or at least are at their best in certain seasons, so don't have your heart set on just one cheese. Tell your cheesemonger what you like, and let him guide you to what's best on the day. When you find a cheese you really like, next time ask your cheesemonger what other cheeses are similar. This way you'll expand the range of cheeses you've experienced.

storing

Store cheeses in the warmest part of the refrigerator, which is usually the vegetable compartment, as they're happiest at 44–59°F. Humidity is important too. Have a large, lidded, plastic container in the fridge reserved just for cheese; bear in mind that if you store blue-veined or bloomy rind cheeses with other cheeses, they may share their mold. It's harmless, however, and can be scraped off any cheeses where it isn't welcome.

Always buy from a specialist cheese shop or delicatessen with busy trade to ensure high turnover.

Pieces of parmesan and other hard grating cheeses should be gouged off using a parmesan knife.

tasting

As with all things, taste is subjective—there are no good or bad cheeses; if you like it it's good. If you don't like it, it might be worth giving it a second chance at a later stage; maybe you tasted a version that wasn't at its best, or maybe your taste buds will "grow into it."

They say we eat with our eyes first—so before you taste a cheese, have a good look at it. Its color, texture, rind, and shape are all part of its unique appeal. Aroma is a big part of taste, so give it a good sniff before putting it in your mouth.

Once it's in your mouth, chew it well to give it a chance to warm up (food has very little flavor when it's very cold or very hot) and think about whether it tastes sweet, salty, sour (tangy), bitter (astringent), or savory (meaty) and also about the texture. Once you've swallowed it, take time to think about the aftertaste, which can be quite different from the initial flavor.

I once asked Dr. Max Lake (winemaker, wine judge, and world authority on taste) how one becomes knowledgeable about wine. This was his reply: "drink wine, talk about it, drink more wine, talk about it and drink more wine." I think the same can be said for learning about cheese. Eat it and discuss it often, then try some more.

accompaniments

The cheese should be the star attraction, so keep any accompaniments simple. Bread is necessary with most cheeses; a crisp white baguette for softer cheeses, fruit and nut breads with bloomy rind or blue-veined cheeses, and thin slices of dark bread with washed rind and hard cheeses. Crispbreads, such as lavash, provide a pleasant textural contrast. Fresh apples, pears, grapes, and figs, and dried muscatels, dates, and figs are good accompaniments, but most other fruits are best avoided. Nuts and chutneys are especially good with harder cheeses, while olives and pickled vegetables work well with white cheeses such as Feta and yogurt cheeses.

serving

Bring cheese to room temperature before serving. Half an hour may be enough for a small or fresh cheese, while a large wheel or wedge of denser cheese may need an hour or two. The length of time also depends on the temperature of the room. Soft cheeses such as brie and other bloomy rind or washed rind cheeses should be warm enough to becoming flowing and supple if that's their nature. Don't pre-slice cheese as it will dry out.

If cutting a large wheel or block of cheese into sections, cut it so that a piece of the rind, or external surface, is attached to each wedge or piece, as flavor often varies between the center and the area closest to the rind.

Avoid putting too many cheeses together on an elaborate cheese platter. It looks more impressive to have one or two whole wheels or large wedges of cheese than small bits of five or six different varieties. If serving more than one cheese, consider serving a selection of two or three related cheeses, such as three different sheep's milk cheeses or three different blue-veined cheeses, one each from cow's milk, sheep's milk, and goat's milk.

Place the wheel or wedge of cheese on a board or platter, preferably with a suitable cheese knife. Knives for soft cheeses have holes in them to help stop the cheese sticking to the flat blade of the knife. Parmesan is best cut with a small parmesan knife, which is used to gouge pieces off the wedge rather than to slice. Butter knives are also suitable for soft cheeses and paring knives for hard cheeses; very soft cheeses may require a spoon. If serving more than one cheese, set a separate knife alongside each cheese.

Serve cheese before dessert, French-style, or after dessert, British-style, but avoid serving too much cheese with pre-dinner drinks as it's a heavy food and will dull your guests' appetite. If serving a cheese suited to red wine, serving it before dessert may be best so as to finish off the red wine served with the main course. If the cheese is better suited to a sweet wine, after dessert may be more appropriate.

If cutting a large wheel into sections, cut it so that a piece of the rind is attached to each wedge.

glossary

Cheese has its own language—and the names of cheeses often tell us a lot about their history and how and where they're made. Understanding a few basic words in French, Italian, Spanish, Portuguese, and German as well as some technical terms, makes the wonderful world of cheese that much more interesting.

The cheese terms listed in this glossary will all resurface in various chapters, so it's easy to flip back and double check if there is anything you don't understand. Some of the sizing or descriptive words have direct opposites, so be sure to look up both words for a little extra cheese knowledge.

affinage: the time taken for a cheese to mature or ripen

affineur: the French term for a professional cheese ripener. Such people usually buy young cheeses from producers and age them in their cellars before selling them; many languages don't have a direct translation and use the French term (in Italian, *stagionatoro*)

affumicato: Italian for "smoked"

almkäse: see alpkäse

alpage (d'alpage): French for "Alpine," used to refer to cheese made above a certain altitude only during the months when the animals graze on the high Alpine pastures (see alpkäse, d'alpeggio)

alpine: meaning "from the Alps," the European mountain range that passes through Austria, France, Germany, Italy, Liechtenstein, Slovenia, and Switzerland

alpkäse: German for "Alpine cheese," used to refer to cheese made above a certain altitude only during the months when the animals graze on the high Alpine pastures, also sometimes called almkäse (compare bergkäse; see alpage, d'alpeggio)

annatto: the pulp of the seed of achiote, a South American tree, often used to dye the rind or interior of cheese a reddish-orange; called *roccou* in French

AOC: *Appellation d'Origine Contrôlée*, France and Switzerland's appellation system (see page 270)

artisan (artisanal): meaning "craftsman;" a term often used to denote a cheese produced by traditional methods by a cheesemaker who generally does not use milk from his own farm (compare farmhouse cheese)

artisano: Italian for "artisan," referring to cheeses produced by traditional methods

bergkäse: German for "mountain cheese," usually refers to an Alpine cheese that's made year-round, usually above a certain altitude (compare alpkäse)

bloomy rind/bloomy-rinded cheeses: cheeses with a soft white or mixed mold growing on their rind, also called white mold or mixed mold cheeses

botrytis: a type of mold that grows on grapes, drawing out moisture and concentrating the flavor, used to produce sweet wines often matched with blue-veined cheeses; such wines are said to be "botrytized"

brebis: French for "sheep" and "sheep's cheese"

brevibacterium linens: the bacteria that give washed rind cheeses their distinctive orange color and pungent aroma

brine: a solution of salt and water often used to store cheese to protect it from bacteria and oxygen without the need to form a rind

cabra: Spanish and Portuguese for "goat"

capra: Italian for "goat" and "goat cheese"

carabao: a breed of water buffalo common in the Philippines

chauri: a yak–cow hybrid

cheddaring: a cheesemaking process in which curds are cut into slabs that are stacked on top of one another to drain (compare stirred-curd)

chèvre: French for both "goat" and "goat cheese"

classica: Italian for "classic," sometimes used to denote a cheese produced in the traditional way

curado: Italian for "cured," referring to a cheese that has undergone some aging (see *mezzano*)

curds: the solid particles (mainly protein and fat) that separate from the liquid whey when milk is curdled (see whey)

d'alpage: see alpage

d'alpeggio: Italian for "of the Alps" or "Alpine," used to refer to cheese made above a certain altitude only during the months when the animals graze on the high Alpine pastures (see alpkäse, alpage)

demi: French for "half," sometimes used to describe a cheese that is half the standard size (see also *petit* and *grand*)

DO: *Denominación de Origen,* Spain's appellation system (see page 270)

DOC: *Denominazione di Origine Controllata,* Italy's appellation system, also *Denominação de Origem Controlada,* Portugal's appellation system (see page 270)

dolce: Italian for "sweet," usually used to describe young cheeses or in blue cheese those with less blue-veining (compare *piccante*)

doux: French for "sweet," usually used to describe young cheeses or in blue cheese those with less blue-veining (compare *piquant*)

duro: Italian for "hard," referring to matured cheeses that are relatively hard (compare *tenero*)

eau-de-vie: French clear fruit-based liquor; literally "water of life"

ekte: Norwegian for "authentic" (compare *faux*)

farmhouse cheese: cheese produced on a farm, usually by traditional methods, using only milk from that farm (compare artisan)

fat content: often referred to as "weight in dry matter," describes the percentage of fat present if the water content of the cheese was removed; the remainder would be largely protein with a very small amount of carbohydrate

faux: French for "false" or "imitation" (compare *ekte*)

formaggio: Italian for "cheese"

fresco: Italian for "fresh"; used to describe cheeses that aren't aged (see *dolce*)

fromage: French for "cheese"

geotrichum candidum: an ivory-colored mold often seen on goat's milk cheeses and other bloomy rind cheeses coated in mixed molds

grand: French for "large," often used to denote the largest variation of a specific cheese (compare *petit*)

jeune: French for "young," referring to a cheese that hasn't been aged for very long (compare *vieille*)

käse: German for "cheese"

lactation cycle: the period of time during which an animal gives milk; most animals don't naturally produce milk year-round

lactate crystals: small, white, crunchy crystals formed by lactose and calcium combining, a natural part of some aged cheeses

lactic aroma: the smell of milk

MUNSTER

COMTÉ

MORBIER

REBLOCHON

PYRENÄEN-
SCHAFS-
KÄSE

BRIE

ROQUEFORT

ZIEGENKÄSE
ROLLE

Ziegenkäse is German for "goat's milk cheese"; Schafskäse is "sheep's milk cheese" (see pages 66 and 244).

Uniform rows of gouda (see page 202) await sale in a cheese rack.

lactic fermentation: fermentation generated by the action of bacteria that eat lactose

lactose: the form of sugar found in milk; bacteria that help form cheese by curdling the milk and fermenting the young cheese use lactose as a food source

marc: see pomace

maturo: Italian for "mature," sometimes used to denote an aged cheese (see *réserve, stagionata, stravecchia, vecchia, velho, vieille*)

mezzano: Italian for "half," sometimes used to refer to a cheese that's aged somewhere between young and old (compare *vecchia, curado*)

mold-ripened cheeses: cheeses such as bloomy rind and blue-veined, which are ripened by the activity of mold

natural-rind: a hard, protective, crusty natural outer surface that develops on a cheese during maturation (compare scraped-rind)

oveja: Spanish for "sheep" and "sheep's cheese" (*ovelha* in Portuguese)

pasteurized: heated above a certain temperature for a specific period of time to kill pathogens, generally 161°F for 15–20 seconds or the equivalent (compare thermized, raw milk)

pecora: Italian for "sheep"

PDO: Protected Designation of Origin, one of three gradings within the European Union's appellation system (see page 270)

penicillium candidum: the white mold used on most commercially produced white bloomy rind cheeses

penicillium camemberti: a strain of *Penicillium candidum*

penicillium roqueforti: the blue mold originating in the French caves of Roquefort; laboratory-produced strains of this are used in most blue-veined cheeses

petit: French for "small," often used to denote the smallest variation of a specific cheese (compare *grand*)

PGI: Protected Geographical Indication, one of three gradings within the European Union's appellation system (see page 270)

piccante: Italian for "spicy," usually used to describe matured cheeses or in blue cheese those with more blue-veining (compare *dolce*; see *picón, piquant*)

picón: Spanish for "spicy," usually used to describe matured cheeses or in blue cheese those with more blue-veining (see *piquant, piccante*)

piquant: French for "spicy," usually used to describe matured cheeses or in blue cheese those with more blue-veining (compare *doux*; see *piccante, picón*)

pomace: skins, seeds, and other grape residue left over from winemaking, sometimes distilled to make a clear liquor called marc; pomace is also called marc in French

propionibacter shermani: the bacteria that create the eyes in "swiss cheese" and give it its distinctive flavor

propionic bacteria: see *Propionibacter shermanii*

queijo: Portuguese for "cheese"

queso: Spanish for "cheese"; *quesucos* is a small cheese

raw milk: milk that hasn't been pasteurized (compare pasteurized, thermized)

rennet: an extract from the stomach of young calves, lambs, or kids, containing enzymes that help break down the protein in milk, forming it into solid curds

réserve: French word sometimes used to refer to a long-aged cheese (see *maturo, stagionata, stravecchia, vecchia, velho, vieille*)

scraped-rind: the outer surface of some cheeses, specifically blue-veined cheeses, is regularly scraped to remove any developing rind or molds. They are therefore rindless and usually sold dipped in wax or wrapped in foil to protect them (compare natural-rind)

semi-skimmed milk (partially skimmed milk): milk that has been partially skimmed, typically by combining skimmed evening milk (left to sit overnight so the cream that rises to the top can be skimmed off) with whole milk from the morning's milking

stagionata: Italian for "aged," sometimes used to denote an aged cheese (see *maturo, réserve, stravecchia, vecchia, velho*)

A pasteurizing machine kills all bacteria, a process which is controversial among some cheese-lovers.

stagionatoro: see *affineur*

stirred-curd: a cheesemaking process in which curds are cooked and stirred in their whey to extract as much moisture as possible (compare cheddaring)

stravecchia/stravecchio: Italian for "very old," used to denote a long-aged cheese (see *maturo, réserve, stagionata, vecchio, velho, vieille*)

surface ripened: cheeses, such as bloomy rind and washed rind, that are ripened by the activity of mold or bacteria growing on their surface

sweet milk: whole or unskimmed milk, this term came about in earlier times when most milk was skimmed so that the cream could be used for buttermaking, the remaining milk being used to make cheese; cheeses made from whole milk were a luxury and called "sweet milk cheeses"

tenero: Italian for "tender," referring to young cheeses that are still relatively soft (compare *duro*)

Italian sheep's milk cheese is called pecorino, from *pecora* (Italian for "sheep").

thermized: heated to 140–149°F for 15–20 seconds, this process reduces potentially harmful bacteria without denaturing all of the enzymes that give raw (unpasteurized) milk its natural flavor (compare pasteurized, raw milk)

truckle: a small drum-shaped cheese, often made with curds left over from making larger cheeses

TSG: Traditional Speciality Guaranteed, one of three gradings within the European Union's appellation system (see page 270)

ultrafiltration: a process in which milk is forced through a series of membranes, extracting protein and removing water, resulting in a silkier mouth-feel and creamier flavor

vache (french); vacca (italian); vaca (spanish/portuguese): "cow" and "cow's cheese"

vecchia/vecchio: Italian for "old," sometimes used to denote an aged cheese (see *maturo, réserve, stagionata, stravecchia, velho, vieille;* compare *curado, mezzano*)

velho: Portuguese for "old," sometimes used to denote an aged cheese (see *maturo, réserve, stagionata, stravecchia, vecchio, vieille*)

vieille/vieux: French for "old," referring to a cheese that has been aged for a long time (see *maturo, réserve, stagionata, stravecchia, velho;* compare *jeune*)

washed–curd: a cheesemaking process in which curds are heated in water, washing off some of the sugars on which bacteria feed, reducing their activity and creating very mild, nonacidic cheeses

washed rind: a type of cheese matured by the action of moisture-loving bacteria on its rind (see *Brevibacterium linens*)

whey: the liquid (mainly water with some dissolved protein and fat) that separates from the solid curds when milk is curdled (see curds)

fresh cheeses

The simplest cheeses are made from curdled, sour milk with the whey drained off to leave a soft curd. They might not sound very appetizing put that way, but farmers have been making "curds and whey" (exactly what Little Miss Muffet was eating in the children's nursery rhyme) for as long as they've been milking cows, goats, sheep, and buffalos.

Milk left too long will be attacked by bacteria and naturally turn sour. If it's the right sort of bacteria, the result can be quite delicious. More often excess milk was deliberately soured with selected bacteria to preserve it, often by adding a little of a previous batch of soured milk product to introduce the desired bacteria (this is how yogurt is traditionally made). Cottage cheese, cream cheese, and Feta are some popular cheeses in this category.

Sometimes milk is left to curdle by the action of these souring bacteria (called "lactic fermentation," see fromage frais, page 50), separating into lumps of milk solids (protein and fat called "curds") and liquid (largely water with some dissolved protein and fat, called "whey"). Other times rennet, a substance from the stomach of grass-eating animals with multiple stomachs (such animals are called ruminants), usually a calf but also sometimes lambs and kids, is used to set the milk into a solid mass (synthetic or vegetarian rennet is also often used these days). Old-fashioned junket tablets, used to make the wobbly jellylike milk dessert called junket, are made from rennet.

Once the "junket" is cut up, whey seeps out, leaving the curds behind. Because these curds still have very high moisture content, they're likely to be attacked by other, less desirable bacteria, so they need to be eaten within a day or two, or further preserved. Meanwhile the remaining protein and fat in the whey can be extracted to make another batch of cheese such as ricotta (see page 54).

Draining off more moisture is one way to further preserve fresh curds, by tying them in a cloth hung in a cool place (see yogurt cheeses, page 64) or by letting them drain in a perforated mold sometimes with gentle pressure. Salting also creates an environment in which bacteria are less likely to grow (see Feta, page 58), as does washing the curds to remove the milk sugars on which bacteria feed (see cottage cheese, page 46).

Fresh cheeses are usually eaten before they develop any sort of rind. Even when they are drained or pressed, they have a higher moisture content than aged cheeses so they often have a soft, moist, refreshing mouth-feel. Their soft, spreadable texture also makes them popular for dips and snacks. Surface molds and bacteria haven't had time to work their magic on these cheeses (see bloomy rind cheeses, page 88, and washed rind cheeses, page 114), so their flavors aren't very complex, usually just milky, slightly tangy, and slightly sweet, making

Maltese ġbejniet tal-bżar are fresh white cheeses coated in pepper, salt, olive oil, and vinegar.

them popular in baking and desserts. They also can be salty, depending on how much salt has been added to the curds. They can be granular, especially if the curds have been washed, or smooth if the curds have been beaten to homogenize the solids and remaining liquids (see mascarpone, page 53).

Fresh cheeses, especially the salted, pressed kind, are often preserved in oil or brine (salted water), sometimes with added herbs and spices for flavoring. They can be coated in various flavorings such as pepper or other spices (see coated cheeses, page 70). Those made from goat's milk are often coated in powdered vegetable ash to help absorb moisture (see fresh goat cheeses, page 66), while in Scandinavia, fresh cheeses are often cooked to further preserve them (see cooked cheeses, page 68).

cottage cheeses

A simple way of preserving milk is to curdle it with lemon juice, vinegar, or soured milk, and then to drain the resulting curds. In cottages all over Europe, a cow was traditionally kept to provide milk and butter for the family; thus, simple "cottage cheese" made from excess milk was among the earliest cheeses. Traditionally made from skim milk, the cream having been used for butter, it became a healthy, high-protein, low-calorie food. Typically not pressed, it retains a moist, semi-liquid texture; pressed into firm, sliceable loaves it's called "farmer's cheese"; when drained to a drier, grainier texture it becomes "pot cheese."

Serve: spread on toast or crackers with salad, seafood, or meat as a quick snack.
Drink: sparkling mineral water to match this cheese's low-cal image.

Cottage cheese on crackers with various toppings is a popular healthy lunch.

🇺🇸 🐄 Cottage Cheese

This slightly molten, granular cheese is found in supermarkets around the world. Today the curds are usually set with rennet, cut into small pieces, heated in whey, and washed to remove any remaining milk sugars that could ferment, giving it a longer shelf life and a bland taste. Usually lightly salted and enriched with a little milk or cream, it's often also flavored.

Size: Various size tubs; Affinage: None

Tasting notes: Firm white "grains" of cheese, ranging from a pea to a large pinhead in size, have a dense, almost meaty texture and bland flavor and aroma, while the surrounding liquid adds a creamy mouth-feel.

Pasteurized: Yes; Country: USA

🇩🇪 🐄 Quark

Made by constantly stirring curds to form a smooth creamy paste, German quark (meaning "curd") is softer than Eastern European versions drained in cheesecloth. A myriad of regional names, from Austrian topfen ("pot cheese") to Polish twaróg, reflect this cheese's wide popularity.

Pasteurized: Either; Country: Germany

➕ 🐄 Raejuusto

Scandinavian cottage cheese—called grynost by Swedish Finns, keso in Sweden, and hytteost in Denmark—is a bland, white, granular, low-fat, high-protein cheese virtually identical to American cottage cheese, popular as a garnish for soups or baked potatoes.

Pasteurized: Yes; Country: Finland, Sweden, Denmark

🇬🇧 🐄 Crowdie

The cottage cheese of Scotland, traditionally made in Highland crofts, was probably introduced by Vikings. The name for this creamy, almost bouncy, slightly sour, fresh cheese (*gruth* in Gaelic) comes from the Lowland Scots word *cruds*, meaning "curds."

Pasteurized: Yes; Country: UK (Scotland)

🇵🇭 🐃 🐄 Kesong Puti

Kesong puti, literally "white cheese," is the only indigenous Filipino cheese. Traditionally, milk from carabao (a local water buffalo used as a draft animal) is curdled with vinegar, producing a smooth, slightly salty, mildly tangy cheese.

Pasteurized: Either; Country: Philippines

greek cottage cheeses

Greece has the highest per capita cheese consumption in Europe. Goats and sheep have long played a major role in this land where climate and geography make cattle-raising difficult. The earliest Greek cheeses were likely made when milk curdled in the hot sun soured by naturally occurring bacteria. Drained in a cloth, it was ready to eat immediately or to be packed into a vessel to age in a cool place, where further bacterial growth preserved it, giving a sharper, more complex flavor. Greece now produces five PDO-accredited fresh spreadable cheeses. Made mostly from goat's or sheep's milk, often combined, they're all produced commercially but are also often homemade.

Serve: spread on a ripe tomato slice sprinkled with oregano.
Drink: a crisp rosé, such as that made from Greek grape agiorgitiko.

Sheep graze in an olive grove in Greece.

Galotyri PDO

One of Greece's most ancient cheeses, Galotyri, literally "milk cheese," is from northern and central Greece where semi-nomadic shepherds once wandered with their flocks. Traditionally a by-product, made from the buttermilk left over after making the whey-cheese mizithra (see page 56), these days it's ripened in jugs rather than the traditional goatskins.

Size: Varies; Affinage: Minimum 2 months
Tasting notes: This smooth, soft, creamy white cheese is not eaten fresh but left to mature a little. The bacteria that ferment it usually give it a pinkish hue, along with the distinct aroma and pleasantly sharp tang.
Pasteurized: Either; Country: Greece (Epirus, Thessaly)

Anevato PDO

This goat's milk cheese from the fertile northwestern region of Macedonia has a slightly granular, ricotta-like texture (see page 54). It is aged at least 2 months until the bacteria fermenting it produce a salmon-pink hue, sharp aroma, and fiery flavor.

Pasteurized: Yes; Country: Greece (Western Macedonia)

Katiki Domokou PDO

This mild, slightly tart cheese from central Greece has the slightly grainy texture of strained yogurt and is eaten in a similar way to yogurt—served fresh with grilled meats. Tsalafouti from Epirus and Macedonia is virtually identical.

Pasteurized: Yes; Country: Greece (Domokos)

Kopanisti PDO

Traditionally aged in clay jugs or small barrels with fresh cheese kneaded into the aging cheese over a month or more, this firm, slightly granular, orangey-pink cheese from the Cyclades has a strong, sour, peppery, salty flavor and spicy aroma.

Pasteurized: No; Country: Greece (Cyclades)

Pichtogalo Chanion PDO

Literally "thick milk from Chania" (a town in western Crete, also called Hania), this smooth, white, slightly salty, tart cheese is made from blended sheep's and goat's milk. It has the consistency of thick yogurt and is eaten fresh.

Pasteurized: Either; Country: Greece (Crete)

fromage frais

Meaning literally "fresh cheese," fromage frais is the cottage cheese of France. Refreshing, with a pleasant mouth-feel, its high moisture content results in a very short shelf life, so it's best eaten as soon as it's produced.

The milk is set without rennet, by a bacterial culture similar to that used for yogurt (lactic fermentation). It is most commonly made from pasteurized cow's milk, though sheep's and goat's milk can be used and a few small, farm-based producers use raw milk. Made all over France, and now all over the world, shapes and textures vary, but it's always snowy white.

Serve: with fresh fruit for a healthy breakfast or dessert.
Drink: a slightly sweet sparkling rosé.

Allison Hooper modeled her Vermont Butter & Cheese Fromage Blanc on the ones she ate in Brittany.

▌▐ 🐄 Petit-Suisse

Invented in 1850 by Madame Herould in Normandy, on the advice of a Swiss dairyman who suggested adding cream to fromage frais curds, producing a richer, softer cheese, petit-suisse ("little Swiss") quickly became popular at the Les Halles market in Paris, at least partly due to the enterprising promotion of Madame's business partner, Charles Gervais.

Size: 1–2oz cylinders; Affinage: None

Tasting notes: These small white cylinders of very soft, creamy cheese have a mousse-like texture and taste of sweet rich milk with a slightly acidic tang. They're now produced throughout France and usually sold in trays of six; quality does vary.

Pasteurized: Yes; Country: France (traditionally Normandy)

▌▐ 🐄 Fromage Blanc

Traditionally sold in small pots, only slightly drained, or further drained and molded into various shapes (hearts are popular), fromage blanc literally means "white cheese." Unsalted, it has an even more delicate sweet-sour taste and softer texture than other fromage frais.

Pasteurized: Either; Country: France

🇺🇸 🐄 Vermont Butter & Cheese Fromage Blanc

Cheesemaker Allison Hooper modeled her fromage blanc on the ones she ate while studying cheesemaking in France. It contains no butterfat and has a slightly tart, fresh milk flavor and a smooth, spreadable texture.

Pasteurized: Yes; Country: USA (Vermont)

▌▐ 🐄 Mandjeskaas (Maquée)

This traditional Flemish cheese is a fresh curd drained in baskets (*mandjes* means "basket"), then packed in small buckets. It may be enriched with cream or butter or flavored with herbs, garlic, or other seasonings.

Pasteurized: Yes; Country: Belgium (Flemish Brabant)

▌▐ 🐐 🐐 Brousse du Rove

Curds are beaten (*brousser* in Provençal), then drained, producing sweet, soft, milky cheese sold in plastic cones. Rove is a town near Marseilles. It's also the breed of goats traditionally used, though nontraditional cow's milk versions are produced.

Pasteurized: No; Country: France (Provence-Alpes-Côte-d'Azur)

cream cheese

While 19th-century British cooking authority Mrs. Beeton described cream cheese as "cream dried sufficiently to be cut with a knife," William Lawrence is credited with inventing American-style cream cheese in 1872 in Chester, New York, while attempting to reproduce French petit-suisse (see page 51). By 1880, cheese distributor Reynolds was selling this thicker, more homogenous product in tinfoil wrappers branded "Philadelphia" (the city was then famous for premium foodstuffs). Phenix Cheese Company bought the trademark and in 1928 merged with J.L. Kraft. Most cream cheeses are made from cream-enriched milk inoculated with lactic acid-producing bacteria (used in yogurt), giving them a pleasant tang. In the USA, "cream cheese" must contain minimum 33% fat.

Serve: mixed with a little sugar and liqueur, such as Grand Marnier, over fresh fruit.
Drink: a nip of the liqueur.

Mascarpone tops coffee and liqueur-soaked biscuits in the Italian dessert tiramisu.

▮▮ 🐄 Mascarpone

Produced around Milan since at least the 16th century from cream skimmed off milk used for making other cheeses, there's much debate as to the origin of the name "mascarpone," though it most likely comes from Cascina Mascherpa, a local dairy farm no longer in existence. It's best known as a key ingredient in the Italian dessert, tiramisu.

Size: Various size tubs; Affinage: None
Tasting notes: Pale cream in color with the smooth spoonable texture of drained yogurt or clotted cream and a rich, creamy flavor and faint tang. When beaten it softens to a supple, slightly elastic consistency perfect for drizzling.
Pasteurized: Yes; Country: Italy (Lombardy)

▦ 🐄 Creole Cream Cheese

A French-inspired specialty of southern Louisiana, fresh curd is enriched with cream to produce a cheese that varies from a thick, sour cream-like texture to set curds in a creamy liquid. Bittersweet Plantation Dairy's version is justifiably renowned.
Pasteurized: Yes; Country: USA (Louisiana)

◈ 🐄 🐃 Requeijão Cremoso

Literally "creamy curd," this soft, mild, white Brazilian cheese is made by stirring cream into fresh curds while heating them. Sold in glasses or plastic cups, Catupiry is a popular brand. Portuguese requeijão is a firmer, stronger-flavored cheese.
Pasteurized: Yes; Country: Brazil

▦ 🐄 American Neufchâtel

With 20–32% fat, this smooth, creamy, slightly tangy, spreadable cheese can't be labeled "cream cheese" in the USA. Firmer than French Neufchâtel (see page 99) and without the bloomy rind, it's very similar to Philadelphia Cream Cheese, though slightly softer and stickier.
Pasteurized: Yes; Country: USA

▦ 🐄 🐃 Chenna (Chhana)

Boiled cow's or buffalo's milk is coagulated with acid or sour whey and drained in a cloth, producing this moist, crumbly Indian cheese like a light cream cheese. Chenna has less moisture and more fat than the similar paneer (see page 61).
Pasteurized: Either; Country: India, Bangladesh, Nepal

ricotta

Ricotta is made from whey left over from producing other cheeses; "ri-cotta" literally means "re-cooked." Whey is reheated, sometimes with a little fresh milk added, until the remaining protein coagulates; it's then collected and drained, producing this delicate, creamy cheese. Ricotta can be made from cow's, goat's, sheep's, or buffalo's milk whey and is most common in southern Italy. Because of its high moisture content, fresh ricotta has a very short shelf life, so various techniques are used to preserve it, including salting, baking, smoking, and souring. It's also relatively low-fat, as most of the fat goes into the initial cheese.

Serve: with fresh fruit for a healthy brunch.
Drink: a slightly spritzy, fruity moscato (low in alcohol, it's perfect for brunch).

Lazio in Italy is the home of traditional Ricotta Romana cheese.

Ricotta Romana PDO

In the reclaimed marshland around Rome (Agro Romano), Ricotta Romana made the traditional way from sheep's milk whey and drained in baskets (traditionally woven from rushes) has a mild, sweet flavor. In Sardinia, another classic ricotta, ricotta gentile, is made from sheep's milk whey left over from making Pecorino Romano (see page 247), so is sometimes incorrectly called Ricotta Romana.

Size: Maximum about 4lb 4oz; Affinage: None

Tasting notes: Fresh ricotta is moist and soft, slightly granular rather than smooth and pasty, with a vaguely sweet, milky, almost eggy taste and fresh milky aroma. Ricotta Romana is whiter than ricotta made from cow's milk and has a finer, softer texture.

Pasteurized: Yes; Country: Italy (Lazio)

Baked Ricotta (Ricotta Infornata)

In Sicily, whey is mixed with sea salt or soured whey, recooked, drained in woven rush baskets, sprinkled with black pepper, and baked in stone ovens. A thin brown skin hides a smooth, creamy pale yellow interior.

Pasteurized: Either; Country: Italy (Sicily)

Salted Ricotta (Ricotta Salata)

Salting and pressing preserves ricotta by removing excess moisture, creating a Feta-like cheese (see page 58), though less salty. It can be eaten as it is or aged until sweet, slightly nutty, and gratable.

Pasteurized: Either; Country: Italy

Smoked Ricotta (Ricotta Affumicata)

All over Italy, ricotta is preserved by smoking—in Abruzzo over juniper wood, in Sardinia over herbs, in Veneto over green conifer wood. The longer it's smoked, the firmer it is and the stronger the flavor.

Pasteurized: Either; Country: Italy

Strong Ricotta (Ricotta Forte)

A specialty of Puglia where it's often used in pasta dishes, this ricotta is soured by naturally occurring bacteria, then regularly stirred over several months, draining off the released whey, to produce a strong-smelling, tangy, spicy cheese.

Pasteurized: Either; Country: Italy (Puglia)

mizithra & other whey cheeses

Farmers don't like waste; they discovered long ago that whey left over from cheesemaking could be reheated and curdled, the remaining proteins coagulating to form a second cheese, often eaten by the family, leaving the primary cheese to be aged and sold. Mizithra is the Greek version of these cheeses and, like the more widely known ricotta (see page 54), has many variations. Fresh mizithra, only available December to June because Greek cheeses are made with seasonal sheep's and goat's milk, is salted, dried, and matured to preserve it. Anthotiro is mizithra made from whey left over from making kefalotyri (see page 253). See also geitost and mesost (page 69).

Serve: spread on dried bread rusks with olive oil as part of a *meze*.
Drink: ouzo with a dash of water, the traditional drink with such snacks.

Herds of sheep often cause traffic jams on the Greek island of Crete where Xynomyzithra Kritis is made.

☰ 🐐 🐑 Xynomyzithra Kritis PDO

Xynomyzithra Kritis translates as "sour whey cheese of Crete," which is exactly what it is. The PDO designation is used only for cheeses made the traditional way from soured whey (*xyno* means "sour"), with the addition of up to 15% whole milk, drained, salted, pressed, and left to ripen in cloth sacks for at least 2 months.

Size: Truncated cones; Affinage: Minimum 2 months
Tasting notes: Goat's and sheep's milk create a purer white cheese than that made from cow's milk. The texture is soft, creamy, and slightly granular, and the taste is sweetish with a tartness from the longer-than-usual aging and soured whey.

Pasteurized: No; Country: Greece (Crete)

☰ 🐐 🐑 Manouri PDO

Made with 25% added milk or cream, this whey cheese from northern Greece is nicknamed "fat mizithra." Shaped into logs, it has a smooth, dense, almost buttery texture and, as it's only lightly salted, tastes sweet and creamy.

Pasteurized: No; Country: Greece (Macedonia, Thessaly)

🏛 🐐 Requesón

This fresh Spanish whey cheese is also called nazurón, brossat, brullo, and gaztanbera. It has a granular, almost sandy texture and slightly sweet taste. Like other ricotta-style cheeses, it's popular for desserts or snacks. Also made in Mexico and Peru.

Pasteurized: Either; Country: Spain, Mexico, Peru

▮▮ 🐐 🐑 Brocciu Corse (Broccio) PDO

This Corsican cheese was France's first *fromage de lactosérum* ("whey cheese") given AOC status. Whole milk is added to the whey, so it tastes like a slightly sweet, rich, milky ricotta. Also sometimes salted and matured (*passu*).

Pasteurized: No; Country: France (Corsica)

 🐐 🐑 Anari

Often made from whey left over from making the more widely known Cypriot halloumi (see page 85), fresh anari is snow white and firm enough to be sliced, with a mild, almost neutral, taste. It can also be dried for grating.

Pasteurized: Either; Country: Cyprus

feta

Although Feta-like cheeses have been made in Balkan countries since antiquity and were introduced around the world by immigrant Greeks, Feta PDO accounts for 70% of all cheese consumed in Greece. Only Greek cheese made to strict guidelines can now be called Feta within the EU (see page 274). The name "Feta," meaning "slice," dates back to the 1600s and refers to the slices of cheese stacked into tins or barrels for aging. Feta can only be made eight months of the year because of sheep milk's seasonal availability. It varies in texture and flavor regionally, with northern versions generally milder, softer, and creamier.

Serve: in a Greek salad with ripe tomatoes, cucumber, and sweet onion.
Drink: a tart Greek white wine such as Assyrtiko from Santorini.

Feta is often included in a Greek salad with tomato, cucumber, bell peppers, and black olives.

Barrel-Aged Feta PDO

Feta stored in wooden barrels is considered the best, as the wood allows some air contact to aid ripening. Milk is coagulated with rennet, drained in circular molds, cut into wedges, salted liberally, and left to dry for 1–2 days, then packed into wooden barrels and topped with brine. Feta must be made from sheep's milk with a maximum of 30% goat's milk allowed.

Size: Various size wedges, rectangles; Affinage: Minimum 2 months

Tasting notes: Pure white and crumbly with small fissures and a moist, glistening surface, this cheese has a richer, deeper flavor than Feta matured in tins. An assertive tang mellows to lemony tartness with a balanced milky sweetness.

Pasteurized: Either; Country: Greece (Epirus, Lesvos, Central Mainland, Macedonia, Peloponnese, Thessaly, Thrace)

Sirene

Bulgaria's most popular cheese was sold as "Bulgarian feta" before Feta's PDO was granted. Traditionally made from sheep's milk, though cow's milk is increasingly used, it's white, crumbly, slightly grainy, moist, and lemony. Known as sirenje in Macedonia.

Pasteurized: No; Country: Bulgaria

Danish "Feta"

Denmark has produced Feta-style cheese since the 1930s, almost exclusively for export. This smooth, creamy, closed-textured cheese, produced using ultrafiltration, is made mainly from cow's milk. It is blander than traditional Feta, though still salty, and cannot be called Feta within the European Union.

Pasteurized: Yes; Country: Denmark

Telemea

Made mainly from cow's and sheep's milk, though goat's and buffalo's milk is sometimes used, this Romanian Feta-style cheese is creamy and tangy when two weeks old, becoming firmer, saltier, and more strongly flavored with age.

Pasteurized: Either; Country: Romania

Kalathaki Limnou PDO

This Feta-style cheese from the Greek island of Limnos can't be called Feta as it's made outside the designated area. Drained in wicker baskets, (*kalathaki* means "little basket") it's matured in brine and is milder, drier, and denser than Feta. It may contain maximum 30% goat's milk.

Pasteurized: Either; Country: Greece (Limnos)

soft and salty cheeses

Earthenware pots found in a pharaoh's tomb suggest that Egyptians made cheese over 5,000 years ago. Similar pots are used today to collect milk to produce laban rayeb, a simple curd eaten fresh, or used to make soft, salty karish and pungent, aged mish. Most traditional soft, salty cheeses are factory-made today, but many are also still homemade. These simple curds, usually pressed and pickled in salty brine, similar to Feta (see page 58), often have names simply meaning "cheese" (Sudanese gibbna), "white cheese," or "Arabic cheese" (jibneh arabieh in English-speaking countries), indicating their fundamental role in the regions' cuisines.

Serve: with flat bread and olive oil.
Drink: fresh fruit juice, such as sour cherry or apricot (these are usually breakfast cheeses).

Cows grazing along the fertile Nile river valley in Egypt produce milk for local white cheeses.

Domiati

Named after the northern Egyptian city of Damietta and also called gebnah beda ("white cheese") and gebnah tariyah ("soft cheese"), domiati has been made for over 2,300 years. Similar to Feta, except that the milk is salted before coagulation, it's occasionally made from goat's or sheep's milk. It is eaten fresh or aged in salted whey for 4–8 months.

Size: Various size cylinders, loaves; Affinage: 0–8 months

Tasting notes: This smooth, white, slightly crumbly, salty cheese is semi-soft when young, firming with age, and becoming light brown, flaky, and brittle when fully aged. Fresh, it has a milky flavor with a slight tang that becomes much more pronounced with age.

Pasteurized: Either; Country: Egypt

Testouri

This fresh, lightly salted, orange-shaped cheese, now most commonly considered Egyptian, is popular throughout the Middle East. It may have originated in the Tunisian city of Testour and been spread by the Ottomans throughout the region.

Pasteurized: Either; Country: Egypt

Beyaz Peynir

The curds for this mild, salty, typically sheep's milk cheese, the name of which means "white cheese," are pressed in cheesecloth, cut into slices, and aged in brine. It's popular for breakfast with olives, tomato, and cucumber.

Pasteurized: Yes; Country: Turkey

Akawi

Disks or wedges of firm, stark white, slightly springy, crumbly, mild, salty cheese are popular in Lebanon, Syria, Palestine, and Jordan. Traditionally made from goat's or sheep's milk, they're usually packed in brine, though unbrined versions are used for sweet dishes.

Pasteurized: Either; Country: Lebanon, Syria, Jordan

Paneer

Mild, pleasantly lactic, moist, and slightly springy, paneer ("cheese" in Hindi) is the most common cheese throughout the Indian subcontinent, though it probably originated in Persia (Iran). Often homemade, it's usually eaten fresh and softens without dissolving when heated.

Pasteurized: Either; Country: India, Pakistan, Iran

yogurt cheeses

Rennet is commonly used to curdle milk for cheesemaking (see page 14), but airborne bacteria will also curdle unrefrigerated milk. Yogurt is traditionally made by mixing fresh milk with a little yogurt from a previous batch, then storing it in a warm place where the bacteria multiply, creating more yogurt. It can then be drained, creating a simple cheese that can be dried, matured, seasoned, or marinated. Sometimes it's said that these "lactic set" cheeses (cheeses set by lactose-loving bacteria) aren't really cheese because they don't contain rennet. They certainly taste like cheese.

Serve: as a snack with olives, pickles, bread, and olive oil.
Drink: arak, raki, ouzo, or similar clear liquor.

Make simple yogurt cheese (labneh) by draining yogurt in muslin or a clean thin cloth overnight.

Arish

Yogurt is heated until it splits, then drained in cheesecloth for 1–2 days until firm enough to shape into small balls or use like thick cream cheese. It's popular for breakfast or as a snack throughout the Arabic world. Labneh (yogurt drained without heating) is similar, as is serat, an Iranian and Afghani mountain cheese smoked and dipped in beeswax.

Size: Typically golfball size; Affinage: None

Tasting notes: These white, crumbly, moist balls of curd are slightly salty with a mild acidic tang, and largely flavored by their herb or spice coating, which is most typically za'atar (a mixture of dried thyme, sesame seeds, and salt).

Pasteurized: Either; Country: Lebanon

Shangleesh

This strong-smelling cheese is made from sun-dried balls of arish ripened by surface molds, which are then removed before the balls are rolled in spices and stored in oil. Syrian sorke (or surke) is similar.

Pasteurized: Either; Country: Lebanon

Serkam

In Nepal, Pakistan, and Mongolia, yogurt made from the milk of yaks or chauris (a yak–cow hybrid) is made into butter. The remaining buttermilk is boiled and drained to make this fresh, slightly granular cheese, called dartsi in Bhutan.

Pasteurized: Either; Country: Nepal, Pakistan, Mongolia

Djamid

These hard cheese balls with a dry interior dotted with salt crystals are traditionally Jordanian. Made from naturally soured buttermilk and shaped by hand, they are salted and sun-dried, then stored in jars for up to 12 months.

Pasteurized: Either; Country: Jordan

Tiroler Graukäse PDO

The mold on the rind of this tangy, sour, spicy Austrian cheese (literally "gray cheese") can penetrate the cream-colored interior as it matures. It is low in fat, because it's made from naturally soured buttermilk.

Pasteurized: Either; Country: Austria (Tyrol)

bryndza

Eastern European shepherds tending flocks in remote mountains add rennet to the sheep's milk, drain the curds in cloth sacks, and take these simple cheeses down to the village dairies once a week, where they're broken up, salted, pressed into blocks, and brined or packed into barrels with salt to make bryndza (from Romanian *brânză* or *brînză* meaning "cheese," also colloquial for "poverty"). Aging varies and goat's and/or cow's milk is sometimes used, so the resulting Feta-like cheeses (see page 58) from Romania, Poland, Slovakia, Hungary, Bulgaria, Russia, Ukraine, and Austria range from mild, soft, and creamy to firm, crumbly, and tangy.

Serve: melted over vegetables or stirred through meat sauces.
Drink: pilsner beer such as Polish Pilsner Urquell.

Slovenská Bryndza is traditionally made with milk from sheep that graze high in the Slovak mountains.

Slovenská Bryndza PGI

Slovakian mountain shepherds traditionally drained and crushed surplus fresh cheese, salting and pressing it into wooden barrels; thus, "barrel bryndza" could be stored for a long time. The first factory to preserve the traditional fresh sheep's cheeses opened in 1787, and its less-salty, spreadable version quickly became popular. It can contain a maximum 49% cow's milk, which must be pasteurized.

Size: Various; Affinage: 8–10 days

Tasting notes: This white, slightly granular cheese with delicate aroma and pleasantly sour taste (slightly less salty than Feta) is sold in plastic tubs or foil containers. It is essential in traditional dishes including pirohy (stuffed dumplings) and halušky (potato dumplings).

Pasteurized: Either (sheep), Pasteurized (cow); Country: Slovakia

Bryndza Podhalańska PDO

Produced May–September in the traditional Podhale region, this Polish sheep's milk cheese dates back 500 years. White, sometimes with a pale green tint, it can contain maximum 40% cow's milk, so flavor, saltiness, and sourness vary.

Pasteurized: No; Country: Poland (Nowotarski, Tatrzański, Żywiecki)

Yarra Valley Dairy Persian Fetta

Creamy white chunks of cheese in a small distinctive tin of oil are flavored with garlic, black pepper, thyme, and juniper. This popular Australian cheese from Victoria's Yarra Valley is soft-textured compared to Greek Feta and only lightly salted.

Pasteurized: Yes; Country: Australia (Victoria)

Brânză de Burduf

Burduf, Romanian for "sack," perhaps refers to the pouch made from sheep's stomach or skin in which this bryndza is often stored for long aging. It also can be stored in a pine bark tube, which imparts a resinous flavor.

Pasteurized: No; Country: Romania (Transylvania)

Ornelle Chevre Salade

Made by ultrafiltration in the style of Danish "Feta" (see page 58), this pure-white, slightly crumbly, creamy cheese from Otago is softer, milder, and less salty than traditional Feta. It won gold at the 2008 New Zealand Cheese Championships.

Pasteurized: Yes; Country: New Zealand (Otago)

fresh goat cheese

People tend to either love or hate goat cheese, often called by its French name, chèvre. Those who hate it may have had a cheese with an unpleasant "goaty" aroma and flavor, usually from poor-quality milk, often during winter. It's worth persevering, as good goat cheese has a mild creamy tang and fine texture. Often sold fresh (in small cylinders, pyramids, or disks), it can also be matured. It is sometimes rolled in ash, which softens the flavor (see page 100), coated in seasonings, or stored in oil, often with herbs and spices. Büscium da cavra is a fresh goat cheese, a specialty of Ticino, Switzerland.

Serve: with crispbread or fresh crusty white bread.
Drink: sauvignon blanc, the classic match (it echoes the cheese's herbal notes).

This homemade fresh goat cheese is hand-ladled into molds.

🇨🇦 🐐 Woolwich Dairy Chevrai (Madam Chèvre)

When cheesemaker Adozinda Dutra moved from Portugal's Azores to Ontario in 1983, she started making Portuguese-style goat cheese as a hobby; demand grew and soon she and her family bought a local dairy. They now produce 50-plus varieties of cheese (several regular American Cheese Society Awards winners) and have three factories, including one in Wisconsin.

Size: 4oz, 10¹/₂oz logs; Affinage: None

Tasting notes: This traditional unripened goat cheese log is pure white with a light, slightly tangy flavor and smooth, firm, sliceable texture. Also available coated in various flavorings: herbs, garlic, dried tomatoes, crushed green and black peppercorns, cranberry, and cinnamon.

Pasteurized: Yes; Country: Canada (Ontario)

🇦🇺 🐐 Meredith Dairy Goat's Cheese

These soft chunks of creamy, lightly salty, Australian goat's curd are stored in extra-virgin olive oil with fresh garlic and thyme. The flavorings impart a subtle taste, but the sweetly tangy flavor of fresh goat's milk shines through.

Pasteurized: Yes; Country: Australia (Victoria)

🐐 St Tola Crottin

These small white nuggets from Ireland's County Clare have a smooth, fine texture and creamy, sweet, slightly salty, herbal flavor when eaten fresh. Matured, they develop a more compact texture; a thin, mottled, cream-colored rind; and more pronounced flavor.

Pasteurized: No; Country: Ireland (Clare)

🇬🇧 🐐 Innes Button

Light, almost soufflé-like, and best eaten very fresh, when the mild, sweet milky flavor and aroma have just a faint lactic tang, this cheese is also available coated in ginger, caraway, or pink peppercorns.

Pasteurized: No; Country: UK (England—Staffordshire)

🇺🇸 🐐 Coach Farm Fresh Goat Cheese

New York's Coach Farm, established in 1983, helped launch local goat cheeses onto the American market. Their hand-ladled fresh, pure white cheeses are produced in a range of shapes: logs, disks, buttons, bricks, and hearts. Also available herb- or pepper-coated.

Pasteurized: Yes; Country: USA (New York)

cooked cheeses

Scandinavia has an interesting tradition of cooking fresh cheeses. Whey left over from cheesemaking is often re-heated to make cheeses such as Italian ricotta (see page 54), but in colder Scandinavia, where milk is scarce throughout winter, whey is boiled to create longer-lasting, fudgelike cheeses. In Finland, fresh curds, sometimes from reindeer's milk, were traditionally preserved by baking in front of an open fire, creating a slightly sweet, brown-flecked crust. These cheeses are eaten as desserts with cream or jam, or put in the coffeepot to soften, perhaps also sweetening the coffee in days when sugar wasn't so common in northern Europe.

Serve: with dark bread and berries (especially cloudberries) or berry jam.
Drink: coffee is traditional; dipping the cheese in the pot is optional.

The Sámi people of northern Scandinavia still herd reindeer and make cheese from their milk.

Geitost

Despite its name, most Norwegian geitost ("goat cheese") is today made from a blend of goat's and cow's milk, cream, and whey. Ekte ("authentic") geitost indicates 100% goat's milk; mysost is 100% cow's milk. Heated until most of the moisture evaporates and the milk sugars caramelize into a brown, sticky mass, it's molded into blocks. Also called gjetost and brunost.

Size: Various size blocks; Affinage: None
Tasting notes: This golden-brown cheese has a firm, smooth, fudgelike texture and appearance, and tastes like a slightly tangy salted caramel. The darker the color, the stronger the caramel flavors and aromas. Ekte geitost is slightly more sour.
Pasteurized: Yes; Country: Norway

Mesost

Smooth, fudgelike, coffee-colored Swedish mesost, made from cow's milk whey, cream, and sugar, is similar to geitost. The similar, softer, goat's milk whey version (mainly from artisan dairies in the mid-north of Sweden) is just called mese (*ost* means "cheese").

Pasteurized: Either; Country: Sweden

Munajuusto

These firm, moist, golden domes of Finnish cheese look like baked ricotta. Traditionally homemade, milk (occasionally reindeer's) is combined with eggs (*muna* means "egg"), heated until it curdles, then pressed into molds. It's sometimes roasted in front of a fire.

Pasteurized: Yes; Country: Finland

Leipäjuusto

This thin, round, white Finnish cheese has a brown-speckled caramelized crust, traditionally made by placing the freshly pressed cheese before an open fire. The mild interior is smooth and creamy. Also called juustoleipä ("bread cheese") and kaffeost ("coffee cheese").

Pasteurized: Either; Country: Finland, Sweden (Lapland)

Bass Lake Juustoleipä

Bass Lake Cheese Factory re-created "Finnish squeaky cheese" for the local Finnish community, who have deemed it the most authentic version in the USA. *Juusto* means "cheese" and *leipä* means "bread," referring to the cheese's flat shape.

Pasteurized: Yes; Country: USA (Wisconsin)

coated cheeses

Processed cheeses are coated in all manner of flavorings, from sun-dried tomatoes to flower petals, generally to add flavor to bland cheeses for people who don't enjoy the taste of cheese; these cheeses are usually best avoided. There are, however, some classic cheeses that traditionally include a light coating of something typical of their region. Ash from burning vines and pomace (skins and seeds left over from winemaking) are common in wine-producing regions, while sheep's and goat's milk cheeses lend themselves well to a light coating of herbs or spices. See also Hereford Hop (page 193) and figue (page 109).

Serve: with simple bread or crackers, as there's already a lot of flavor.
Drink: a soft Beaujolais-style red, or wine from the grape used in a pomace coating.

Highland cattle are a hardy breed, accustomed to the high rainfall and strong winds of Scottish winters.

🏴󠁧󠁢󠁳󠁣󠁴󠁿 🐄 Caboc

Mariota de Ile, daughter of MacDonald Lord of the Isles, sent to Ireland in the 15th century to avoid an unwanted marriage, returned with the recipe for Scotland's oldest named cheese. Her descendant, Susannah Stone at Highland Fine Cheeses, revived it in the 1960s, adding the fine, toasted oatmeal coating, because oatcakes, the traditional accompaniment, were rarely seen outside Scotland then.

Size: 3¹/₂oz logs; Affinage: Minimum 2 months
Tasting notes: Pale yellow with a smooth, firm, slightly granular texture, which melts on the tongue like butter, this double cream cheese (see page 104) has a rich flavor, distinct lemony tang, and nutty finish from the oatmeal coating.
Pasteurized: Yes; Country: UK (Scotland—Ross-shire)

▮▮ 🐐 🐑 Brin d'Amour

Coated in local rosemary and thyme, with a thin dusting of white mold, this Corsican cheese can look intimidating, but the firm ivory interior is mild with an herbal tang. Fleur du Maquis, also from Corsica, is almost identical.
Pasteurized: Either; Country: France (Corsica)

▮▮ 🐑 Cacio a Forma di Limone

This fresh white cheese is a specialty of the Metauro Valley in the central-eastern Italian region of Marche. Drained in lemon-shaped molds, it's coated with grated lemon zest, producing a mild, slightly salty, lemony flavor.
Pasteurized: Either; Country: Italy (Marche)

▮▮ 🐄 🐐 Aromes au Gène de Marc

For this specialty of France's Rhône-Alpes region, ripe Picodon (see page 109), rigotte (see page 151), or similar cheeses are stored in pomace (*marc* in French) for at least a month, then coated in it, producing a strong, bittersweet, yeasty taste and aroma.
Pasteurized: Either; Country: France (Rhône-Alpes)

▮ 🐐 🐑 🐄 Ġbejna

Malta's national cheese, from the island of Gozo, is available fresh, dried, or coated liberally in crushed black pepper and seasoned with salt, olive oil, and vinegar (ġbejniet tal-bzar). These small, cream-colored, mild disks are usually made by farmers' wives.
Pasteurized: Either; Country: Malta (Gozo)

stretched-curd cheeses

These cheeses, also called spun-curd, *pasta filata*, or string cheese, are a special subgroup of fresh cheeses, though some are aged and more closely resemble the semi-hard cooked cheeses of later chapters.

These cheeses begin like any other, with soured milk being set into curds and whey. After the whey is drained off, the curds are mixed with water and heated to form a pliable mass, which is then pulled and stretched in the hot water to expel extra whey and form stretchy, resilient strands of cheese. This is traditionally done by hand, though machines are often used today for factory-produced versions. When the texture is stretchy enough, a section of cheese is torn or cut off and sealed in cold water.

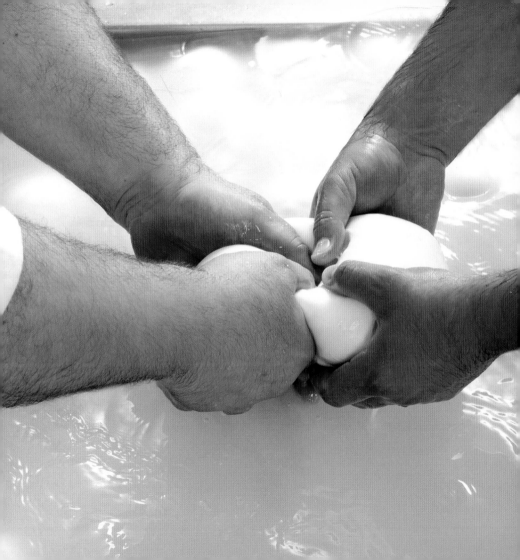

There are three main types of stretched-curd cheeses:

• Fresh versions, such as mozzarella (see page 76), where the sealed skin coats a moist, supple interior of soft layered fibers, are often sold in whey (or brine) and should be consumed as soon as possible. Like all fresh cheeses, they have a simple, mild flavor of sweet fresh milk with a slight tang. Their texture, both raw and melted, is their most distinctive quality, and they marry well with other flavors such as sweetly tart tomatoes or salad dressings.

• Aged versions, such as caciocavallo (see page 80), are similar to other semi-hard, cooked cheeses such as edam and gouda (see page 202); the hot water in which the curds are melted washes away a lot of the lactic acid, leaving a mild, supple cheese. The curds are heated for longer than for the fresh version and the warm pliable curds are kneaded more vigorously, expelling more moisture. The resulting smooth mass is formed into many different shapes. They're sometimes waxed before being aged for several months to a year or longer. They start out simple, buttery, and slightly sweet, but over time develop more complex, sharper, spicy flavors. Young, they're good for sandwiches and snacks, while older ones are better used in cooking.

• Frying cheeses, such as halloumi (see page 85), are worked most vigorously to extract as much whey as possible, and then often aged in brine to prevent a rind forming. This creates hard, rubbery, salty cheeses that really only come into their own when heated.

All stretched-curd cheeses share similar properties. The curds are firm enough so they don't have to be put into molds to form their shape, but they can be shaped by hand into a large variety of forms including braids, balls, sheets (see Shaw River Farcita, page 79), and giant sausages (see provolone, page 82). They can also be shaped around a filling such as butter or cream (see burrata and manteca, page 77), or even pieces of ham or truffle. They have

Caciocavallo means "cheese on horseback," as pairs of cheeses are suspended over a rod to age.

a mild flavor and firm, supple texture, and they melt into long stretchy strings when fresh or, when aged, a soft yielding mass that holds its shape and doesn't turn greasy. This makes them popular for snacks ranging from kids' string cheese sticks (see page 157), through pizza toppings and fillings for rice balls (Italian *suppli* and *arancini*), to fried provoleta at South American barbecues (see page 83). They are also often smoked to add a little extra flavor, creating an attractive, shiny, smooth, golden-brown rind and supple pale golden interior, (see Oscypek, page 263).

fresh italian mozzarella

Mozzare means "to cut off" in Italian, referring to the chunks of cheese cut off in the stretched-curd cheesemaking process (see page 72). Originally made from buffalo milk, mozzarella was first possibly mentioned in the 1200s when monks were recorded giving bread and "mozza" to visiting pilgrims. Popularity increased in the 1800s when mozzarella was combined with tomatoes and basil to make the classic pizza margherita, and soon cow's milk versions were produced to meet demand. The firmer, bland, pale yellow, industrially produced cheese that's also called mozzarella is a far cry from the sweet, fresh versions.

Serve: at room temperature, torn into chunks as a salad with tomato and basil.
Drink: the faint grassy notes of an Italian sauvignon blanc, such as Collio, are a perfect match.

Insalata Caprese, fresh mozzarella with sliced tomato and basil, is named for the Italian Isle of Capri.

▮▮🐃 Mozzarella di Bufala Campana PDO

Indian water buffalo were introduced as draft animals to the swampy plains near Naples in the 6th or 7th century. This cheese is best stored at room temperature and eaten the day it's made; however, industrially produced balls chilled in whey and air-freighted around the world are still delicious. It's also produced as braids (*treccia*), small balls (*bocconcini*), and sheets *(sfoglia)*.

Size: Typically 7oz balls; Affinage: None

Tasting notes: A thin, slippery skin encases a slightly springy, almost melting interior of layered curds that release droplets of whey when cut. Produced only in southern Italy, it is porcelain white, with a sweet, lactic tang, grassy aroma, and fresh aftertaste.

Pasteurized: Either; Country: Italy (Campania, Lazio, Puglia, Molise)

▮▮🐄 Mozzarella TSG

Italian cow's milk mozzarella made using a traditional starter of heat-resistant lactic bacteria is similar to Mozzarella di Bufala, but slightly firmer with a milder flavor. Cow's milk mozzarella is also called fior di latte ("flower of the milk").

Pasteurized: Yes; Country: Italy

▮▮🐄🐃 Burrata

Created in the 1920s from buffalo milk (cow's milk versions now exist), this specialty of Puglia is fresh mozzarella balls filled with cream and fresh curd and twisted closed. Gioia Cheese Company produces a good cow's milk version in California.

Pasteurized: Either; Country: Italy (Puglia)

▮▮🐄🐃 Bocconcini

Walnut-sized balls of mozzarella are called bocconcini ("little mouthfuls"). Usually made from cow's milk, they're bland, springy little nuggets that add texture to salads and melt beautifully into pasta. Ciliegini, or "cherry bocconcini," are smaller versions.

Pasteurized: Yes; Country: Italy

▮▮🐄🐃 Manteca

Fresh buffalo's or cow's milk mozzarella, or the similar, slightly drier scamorza (see page 81), is shaped around a lump of cold butter. It may be smoked, aged for a few weeks, or waxed for export. It is also called burrino.

Pasteurized: Either; Country: Italy (south)

other mozzarella

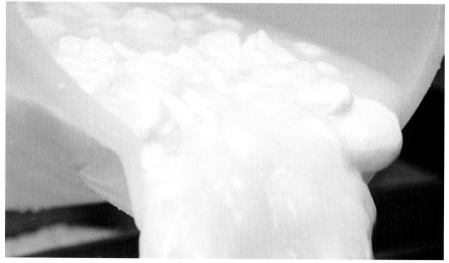

The delicious simplicity of fresh Italian mozzarella has inspired cheesemakers around the world. In Italy, as well as elsewhere, variations such as burrata, manteca (see page 77), and mozzarella affumicata are produced. Outside Italy, producers such as Australia's Shaw River have established herds of dairy buffalo, while others, such as South Africa's Sue Smallwood, work with cow's milk. In the USA, Paula Lambert adds her own spin by creating a mozzarella from blended cow's and goat's milk as well as making an excellent version of the traditional Mexican mozzarella-style cow's milk cheese, queso oaxaca.

Serve: melted through pasta or on pizzas.
Drink: crisp unoaked chardonnay, such as Pio Cesare L'Altro from Piedmont.

Mozzarella curds are drained before being stretched in hot water into shapes such as balls and braids.

Capriella

Artisan cheesemaker Paula Lambert started the Mozzarella Company in Texas in 1982 after discovering fresh mozzarella on a trip to Italy. She now distributes over 98 tons of cheese throughout the USA annually, while maintaining her artisanal quality. Her Capriella is a fresh mozzarella handmade from 50% cow's milk and 50% goat's milk (*capri* is Latin for "goats").

Size: 7¾oz balls; Affinage: None

Tasting notes: These soft, moist, pure-white orbs have the typical layered texture of fior di latte (see Mozzarella TSG, page 77), without quite the same milky sweetness as mozzarella made from 100% cow's or buffalo's milk. Instead, there's a pleasant tang from the goat's milk.

Pasteurized: Yes; Country: USA (Texas)

Mozzarella Affumicata

Traditionally a winter cheese, now produced year-round, large balls of fresh mozzarella are smoked over smoldering straw for 15–20 minutes, producing a brown exterior covering a firmer, pale golden interior with a mildly smoky aroma and taste.

Pasteurized: Yes; Country: Italy

Queso Oaxaca

Also called Mexican mozzarella, this mild, sweetly milky, stretched-curd cheese originated in Oaxaca in southeastern Mexico. It is traditionally long, wide ribbons wound up like balls of wool. Similar to asadero (see page 87), it's popular in quesadillas.

Pasteurized: Yes; Country: Mexico (Oaxaca)

Bronberg Organic Mozzarella

Firmer than fresh mozzarella, with a longer shelf life, this off-white, mild, creamy, slightly salty, semi-soft cheese from South Africa is made from organic cow's milk and shaped into 5oz sliceable blocks rather than the traditional balls.

Pasteurized: Yes; Country: South Africa (Gauteng)

Shaw River Mozzarella Farcita

Shaw River (then Purrumbete) established Australia's first dairy buffalo herd in 1995 in Victoria. As well as mozzarella balls, they produce thin sheets of springy white mozzarella perfect for filling, rolling, and slicing (*farcita* means "stuffed" in Italian).

Pasteurized: Yes; Country: Australia (Victoria)

caciocavallo

Caciocavallo, meaning "cheese on horseback," comes from the practice of aging cheeses dangling in pairs on either side of a rod, as if astride a horse. Many variations of this stretched-curd cheese exist throughout southern Italy in a wide range of shapes and sizes, as with the similar provolone (see page 82). Caciocavallo podolico from Campania and the best Caciocavallo Silano are made with milk from rare-breed Podolica cows. Caciocavallo di agnone from Molise is cave-aged for up to a year and Sicilian caciocavallo palermitano is brick-shaped. Caciocavallo *affumicato* indicates smoked caciocavallo. Turkish kaşar peyniri and Lebanese kashkawan are similar.

Serve: on crusty bread with chutney or pickles.
Drink: a soft Italian red wine such as dolcetto.

Caciocavallo Silano is named for the Sila Plateau in Calabria, southern Italy.

Caciocavallo Silano PDO

Produced in the southern Italian regions of Calabria, Campania, Molise, Puglia, and Basilicata since ancient times and named after Calabria's high Sila Plateau, Caciocavallo Silano has perhaps the widest geographic range of any Italian PDO cheese. Both artisan and factory versions are produced, some with a tasteless, transparent coating to prevent yeast or mold growth and to increase shelf life.

Size: 3–5½lb spheres; Affinage: Minimum 30 days
Tasting notes: Typically shaped like a full sack tied at the neck, the smooth, shiny, hard, ivory-colored rind ages to yellowy-brown. The pale yellow interior is stretchy when young, with a slight tang, darkening and becoming crumbly and stronger-tasting when aged.

Pasteurized: No; Country: Italy (Calabria, Campania, Molise, Puglia, Basilicata)

Caciobufala

Casa Madaio, a family firm of *stagionatori* ("cheese-agers" or *affineurs*), buys this log-shaped buffalo's milk caciocavallo from one farm in Campania and ages it in their caves for 8–12 months. It's mild and sweet, even when fully aged.

Pasteurized: No; Country: Italy (Campania)

 Kashkaval

This salty, sharp, slightly bitter, traditionally sheep's milk cheese, popular in Bulgaria, Romania, Serbia, Slovakia, and Macedonia, is thought to be the original caciocavallo. Referred to as "the cheddar of the Balkans," it's also called katschkawalj or caşcaval.

Pasteurized: Either; Country: Bulgaria, Romania, Serbia, Slovakia, Macedonia

Ragusano PDO

Raw milk from cows grazing on herb-rich pastures around Ragusa, in southeastern Sicily, has been used to produce this huge (26½–35lb), step-shaped caciocavallo for centuries. The pale rind darkens with age and the elastic interior becomes harder and tangier.

Pasteurized: No; Country: Italy (Sicily)

Scamorza

This mild cheese made in southern Italy has caciocavallo's typical gourd shape and elastic stretched-curd body. It was traditionally produced for quick sale while caciocavallo was aging. The dark brown, smoked version is most popular.

Pasteurized: Either; Country: Italy (Puglia, Abruzzo, Basilicata, Molise)

provolone

A traditional stretched-curd southern Italian cheese, the popularity of which spread to the lush, cattle-rearing north by the 18th century, the name provolone likely derives from Neapolitan dialect *pruvà*, meaning "taste." The four basic shapes have many size variations with their own descriptive names, such as sausage-shaped *pancettone* and *salamino*; melon-shaped *mandarino* and *provoletta*; truncated cones called *gigante* and *gigantone*; and pear-shaped, or bottle-shaped, *fiaschetta*. Typically looped with string and tied at the top so they can be hung to age in pairs in the same way as the similar caciocavallo (see page 80), provolone has a higher fat content and matures more slowly than caciocavallo.

Serve: with Italian mustard fruits (*mostarda di frutta*) and crusty bread.
Drink: a full-bodied red, like Nebbiolo, with *piccante*; a softer Beaujolais-style red with *dolce*.

Provolone cheese is made by stretching the curds while they are still warm.

Provolone Valpadana PDO

Provolone has become so entrenched in Italy's north that the first PDO provolone hails traditionally from Lombardy (also made in Emilia Romagna, Trentino-Alto Adige, and Veneto). There are two variations: *dolce*, made with calf's rennet, is eaten young, while *piccante*, containing lamb's or kid's rennet, is aged for at least three months; either may be smoked. Sizes range from 1lb to 220lb.

Size: Various shapes/sizes (see above); Affinage: *dolce* **1–3 months**

Tasting notes: A thin, smooth, pale yellow to old-gold-colored rind covers a smooth, supple, off-white interior, which may have a few scattered eyes and become slightly flaky with age. Dolce, usually eaten sliced or melted, is mild; piccante, usually grated, is tangier.

Pasteurized: Either; Country: Italy (Emilia Romagna, Lombardy, Trentino-Alto Adige, Veneto)

Provolone del Monaco DOC

A hard, smooth, slightly cracked rind covers a firm, off-white interior with small eyes. These 4½–11lb orbs from Campania, mild and sweet when young, become slightly spicy with age. Previously called caciocavallo del monaco, a PDO application has been filed.

Pasteurized: No; Country: Italy (Campania)

American Provolone

BelGioioso Cheese Inc. produces provolone in a range of shapes (from 7¾oz balls to 198lb sausages), and strengths (mild, medium, sharp, and extra-sharp), which have won many American Cheese Society Awards. American provolone is sometimes called provola.

Pasteurized: Either; Country: USA (Wisconsin)

Provola delle Madonie

This pear-shaped provolone from Sicily weighs 2lb and is aged for 10–15 days. The smooth, thin, yellow rind covers a mild, firm, supple, pale yellow interior. Up to 20% sheep's or goat's milk may be mixed with the cow's milk.

Pasteurized: Either; Country: Italy (Sicily)

Provoleta (Provolone Parrillero)

Provoleta, an Argentinian brand of sausage-shaped provolone, has become a generic name for provolone parrillero. Sliced into disks and grilled at the beginning of an *asado* ("barbecue"), it's often seasoned with chile or oregano and served with *chimichurri* (a kind of green sauce).

Pasteurized: Yes; Country: Argentina, Uruguay

saganaki—frying cheeses

Saganaki, a small two-handled Greek frying pan, has given its name to
any dish of fried cheese, as it's the vessel often used to prepare this popular
Greek snack. Any cheese can be coated and fried, but those low in moisture or previously subjected
to high heat hold together even without a coating. Often bland in their raw state, they come into
their own when heated. Stretched-curd cheeses such as Kasseri (see page 87) and halloumi—firmer
cousins of mozzarella (see page 76), where the curds are worked more strenuously to expel more
whey—are classic frying cheeses, as is kefalotyri (see page 253).

Serve: pan-fried to a crisp golden skin and soft interior, with a squeeze of lemon.
Drink: an aromatic Greek moschofilero or dry rosé.

Halloumi curds are drained before being stretched in hot water.

 Halloumi

Traditionally made from sheep's, or blended sheep's and goat's milk, Cyprus' national cheese increasingly includes less-seasonal cow's milk. Also popular throughout Greece and the Middle East (hâlûm in Egypt, hellim in Turkey, "kebab cheese" in Lebanon), in the USA and Canada the name "halloumi" can be used only for the Cypriot cheese. A PDO application has been filed.

Size: Flat block, about 9oz; Affinage: None to 1 month

Tasting notes: White, springy, bland, and squeaky when raw, it fries to a pliable texture with a mellow, slightly lactic tang, pleasant saltiness, and subtle herbal notes from the central vein of dried mint. Cow's milk versions turn rubbery quickly as they cool.

Pasteurized: Either; Country: Cyprus

Formaella Arachovas Parnassou PDO

Originally made by shepherds on Greece's Mount Parnassus, the curd is shaped in wicker cylinders and immersed in hot whey. This mild, dense cheese can be aged for grating or fried, releasing milky aromas and sweet savory flavors.

Pasteurized: Either; Country: Greece (Boeotia)

Batzos PDO

The curd for this semi-hard to hard, brined northern Greek cheese is stirred and reheated, expelling excess whey and butterfat, producing a firm, dry texture. It is salty and slightly sour with a buttery aroma when fried.

Pasteurized: No; Country: Greece (Thessaly, Macedonia)

Sfela PDO

The curd for this southern Greek Feta-like cheese (see page 58) is finely cut, then reheated, giving it a denser texture than Feta and the nickname *Feta tis Fotias* ("Feta of the Fire"). Saltier than Feta, its tangy, creamy taste is stronger when fried.

Pasteurized: Either; Country: Greece (Peloponnese)

Queso Blanco

This large family of firm, salty fresh white cheeses, also called queso fresco, are found all over Latin America. Probably introduced by Spanish settlers, many have curds pressed and scalded sufficiently to hold their shape when heated—ideal for frying.

Pasteurized: Either; Country: Mexico, Peru

other stretched-curd cheeses

Stretched-curd cheeses, also called "string cheese," are made all over the world. Many, however, are traditionally from Italy (including mozzarella, see page 76; caciocavallo, page 80, and provolone, page 82) so the Italian name, *pasta filata* (literally, "spun paste") is often heard. Many can be grilled or fried without melting away into an oily mass, as they've already been heated during their manufacturing process. They soften beautifully while still retaining some shape; the softer, moister ones, such as mozzarella, form delicious strings, while the firmer ones, such as halloumi (see page 85), wilt but remain firm, developing a crisp outside and yielding center.

Serve: with crispbread or crackers.
Drink: a brown ale or full-bodied white wine such as viognier.

The cheese-producing town of Metsovo lies in the mountainous region of Epirus.

Metsovone PDO

A recently created smoked Greek cheese and one of the few made primarily from cow's milk (with up to 20% goat's or sheep's milk), Metsovone derives its name from the Vlach-speaking mountain town of Metsovo (in northwestern Greece) combined with Italian "provolone," on which it was modeled when local boys were sent to Italy in the 1950s to learn cheesemaking.

Size: 3–10lb sausages; Affinage: Minimum 3 months

Tasting notes: The pale yellow interior darkens toward the smoked rind; the campfire aroma and salty, smoky flavors meld with the milky, savory notes, which become slightly peppery with age. The distinctive sausage shape is coated in paraffin wax.

Pasteurized: No; Country: Greece (Epirus)

Kasseri PDO

From northwestern Greece and the island of Lesvos, the best are pure sheep's milk, though some contain up to 20% goat's milk. Young wheels or loaves are semi-hard, sweet, and slightly tangy, becoming firmer, saltier, and spicier with age.

Pasteurized: Either; Country: Greece (Macedonia, Thessaly, Thrace, Lesvos)

Asadero

This Mexican cheese comes in varied sizes and shapes, including bricks, balls, and braids. A thin, pale rind encloses a firm, smooth, off-white interior with a few small eyes and mild, buttery, slightly tangy flavor. Similar to queso oaxaca (see page 79).

Pasteurized: Yes; Country: Mexico (Oaxaca)

Slovenská Parenica PGI

This fresh, white, Slovakian sheep's milk cheese is stretched into long strips, wound from either end into s-shaped spirals, tied and lightly smoked, producing a salty, slightly tangy, smoky flavor. Most commercial non-PGI versions are cow's milk and oval-shaped.

Pasteurized: No; Country: Slovakia (Pohronie)

Stracciata

In Italy's Abruzzo and Molise, ribbons of white stretched-curd cow's milk cheese are folded into blocks resembling large halloumi (see page 85) and eaten immediately or aged for a week to a spreadable consistency. Puglia's buffalo milk stracciatella di bufala is similar.

Pasteurized: No; Country: Italy (Abruzzo, Molise)

bloomy rind cheeses

There are three subgroups of cheese with bloomy rinds:

• those with a snowy covering of white mold, called *duvet blanc* ("white down") in French, such as camembert (see page 96)

• those with a mottled coating of mixed blue, gray, green, and white molds; often goat's milk cheeses (see page 110)

• washed rind cheeses (see page 114) that also grow a dusting of white mold over their orange rind, such as Pont-l'Évêque (see page 137)

Camembert and brie (see pages 92 and 96), the best-known examples of this large family of cheeses, are most people's introduction to surface-mold-ripened cheeses. While modern food science has taught us to fear the combination of mold and food, many traditional fermented foods and drinks (such as bread, salami, sauerkraut, vinegar, beer, and wine) are created by harnessing the beneficial effects of molds and related yeasts. Have you noticed how the rind of brie smells mushroomy? That's because mushrooms are a fungus, a type of mold.

Like many ancient foods, cheeses ripened with surface molds were probably discovered by accident. Cheese, invented long before refrigeration, was traditionally stored in cellars or caves, which often have a distinctly moldy smell. Airborne molds living in these cool, damp places settled and grew on the surface of cheese stored there, and when eaten (out of necessity), they were found to have an appealing soft texture and delicious taste.

The first surface molds used in cheesemaking were the mixed blue-gray variety, including strains of ivory-colored *Geotrichum candidum*, common on goat cheeses, and blue *Penicillium roqueforti*, used in most blue-veined cheeses. Only relatively recently have scientists isolated *Penicillium candidum* and the related *Penicillium camemberti* and cultivated them, enabling cheesemakers to create an attractive, pure white, bloomy mold rind.

Selected molds are usually added to the fresh milk (though they can also be sprayed onto the formed cheeses later), then, as for all cheeses, the solid curds are separated from the liquid whey. This is usually done quite gently when making surface-ripened cheeses, to avoid breaking up the curds more than necessary, retaining as much moisture as possible in them. The drained cheeses are removed from their hoops, salted (either with dry salt or in brine) to partially seal the surface, and left to ripen in a cool, humid environment.

Within four or five days, a bloomy white or mottled blue-gray mold develops on the surface. The mold then sends shoots (or spores) from the surface toward the center of the cheese,

Penicillium candidum mold is used to create the characteristic soft, white rind of bloomy rind cheeses.

slowly breaking down the firm interior to the oozy, yielding mass characteristic of fully ripe brie. The cheese ripens from the outside in, and when only half-ripe will have a soft creamy paste just under the rind with a distinct chalky center. The molds break down the firm cheese, creating the creamy, buttery flavor and texture that makes cheeses such as brie a great introduction to surface-ripened cheeses.

By the time it's very ripe, a surface-ripened cheese may have a mottled patchy rind and a slight smell of ammonia. How ripe you like your bloomy rind cheeses and whether or not you want to cut the rind off before eating them is a matter of personal taste. If you're unsure, start with the firmer, whiter cheeses and work your way up to the more feral-looking mixed mold versions. But do give them a try; remember, we wouldn't have bread, vinegar, or wine if it weren't for helpful molds and yeasts.

french brie

To many people "bloomy rind cheese" means brie and camembert (see page 96), and they consider the two synonymous. While they're certainly closely related, a number of key differences, notably the region of production and size, distinguish them. Authentic brie, usually in large wheels (11–15in in diameter and 2–6½lb), comes from the region around Paris (the Île-de-France) and is generally named for the town in which it's made, while camembert, a later development, comes from farther north in Normandy. Traditionally made from raw milk, brie's barely cut curd is hand-ladled into molds (using a "brie shovel"), before being sprayed with *Penicillium candidum* and aged for 4–10 weeks.

Serve: with crisp baguette and dried muscatel grapes.
Drink: an Australian chardonnay or French Vouvray to match the rich buttery flavor.

Brie de Meaux ripens in the cellar of cheesemaker Marie France Ganot.

■ ■ 🐄 Brie de Meaux PDO

This classic raw-milk brie has been produced around Meaux, 31 miles east of Paris, since at least the 8th century. Meaux's proximity to the Paris market helped secure a place in history for its cheese, named the "king of cheeses" at the Congress of Vienna tournament in 1815. Fromage de meaux is a pasteurized version made for export.

Size: 5½–6½lb disks, 14–15in diameter; Affinage: 8 weeks
Tasting notes: The velvety white rind develops reddish-brown streaks as it ages and, when fully ripe, the smooth, straw-colored interior oozes and won't hold its shape. A slightly mushroomy, smoky aroma is echoed in a rich, sweet, creamy, almost nutty flavor.
Pasteurized: No; Country: France (Île-de-France)

■ ■ 🐄 Brie de Melun PDO

The only other PDO brie, this smaller (10½–11in) raw milk cheese is saltier, sour from lactic fermentation (Meaux is rennet-curdled), and stronger-flavored, with a redder rind from longer aging (up to 10 weeks). Pasteurized fromage de melun is exported.
Pasteurized: No; Country: France (Île-de-France)

■ ■ 🐄 Le Fougerus

Originally farm-produced for family consumption, commercial production began in the early 1900s. The decorative fern leaf (*fougère*) lightly scents this 6in raw-milk brie-like cheese from Île-de-France, matured for 4 weeks with a supple, sweet, slightly salty interior.
Pasteurized: No; Country: France (Île-de-France)

■ ■ 🐄 Brie de Coulommiers

Some say this smaller (9in) brie is the original one. It's typically eaten young and firm, with a thick white rind and sweet, strong mushroom aroma. A 5½in version, called simply coulommiers, may use pasteurized milk.
Pasteurized: No; Country: France (Île-de-France)

■ ■ 🐄 Brie Noir

"Black" brie, aged for up to a year and rarely seen outside Île-de-France, shrinks to a 12in-wide, ¾in-thick disk with brown, crumbly rind; dense, dark golden interior; and thick, velvety consistency. Locals dunk it into café au lait for breakfast.
Pasteurized: No; Country: France (Île-de-France)

other bries

Terroir (climate, soil, vegetation), breed of cattle, and production method all contribute to the distinctiveness of European cheeses. Their beauty, like that of classic wines, lies in the fact that they cannot be duplicated elsewhere, so the EU has protected many of their names (see page 270). But enthusiastic cheesemakers all over the world have used such classics as benchmarks, producing similar but distinctive cheeses. Size is a common variable among non-French bries, and there's a lot of overlap between what's called brie and what's called camembert (see page 96). Still, some fine cheeses have been created, many acknowledging their inspiration by using "brie" in their name.

Serve: with fresh crusty bread and a little fruity chutney or quince paste.
Drink: soft, fruity red wine, such as Beaujolais nouveau or dolcetto.

Brie can be enjoyed simply with a crusty baguette and good wine.

Somerset Brie

The Lubborn Creamery, in the county of Somerset in England's lush southwest, produces both organic and non-organic brie, as well as cow's and goat's milk camembert, all with milk sourced from local farms. Somerset Brie is one of the UK's best-selling soft cheeses; the organic version won Best Organic Cheese at the 2008 British Cheese Awards.

Size: Small 2lb, large 5lb; Affinage: 4 weeks

Tasting notes: Not released until it's fully mature, this cheese has a firm, bloomy white rind and flowing, custardy, straw-yellow interior. The mild, fresh, sweet flavor is fuller and richer in the larger cheeses, but still less robust than a French brie.

Pasteurized: Yes; Country: UK (England—Somerset)

Cooleeney

Thick-rinded raw-milk Cooleeney from County Cork in the south of Ireland is camembert-like when young, but the patchy white and red rind, soft creamy interior, full rich flavor, and slightly grassy aftertaste of the ripe cheese are definitely brie-like.

Pasteurized: No; Country: Ireland (Cork)

Comox Brie

The soft, creamy interior and rich buttery flavor won this Canadian brie from British Columbia a gold medal at the 2008 World Championship Cheese Contest. It's slightly smaller, thicker, softer, and milder than Comox's award-winning camembert.

Pasteurized: Yes; Country: Canada (British Columbia)

Marin Rouge et Noir Brie

America's oldest continually operating cheese producer—California's Marin French Cheese—produces this naturally ripened brie. The creamy texture, delicate and buttery flavor, and lingering aftertaste intensify with age.

Pasteurized: Yes; Country: USA (California)

Pakipaki Goats' Milk Brie

Named for the white limestone hills around Pakipaki in the wine region of Hawkes Bay on New Zealand's North Island. Goat's milk gives this Te Mata Cheese Company brie a silky, stark white interior and pleasantly tangy flavor.

Pasteurized: Yes; Country: New Zealand (Hawkes Bay)

camembert

To many, brie (see page 92) and camembert are synonymous: mild, French-style cheeses with a white bloomy rind. They're certainly close cousins, both traditionally made from raw milk, the barely cut curds hand-ladled into molds and sprayed with *Penicillium candidum* (or *Penicillum camemberti*, a strain of the same mold). There are, however, a few differences, including region of production and size. Camembert comes from Normandy (in France's northwest), famous for apples, especially cider and Calvados (apple brandy); brie comes from Île-de-France (around Paris). Camembert is generally smaller and shorter-aged, rarely reaching the oozing ripeness of brie, remaining firmer with a supple, not flowing, interior.

Serve: with redcurrant jelly and slices of soft baguette.
Drink: hard apple cider.

Roydon Camembert is produced on Fairview wine estate near Cape Town, South Africa.

▪ ▮ 🐄 Camembert de Normandie PDO

Legend says that Abbé Gobert, a priest fleeing Meaux during the French Revolution, taught Marie Harel of Camembert, a tiny village in Normandy, to make brie-style cheese. The innovation of wooden cheese boxes around 1890 (see page 136) made transportation easier and its popularity spread. Non-PDO camembert is made by ultrafiltration for export.

Size: Minimum 5oz, 4in diameter; Affinage: Minimum 21 days

Tasting notes: Locals often prefer camembert 2–3 weeks old, with an intact, velvety, white rind; occasional orange-reddish stripe; and mushroom aroma. Moitié affiné (half-aged), the pale cream-colored center is firm with soft, creamy edges, giving two textures and flavors in each mouthful.

Pasteurized: No; Country: France (Normandy)

▪ ▮ 🐄 Camembert au Calvados

This cheese combines Normandy's famous cheese and apples. The rind is peeled off a young camembert and the naked cheese is soaked in Calvados, then coated in fresh breadcrumbs, producing a soft cheese with a distinct apple-brandy flavor.

Pasteurized: No; Country: France (Normandy)

🇿🇦 🐄 🐐 Roydon Camembert

Produced on Fairview wine estate near Cape Town in South Africa, from cow's milk and cream with 25% goat's milk, this creamy, supple cheese with slight "barnyard" flavors has repeatedly won gold medals at the World Cheese Awards.

Pasteurized: Yes; Country: South Africa (Western Cape)

▪ ▮ 🐄 St. Killian

These 9oz hexagonal cheeses are made by a French cheesemaker in Ireland's County Wexford with milk from the farm's own herd. With a strong mushroomy aroma, buttery and faintly herbal flavor, and velvety white rind, they closely resemble the real thing.

Pasteurized: Yes; Country: Ireland (Wexford)

🇺🇸 🐄 🐑 Hudson Valley Camembert

New York's Old Chatham Shepherding Company combines its sheep's milk with local cow's milk and cream, producing small, square cheeses with a velvety, white rind. Aged for 3 weeks, they're mild and buttery with a semi-firm interior.

Pasteurized: Yes; Country: USA (New York)

other french white mold cheeses

French cheese has been ripened under white and gray molds for many hundreds of years. Each area has its specialties, most named for a village or town near which they're made, such as Bougon, Olivet, Chaource, and Dreux. Some such as brie (see page 92) and camembert (see page 96) have become famous and imitated worldwide; some of the lesser-known ones are exported and worth seeking out at home; while others are a treat to discover when visiting France. White-rinded cheeses come in a range of shapes beyond the usual disks, including *bonde* ("cylinder"), *carré* ("square"), *briquette* ("small loaf"), and *coeur* ("heart").

Serve: with crusty French bread.
Drink: Chablis; the natural acidity will cut through the richness of these creamy cheeses.

A traditional painted plate from Picardie depicts the local Neufchâtel cheese.

■ ■ 🐄 Neufchâtel PDO

This ancient cheese from just north of Paris was being exported to Britain by the late 1700s. A little ripe cheese is kneaded into the curd, making it slightly grainy, before it's formed in cylindrical, square, brick, or heart-shaped molds. Eaten relatively young, usually after 3 weeks, it inspired American Neufchâtel (see page 53).

Size: Usually 3½–7oz; Affinage: Minimum 10 days
Tasting notes: The dry, velvety, white rind smells of mushrooms and is quite salty, developing patches of red with age, while the smooth, firm, cream-colored interior has a distinctive graininess, tasting savory and becoming spicier with age.

Pasteurized: Either; Country: France (Upper Normandy, Picardie)

■ ■ 🐄 Chaource PDO

With a higher fat content than many similar cheeses, these light-textured drums from Champagne and Burgundy have melt-in-the-mouth texture, runny edges, and smooth, buttery flavor when aged, but are often eaten young (2–4 weeks) when still chalky-centered, mild, and milky.

Pasteurized: Either; Country: France (Champagne-Ardenne, Burgundy)

■ ■ 🐄 Olivet Cendré

A dusty, pale-gray cheese from the Loire, rolled in ash to preserve it while it ripens over 3 months (*cendre* means "ash"). The supple interior has a somewhat pungent, spicy aroma. Recent versions scent the rind with hay or pepper.

Pasteurized: Yes; Country: France (Loire)

■ ■ 🐄 Dreux a la Feuille

Produced in the town of Dreux, not far from the classic brie region, these camembert-sized cheeses are ripened with chestnut leaves between them to prevent them sticking (*feuille* means "leaf"). The leaves impart a faintly nutty aroma and flavor.

Pasteurized: Either; Country: France (Centre)

■ ■ 🐐 Bougon

This camembert-like cheese is made by a cooperative in Bougon in the area of La Mothe-St.-Heray in western France. It has a firm white interior and grassy flavor typical of goat's milk. A pasteurized version, La Mothe, is exported.

Pasteurized: No (thermized); Country: France (Poitou-Charentes)

ashed white mold cheeses

French goat cheeses were traditionally coated in salt mixed with ash from burnt grapevine clippings to preserve them through winter. The ash provides a protective coating, absorbs excess moisture, and neutralizes surface acidity, enabling a bloomy rind to develop. Many classic goat cheeses, such as Sainte-Maure de Touraine (see page 107), have a coating of ash under their mottled surface. Recently cheesemakers have utilized ash, usually from burnt dried vegetable matter, to create a point of difference for all sorts of cheeses. Mainly decorative, it tends to soften the slightly acidic taste of fresh goat cheeses. See also Humboldt Fog (page 141) and Olivet Cendré (page 99).

Serve: with chilled fresh grapes.
Drink: Mâconnais or other white Burgundy.

Though milk is sourced from domestic breeds, Jim Schott named his dairy after Colorado's mountain goats.

Haystack Peak

Colorado's Haystack Mountain Goat Dairy, started by Jim Schott in 1989, was at the forefront of the introduction of goat cheese in the USA. The company, now part-owned by employee-shareholders, no longer produces its own milk, but purchases it locally and still maintains artisanal cheesemaking traditions. Its flagship, Haystack Peak, is named after a local mountain.

Size: 2lb truncated pyramid; Affinage: About 14 days

Tasting notes: Coated in vegetable ash and covered with bloomy white mold, this truncated pyramid has a firm, smooth, delicately flavored, off-white interior with a slight tang and hint of minerality, becoming runny around the edges as it ages.

Pasteurized: Yes; Country: USA (Colorado)

Crow's Ash Brie

This organic Australian cheese from Queensland won silver at the 2008 World Cheese Awards. A thin layer of ash with patches of white mold covers a firm, pale yellow, buttery interior with smoky, nutty, mushroom flavors and aromas.

Pasteurized: Yes; Country: Australia (Queensland)

Dorstone

These short cylinders from England's Herefordshire have a delicate, wrinkled, mixed mold rind over a coating of charcoal ash and a light, fragile interior with a sweet, very mild, fresh flavor, perfect for people new to goat cheese.

Pasteurized: No; Country: UK (England—Herefordshire)

Cendré de Lune DuVillage 1860

This ash-coated triple-cream (see page 102) cylinder from Quebec has a fine velvety coating, mushroomy aroma, and slightly peppery flavor. It has a slightly acidic, chalky center when young, becoming creamier and buttery with age.

Pasteurized: Yes; Country: Canada (Quebec)

Tymsboro

Truncated pyramids of raw sheep's milk cheese made by Somerset's Sleight Farm from March to November, the white mold rind may have greenish-gray tinges or rusty red patches. The firm, delicate interior is rich, lemony, and sweet.

Pasteurized: No; Country: UK (England—Somerset)

triple-cream cheeses

Decadent triple-cream cheeses were created in the early 1900s in Normandy by diverting precious cream from buttermaking to cheesemaking, adding it to milk to raise the fat content to 75%. They became more common in the 1950s when intensive dairy farming made butter a commodity. Not all triple-creams grow white mold, but those that do, such as St. André, are usually very fluffy, so they are often left unwrapped to keep the snowlike mold unmarked. Usually thick disks or cubes with a firm yet supple texture and mild, buttery flavor, the best cut through the richness with slight acidity. They're sometimes decorated with herbs or spices.

Serve: with sourdough baguette.
Drink: yeasty vintage Champagne, matching luxury with luxury.

Milk from cows in the Normandy region of France was traditionally used to produce Brillat-Savarin.

■ ▮ 🐄 Brillat-Savarin

First made in Normandy in the 1930s, and based on a 19th-century cheese, l'Excelsior, most Brillat-Savarin is now made around Paris by both factory and artisan producers. Named for 19th-century French gastronome Jean Anthelme Brillat-Savarin, who said, "a meal without cheese is like a beautiful woman with one eye."

Size: Squat, 15oz–1lb cylinders; Affinage: 1–2 weeks

Tasting notes: The soft, white mold and firm, moist interior slowly break down over 5–6 weeks to show hints of yellow rind and a smooth, unctuous texture. It has a rich, sweet, buttery taste, with a slight, pleasant tang.

Pasteurized: Either; Country: France (Normandy, Île-de-France)

■ ▮ 🐄 Explorateur

Factory-made near Paris in small and large drum-shapes and named for the first US satellite, Explorer 1. A downy mold covers a firm, moist, creamy, off-white interior with mild, buttery, salty, vaguely mushroomy flavors, ripening to a pleasant nuttiness.

Pasteurized: Either; Country: France (Île-de-France)

▦ 🐄 Jindi Triple Cream

This artisanal block from Victoria is Australia's best-known triple-cream. A thick, fluffy, white mold rind covers a smooth golden-yellow interior with a moist, supple, cakey texture and rich, smooth, buttery taste, developing mushroomy and slight ammonia characters with age.

Pasteurized: Yes; Country: Australia (Victoria)

■ ▮ 🐄 Pierre Robert

This artisan cheese from Fromagerie Rouzaire near Paris has a downy mold; lightly straw-colored, soft, moist interior; and typical, sweet, buttery taste with a slight tang. Fully mature, the texture is mousse-like and the rind can become thick and hard.

Pasteurized: Either; Country: France (Île-de-France)

▤ 🐐 🐄 Minuet

Enriched with cow's milk crème fraîche, California's Minuet combines the richness of traditional triple-creams with the tanginess and fine texture of goat cheese. Under the soft white mold, the interior matures from firm and cakey to almost molten.

Pasteurized: Yes; Country: USA (California)

double-cream cheeses

Like their triple-cream close cousins (see page 102), double-cream cheeses
are mild, creamy, and smooth. Many are rindless, while others grow a white
mold rind. Generally made from milk enriched with cream (Pavé d'Affinois
is an exception), their fat content is between 60% and 74% (at 75% they
become triple-creams). They have a broad appeal due to their soft, sweet interior
and mild aroma. They are eaten quite young and may be flavored with seasonings such as herbs or
pepper. Many are industrially produced, and ironically, many now have low-fat versions.

Serve: with candied fruits or fruit pastes.
Drink: chenin blanc; its lushness matches these rich cheeses well.

Several popular double cream cheeses are produced in the Rhône-Alpes region of southeastern France.

▮▮ 🐄 🐐 🐑 Pavé d'Affinois

This was the first cheese made by ultrafiltration, a process in which milk is forced through a series of membranes, extracting protein and removing water, resulting in a silkier mouth-feel and creamier flavor. Goat's milk, sheep's milk, and low-fat versions are now also produced in a wide range of sizes.

Size: Thick, 1oz–4½lb squares; Affinage: About 2 weeks
Tasting notes: Often compared to a triple-cream cheese because of its rich flavor and mouth-feel. The cream-colored interior is soft and smooth with a short, creamy, delicate flavor, while the white mold rind has a slight aroma of mushrooms.
Pasteurized: Yes; Country: France (Rhône-Alpes)

▮▮ 🐄 Boursault

Tasting somewhat like a mild, dense brie (see page 92), this small, thick, factory-produced disk is soft and creamy with a slightly acidic tang and very faint mushroom aroma from its thin dusting of white mold.

Pasteurized: Either; Country: France (Île-de-France)

▮▮ 🐄 🐐 Saint Felicien

When ripe, these small, soft, pale disks, protected in a stoneware crock, taste slightly nutty and are spoonable at room temperature. The wrinkled yellow rind has a light dusting of white mold. Goat's milk versions are occasionally seen.

Pasteurized: Either; Country: France (Rhône-Alpes)

▮▮ 🐄 Gratte-Paille

This loaf-shaped artisan cheese from the region around Paris has a firm, white mold rind with a rich, dense, almost oily texture; custard-colored interior; and rich, sweetly creamy flavor.

Pasteurized: Either; Country: France (Île-de-France)

▮▮ 🐄 Boursin

These small, tasty disks from Upper Normandy, in their familiar white and green boxes, are creamy and rindless with a good shelf life. Flavorings such as the original garlic and herbs or black pepper give them broad appeal.

Pasteurized: Yes; Country: France (Upper Normandy)

chèvre de la loire

The most famous goat cheeses (chèvre in French) come from
the fertile plains along the River Loire (in the regions of Loire,
Poitou-Charentes, Centre, and Burgundy), where Arabs from Spain
introduced goats in the early Middle Ages. The Arabs were repelled,
but their goats and tradition of goat cheesemaking spread throughout France. Six very similar
PDO-accredited chèvres, distinguished mainly by their shapes, are produced in different villages
along the Loire. The name of the cylindrical Chabichou du Poitou PDO comes from *chebli*, Arabic
for "goat," as it was made by Arabs who remained in the hills near Poitiers after the Moors' defeat.
Chèvre holds its shape well when heated.

Serve: on a salad of bitter greens (such as endive) with walnuts.
Drink: Sancerre, Pouilly fumé, or any sauvignon blanc; they're classic goat cheese wines.

Crottin de Chavignol has a hard, wrinkled surface and develops an almost meaty texture with age.

▮ ▮ 🐐 Sainte-Maure de Touraine PDO

This ashed, log-shaped cheese, from the regions of Poitou-Charentes and Centre, has a wheat straw through the middle to help hold the fresh curd together and aerate the center, assisting ripening. A widely copied cheese, the name "sainte-maure" can be used for any goat cheese log, and pasteurized non-PDO versions are produced with the distinctive straw. Usually aged for 2–4 weeks.

Size: About 9oz; Affinage: Minimum 10 days
Tasting notes: The most "goaty" tasting of the Loire chèvres is usually aged until gray and white mold mottles the rind and the smooth, firm interior becomes dark ivory with a balanced salty sourness and walnut aroma. Sometimes eaten before a rind develops.
Pasteurized: No; Country: France (Centre, Poitou-Charentes)

▮ ▮ 🐐 Crottin de Chavignol PDO

These drum-shaped cheeses with a hard, wrinkled surface and balanced, salty, sweet-sour flavor are made in the regions of Loire, Centre, and Burgundy. With age they develop an almost meaty texture. Crottin de champcol is a similar, pasteurized, non-PDO cheese.

Pasteurized: No; Country: France (Burgundy, Loire, Centre)

▮ ▮ 🐐 Pouligny-Saint-Pierre PDO

Nicknamed "Eiffel Tower" for its tall, thin, pyramid shape with flattened tip, this chèvre from Centre is often aged for 4–5 weeks until the multihued rind becomes knobby and the white interior develops a salty sweetness and pleasantly sour aftertaste.

Pasteurized: No; Country: France (Centre)

▮ ▮ 🐐 Selles-sur-Cher PDO

These 3in charcoal-coated disks from Centre are often eaten a little younger than other chèvres, rind and all. Aged to 4 weeks, the blue-gray rind becomes knobby and the moist, almost claylike interior, salty and sour with a slight sweetness.

Pasteurized: Either; Country: France (Centre)

▮ ▮ 🐐 Valençay PDO

It's said that this ashed truncated pyramid from Centre lost its top to Napoleon's sword because it reminded him of his failed Egyptian campaign. The rind is blue-gray after 3 weeks and the firm, moist interior is salty and tangy.

Pasteurized: No; Country: France (Centre)

other french chèvres

Small, agile, and willing to eat almost anything, goats provide milk in areas inhospitable to cows. France produces hundreds of goat's milk cheeses; some are eaten fresh, while others are aged to develop a mottled rind and coated in ash, herbs, or spices, or preserved in oil. Many names derive from ancient regional languages or dialects, showing their ties to earlier times. All are produced seasonally, from early spring to late autumn, or in reduced quantities from October to February during kidding season. Usually small (2–9oz), they come in a range of shapes: drum (*crottin*, meaning "dung," referring to the flat disk shape), disk, cylinder (*bonde* meaning "plug"), log, pyramid, and truncated pyramid.

Serve: with lightly blanched asparagus dressed with olive oil.
Drink: French rosé such as rosé d'Anjou.

Chèvre soufflé and asparagus with pine nuts makes an excellent appetizer.

▋▋🐐 Rocamadour PDO

Cabécou, meaning "small goat" in the Langue d'Oc, the old language of southern France, refers to small disks of goat cheese from this area. The most prized, praised in 15th-century documents, is cabécou de Rocamadour, from the milk of goats grazing on the plains near the town of Rocamadour, built into the rocky side of a deep canyon.

Size: 1–1¹/₂oz; Affinage: 1–4 weeks

Tasting notes: The thin white rind becomes mottled and dark beige with age, developing occasional patches of blue-gray mold. The very soft, creamy interior smells faintly of milk and mushrooms and has a light, sweetly milky flavor with a hint of hazelnut.

Pasteurized: No; Country: France (Midi-Pyrénées)

▋▋🐐 Figue

Draining in a twisted cloth gives these fist-sized cheeses from southwestern France their distinctive fig shape. A thin white mold grows on the uneven surface, which may be coated in ash, herbs, or paprika. The mature interior is crumbly.

Pasteurized: No; Country: France (Aquitaine)

▋▋🐐🐄 Mâconnais

These small, tapered cylinders from Burgundy, also called chevreton de Mâcon, may also be made from cow's milk or a blend of cow's and goat's milk. The dense interior has faintly herbal aromas. A PDO application has been filed.

Pasteurized: No; Country: France (Burgundy)

▋▋🐐 Picodon AOC

Picodon means "spicy" in the old language of the south, as goats in southeastern France graze on aromatic plants that scent their milk. There's a range of small, hard, puck-shaped Picodons, including Picodon l'Ardeche PDO and Picodon de la Drôme PDO.

Pasteurized: Either; Country: France (Rhône-Alpes, Provence-Alpes-Côte-d'Azur, Languedoc-Roussillon)

▋▋🐐 Pélardon PDO

Goat's milk cheeses have long been known as Pélardon in Languedoc. Similar to Picodon, they have a thin rind that changes from cream to beige with age and a firm interior with a nutty flavor.

Pasteurized: No; Country: France (Languedoc-Roussillon)

mixed mold cheeses

Soft goat cheeses, often called chèvre, meaning "goat" in French, are usually set naturally with very little rennet. The curds are neither cooked nor pressed, producing a very fine-textured cheese. They're often coated in salted ash, which encourages a rind of mottled blue-gray molds rather than the pure white rind often seen on cow's milk cheeses. While this can look intimidating, the fine-textured, pure white cheese underneath is usually quite firm and mild, with the distinctive herbal tang of goat's milk. Ashed cheeses tend to be saltier than those not ashed, as the ash is usually mixed with salt.

Serve: with crusty bread, olives, and jamon (Spanish raw ham) or prosciutto (Italian raw ham).
Drink: fruity white wine such as gewürztraminer or soft fruity reds like Chilean merlot.

Prosciutto and olives are good accompaniments to these mixed mold cheeses.

Monte Enebro

Made by Rafael Baez in Castile-Léon in northwestern Spain, this cheese was voted one of the Best Spanish Cheeses of 2007 by the Spanish government. The curds are inoculated with blue mold, but not pierced, as most blue-veined cheeses are (see page 160), so the mold grows only on the surface without creating veining through the cheese.

Size: Brick-shaped with rounded corners; Affinage: About 3 weeks
Tasting notes: The thin, ash-coated rind grows a mottling of white, brown, and blue-gray mold. The firm, dense, chalky, creamy interior is off-white with creamy, lemony, herbal flavors that intensify, becoming more goaty and pungent with age.
Pasteurized: Yes; Country: Spain (Castile-Léon)

Gamalost

The blue-brown mold on the hard, wrinkled rind of this Norwegian cheese gives it its name (which means "old cheese"). The brown-yellow interior with streaks of blue is soft when young, becoming hard and used for grating when aged.
Pasteurized: Either; Country: Norway

Garrotxa

A traditional cheese revived by a cooperative of young farmers in Catalonia in southeastern Spain. The gray-brown suede-like rind, dotted with white and pink mold, covers a smooth, firm, moist, cream-colored interior with buttery, slightly nutty flavors and milky aroma.
Pasteurized: Either; Country: Spain (Catalonia)

Saint-Marcellin

The mild, creamy interior of these small, traditionally goat's milk, disks from southeastern France becomes molten with age, the thin, wrinkled rind developing patches of white and blue-gray mold. Le pitchou is young saint-marcellin marinated in grapeseed oil with herbes de Provence.
Pasteurized: Either; Country: France (Rhône-Alpes)

Queijo Serpa PDO

When fully ripe, the bulging, thin, leathery rind of this Portuguese sheep's milk cheese is dusted with white and blue-gray mold. The top is cut open and the ivory-colored, buttery, sweet-sour interior, with its bitter, fruity notes, is scooped out.
Pasteurized: No; Country: Portugal (Alentejo)

leaf-wrapped cheeses

Before modern packaging, leaves were used to wrap food for transport or storage; this tradition has remained with some classic cheeses and been adapted to create new ones. Wrapping helps preserve cheeses by insulating them from air and sometimes because of the tannin in certain leaves; the leaves can also scent and flavor the ripening cheeses. Italian robiolas (see page 146) are often wrapped in leaves as diverse as fig and cabbage while a number of US dairies have created modern wrapped cheeses, including Rogue River Blue, wrapped in pear brandy-dipped vine leaves, and Sally Jackson Sheep wrapped in local chestnut leaves. See also Queso de Valdeón (page 175).

Serve: with walnuts, apple slices, and plain crackers.
Drink: Belgian fruit beer or Alsatian pinot blanc.

Carol Gray, the founder of Cornish Yarg, named her cheese by spelling her name backwards.

■ ■ 🐐 Banon PDO

As with many AOC wines, the rules for making this ancient cheese (named for a town in Provence in southeastern France) are quite strict, dictating the breed of goats, maximum yield of milk, and animals' eating regime. Young cheese is wrapped in brown chestnut leaves, which may be soaked in eau-de-vie, then tied with raffia and ripened.

Size: 3¹/₂oz, 3in-wide disks; Affinage: Minimum 15 days

Tasting notes: Beneath the brown leaves, the thin, wrinkled, creamy yellow rind develops patches of blue-gray mold as it ages. The firm, crumbly, white interior softens to a creamy, velvety texture with age as its milky, slightly tangy, nutty flavor becomes more complex.

Pasteurized: No; Country: France (Provence)

■ ■ 🐐 Caciotta Capra Foglie di Noce

The name of this 5¹/₂lb disk from Italy's Veneto region (literally "goat cheese walnut leaves") says it all. Covered in browned walnut leaves, the firm, ivory-colored interior has a robust flavor and distinct taste and aroma of walnuts.

Pasteurized: No (thermized); Country: Italy (Veneto)

🏴󠁧󠁢󠁥󠁮󠁧󠁿 🐄 Cornish Yarg

This cow's milk cheese from England's southwest is covered in local nettle leaves, which develop a dusting of white mold. The semi-hard, slightly crumbly, ivory-colored interior tastes buttery and lemony, becoming creamier near the rind with age.

Pasteurized: Yes; Country: UK (England—Cornwall)

🇦🇺 🐐 Vigneron

The family behind Woodside Cheese Wrights in South Australia also owns Coriole winery. They wash small disks of fresh goat cheese in chardonnay and wrap them in vine leaves, producing a mild, velvety, earthy cheese with a fruity aroma.

Pasteurized: Yes; Country: Australia (South Australia)

🇺🇸 🐐 O'Banon

One of the first American dairies to produce leaf-wrapped cheeses, Capriole Goat Cheese wraps small disks of cheese in bourbon-soaked chestnut leaves, producing a dense, creamy, savory cheese named for the late Indiana governor Frank O'Bannon.

Pasteurized: Yes; Country: USA (Indiana)

washed rind cheeses

Washed rind cheeses, also called smear-ripened or surface-smear cheeses, are immediately recognizable by their distinctive orange rind. This group of surface-ripened cheeses is similar to bloomy rind cheeses (see page 88) in that they ripen from the outside in toward the center. They differ in that the organism aiding the ripening isn't a mold but a bacterium, *Brevibacterium linens*, which is responsible for the distinctive color and pungent aroma. Some popular cheeses in this category include Port Salut, Munster, and limburger.

Brevibacterium linens thrives in humid environments. To encourage its growth, these cheeses are frequently washed, brushed, or rubbed with liquid, typically water or brine, but also sometimes whey or alcohol (see page 122). The wash is also sometimes infused with herbs and spices or colored, most commonly with annatto (*roccou* in French), the pulp of the seed of achiote, a South American tree. As well as creating a humid environment for the bacteria to grow, the washing can remove excess bacteria, controlling its spread and stopping the rind from becoming too sticky or stinky.

Aroma is the other distinctive quality of these cheeses. Often referred to as gamey or feral, or even likened to smelly socks or gym lockers, the aroma (caused by the action of the bacteria on the rind) can initially intimidate the cheese novice. The interior, however, is often quite mild in smell and flavor, usually with a rich, buttery texture. As with bloomy rind cheeses, you may choose to cut off the rind or just scoop the rich center out of the rind.

Like young mold ripened cheeses, young washed rind cheeses have a creamy soft paste near the rind and a firm chalky center that slowly ripens over a month or more as the bacteria break down the surface of the cheese and work their way toward the center. These cheeses come in a wide range of textures; some such as vacherin (see page 134) breaking down to such an oozy creamy paste that they need to be packaged in wooden boxes to hold their shape, while other larger wheels such as Saint-Nectaire (see page 207) soften without ever becoming runny and are discussed with the semi-hard cheeses of later chapters. Some, such as Pont-l'Évêque (see page 137), are surface-ripened by a combination of both mold and bacteria, developing a dusting of white or mixed mold over their orange rind.

Apart from their distinctive color and aroma, washed rind cheeses tend to have a few other qualities in common. They're usually large, flat wheels or squares, with as much surface area as possible for the bacteria to work on, and they are almost always made from cow's milk. They're generally thought to have been developed in monasteries more than 1,000 years ago.

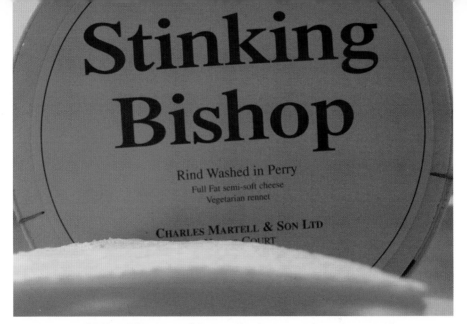

Stinking Bishop has a milder taste than its name and aroma suggest.

Monasteries generally had large landholdings and kept large herds of cows, which provided enough milk from one milking to make a batch of cheese. When cheese is made from such fresh milk, it's quite low in acid and bacteria grow readily on its surface. In contrast, the small peasant farms that grew up around these large medieval monasteries usually kept only one or two cows to provide milk for the family, so in order to make cheese they had to collect milk over several days. The milk from their earlier milkings soured slightly in storage and created a natural "starter" to ferment the warm fresh milk from the most recent milking. Mold is more acid-resistant than bacteria and tended to form on the cheeses made from this more acidic milk. Thus, when monks shared their cheesemaking skills with local peasants, bloomy rind cheeses developed on farms alongside the monastic washed rind cheeses.

trappist cheeses

Trappist monks live "by the work of their hands," selling goods they produce to support themselves. Such monasteries, particularly in France, Belgium, and Switzerland, have produced cheeses since medieval times.

Early monastic codes often forbade red meat or had many meat-free days, so flavorful cheeses provided a satisfying alternative source of protein, and savory, salty, almost meaty-tasting washed rind cheeses became known as "white meat." Trappist-style cheeses spread around Europe and to the New World when monks fled the French Revolution, while those returning after the revolution brought new cheesemaking techniques back with them. See also Abbaye de Belloc (page 245) and Port Salut (page 120).

Serve: with slices of dark or wholegrain bread.
Drink: a Trappist beer such as Chimay.

Huguenot cheese was named for French Protestants who took their cheesemaking skills to South Africa.

Chimay

The Abbey of Notre Dame de Scourmont in Belgium began making cheese in 1876. Today one of only seven monasteries worldwide with Vatican approval to label their products "Trappist," they gather milk from 250 local farms to make three cheeses of different ages (the oldest is over 6 months), plus one washed in their famous Chimay Trappist beer.

Size: 12oz and 5lb wheels; Affinage: Minimum 4 weeks

Tasting notes: The thin orange rind and smooth interior darken with age. The distinct aroma becomes more pungent, though the flavor remains quite mild. When young it's creamy and milky, becoming fruity with a touch of hazelnut and bitterness when fully aged.

Pasteurized: Yes; Country: Belgium (Hainaut)

Maredsous

Originally produced at Belgium's Maredsous Abbey, now made under license by Bel Group in Belgium using French milk, these 2–5lb bricks have a firm, brownish-orange rind dusted with white mold and a mild, pale, supple interior with a hint of smokiness.

Pasteurized: Yes; Country: Belgium

Oka Classique

Named for a Québécois village where French refugee monks established a monastery in the 1890s, these 5lb wheels are now commercially produced in the abbey's original dairy. A pungent, moist, orange rind covers a mild, creamy, slightly nutty interior.

Pasteurized: Yes; Country: Canada (Quebec)

Maroilles (Marolles) PDO

The ancestor of all Trappist cheeses, created in the 10th century at Maroilles Abbey in northern France (burial place of St. Hubert, patron saint of cheesemakers), these thick, red squares are among the most pungent washed rind cheeses.

Pasteurized: Either; Country: France (Picardie, Nord-Pas-de-Calais)

Huguenot

Large, golden-orange wheels named for French Protestant refugees who brought their cheesemaking skills to South Africa in the late 1600s. These repeated World Cheese Awards gold medal winners have a mild, nutty, pale, semi-hard interior with scattered eyes.

Pasteurized: Yes; Country: South Africa (Western Cape)

port salut

The Trappist Abbaye Notre Dame du Port-du-Salut, built in Entrammes
in the Loire Valley in 1815 by monks returning to France after the French
Revolution, initially produced cheese with milk from its own herd. By the
1850s it became so popular that milk was bought from surrounding farms.
The trademark Port-du-Salut was registered in 1874, with imitations, already in existence, adopting
the name Saint-Paulin. Demand for the abbey cheese eventually grew too large for the monks'
facilities and in 1959 they sold the Port-du-Salut brand to a farmers' cooperative, SAFR, later
bought by Bel Group, who produce the industrial version known worldwide today. See also Queso
Nata de Cantabria (page 151) and Esrom (page 261).

Serve: with rye bread and pickles or relish.
Drink: blonde (or golden) ale.

Tamié can be found for sale at local markets in eastern France.

▌▐ 🐄 Mont des Cats

After 1959 the Port-du-Salut monks continued producing an artisanal version of their original cheese, called Fromage de l'Abbaye, but EU regulations governing unpasteurized cheeses became too cost-prohibitive in the 1990s and production ceased. Other abbeys, such as Mont des Cats in northern France, making cheese from the Port-du-Salut recipe since 1850, managed to mechanize sufficiently to continue the tradition.

Size: 4½lb and 1lb wheels; Affinage: About 4 weeks

Tasting notes: Washed and turned by hand in the abbey's cellars, these wheels closely resemble the original cheese from Abbaye Port-du-Salut. A slightly sticky orange rind with traditional barnyard aromas covers a pale, firm, supple interior, with mild, slightly sweet, nutty flavors.

Pasteurized: Yes; Country: France (Nord-Pas-de-Calais)

▌▐ 🐄 Tamié

Another French abbey-produced cheese, made at the ancient Monastery of Tamié in Savoy, founded in 1131. This mild cheese resembles a large Reblochon (see page 125) and is sold wrapped in blue paper decorated with a white Maltese cross.

Pasteurized: No; Country: France (Rhône-Alpes)

▌▐ 🐄 Port Salut

Rather than being washed to encourage the growth of *Brevibacterium linens*, which gives washed rind cheeses their traditional color and aroma, the edible orange rind of this mild industrial version is colored with beta-carotene. Texture is supple and slightly springy.

Pasteurized: Yes; Country: France

▬▬ 🐄 Ridder & Riddar

Swedish Riddar, invented in 1950 in Hova, was named for the annual *Riddarvecka* ("knights' week") tournament. The more widely known Norwegian Ridder followed in 1969. An annatto-colored rind covers a pale, mild, supple, buttery, sweet-savory interior.

Pasteurized: Yes; Country: Norway, Sweden

▌▐ 🐄 Saint-Paulin

Produced all over France and based on the early imitations of the abbey-produced Port-du-Salut, most are virtually identical to today's industrial Port Salut. The best are supple beneath a smooth, thin, orange rind, with a mild lactic aroma and flavor.

Pasteurized: Either; Country: France

alcohol-washed rind cheeses

Fermentation, an ancient form of preservation, produces alcohol and cheese, often in the same region. So it seems natural to wash cheeses in locally produced alcohol, sometimes throughout their ripening, sometimes just in the final washes to add flavor. Wine and beer are the most typical choices, but any alcohol can be used, including cider, perry (pear cider), and spirits. Stinking Bishop from Gloucester, named after a local pear, has a perry-washed rind, while the unrelated Bishop Kennedy is washed in Campbelltown Loch whisky in its final week of ripening. See also camembert au Calvados (page 97), soumaintrain, Époisses (page 137), and Chimay (page 119).

Serve: with dried fruits such as dates, muscatels, or raisins.
Drink: a glass of the alcohol used to wash the rind.

Alcohol-washed rind cheeses pair well with dried fruits such as dates.

🏳️ 🐄 Fromage de Herve PDO

Produced since at least the 15th century, Belgium's best-known cheese is today made in three strengths: *doux* (sweet, aged 4–6 weeks), *piquant* (spicy, aged 5–7 weeks), and the strongest, Remoudou (aged 2–3 months, see page 129). Although Fromage de Herve is typically water-washed, Herve Affiné à la Bière ("matured with beer") is Herve Doux washed in Belgium's famous abbey-brewed beer.

Size: 2oz, 3½oz, 7oz, 14oz cubes; Affinage: 4 weeks–3 months

Tasting notes: These distinctive bright rust-orange cubes have a fudgelike golden interior, relatively sweet taste, and yeasty aroma. Piquant has a spicier flavor and aroma, while the beer gives Affiné à la Bière a hoppy scent and taste.

Pasteurized: Either; Country: Belgium (Liège)

🏳️ 🐐 Saint Vernier

Named for the patron saint of winemakers, and washed in savagnin Arbois wine, this cheese from eastern France has a moist, wrinkled, brownish-orange rind and creamy yellow interior with slightly sour, fruity flavors and a fruity, sometimes slightly ammoniated, aroma.

Pasteurized: Yes; Country: France (Franche-Comté)

🏴󠁧󠁢󠁥󠁮󠁧󠁿 🐐 Stinking Bishop

This flattened disk from England's Gloucestershire is washed with perry (pear cider), developing a pungent aroma and sticky orange rind. Milder tasting than the name and aroma suggest, the pale interior is supple, almost spoonable, when fully ripe.

Pasteurized: Yes; Country: UK (England—Gloucestershire)

🏴󠁧󠁢󠁳󠁣󠁴󠁿 🐄 Bishop Kennedy

Named for a 15th-century bishop of St. Andrews, this Scottish whisky-washed cheese looks like a washed rind brie (see page 92). An orange rind with white mold patches covers a dense, golden, almost oozing interior with smoky, spicy aftertaste.

Pasteurized: No; Country: UK (Scotland—Argyll and Bute)

🏳️ 🐄 Langres PDO

This squat cylinder from France's Champagne, Lorraine, and Burgundy regions, sometimes washed with marc de Champagne, has a pungent, sticky, orange rind and salty, fruity flavor. Sometimes served with champagne poured into the top.

Pasteurized: Either; Country: France (Champagne-Ardenne, Lorraine, Burgundy)

reblochon & taleggio

Not all washed rind cheeses are wildly pungent; two of the most
famous are relatively mild mountain cheeses. A third of all Taleggio
(one of Italy's few washed rind cheeses) is cave-ripened in the
mountains near Val Taleggio in Lombardy, where it originated in the 11th century, while Reblochon
de Savoie, from just across the French border, is nicknamed "the mountain dwarf" because of
its diminutive size among Alpine cheeses; fromage de savoie, a pasteurized non-PDO version,
is exported. Chevrotin, the semi-hard goat's milk cheeses of the Savoy Alps, are among the few
washed rind goat's milk cheeses.

Serve: melted into risotto or polenta, in crepes, or over boiled potatoes.
Drink: a soft red wine such as Beaujolais, gamay, or fruity pinot noir.

Reblochon is one of the cheeses often melted over potatoes to make a classic gratin savoyard.

■ ■ 🐄 Reblochon de Savoie PDO

The name of this cheese from France's Savoy Alps allegedly derives from *reblocher* ("re-pinch the udders") due to the farmers' practice of partially milking their cows, declaring that milking to their landlords for tax purposes, then surreptitiously taking a second milking to produce the richer milk used to make this cheese (see Remoudou, page 129).

Size: 1lb 3oz and 8½oz disks; Affinage: 2–4 weeks

Tasting notes: The thin orange–pink rind is usually coated in a film of white mold, giving a mushroomy aroma. The moist, smooth, supple interior, with occasional eyes, has a creamy, delicately nutty flavor and salty, almost meaty, aftertaste.

Pasteurized: No; Country: France (Rhône–Alpes)

■ ■ 🐄 Beaumont

One of the first industrial raw milk cheeses, this factory-produced version of Tamié (see page 121) created at Beaumont in France's Savoy Alps in 1881 has a Reblochon-style, white mold-dusted, pink–orange rind and supple, straw-colored interior with occasional eyes.

Pasteurized: No; Country: France (Rhône–Alpes)

■ ■ 🐄 Taleggio PDO

The thin, wrinkled, yellowy-pink rind on these thick, 4½lb squares from northern Italy is often dusted with white mold. The meltingly soft, pale interior has buttery, yeasty, nutty, slightly salty flavors, becoming tangier and richer with age.

Pasteurized: Either; Country: Italy (Lombardy, Piedmont, Veneto)

■ ■ 🐐 Chevrotin PDO

Farm-produced in France's Savoy Alps, and modeled on Reblochon, this smooth, mild, goat's milk cheese has a moist, yellow–orange rind with patches of white mold. It was previously known as chevrotin des aravis.

Pasteurized: No; Country: France (Rhône–Alpes)

■ ■ 🐄 Robiola Lombardia

Unlike the round Piedmont robiolas (see page 147), Lombardy's robiolas are square, like small Taleggios, with ridged, brick-red rinds; pale, creamy interiors; and meaty, fruity, salty flavors. Robiola Vecchia Valsassina is an unpasteurized version and Artavaggio a pasteurized one.

Pasteurized: Either; Country: Italy (Lombardy)

pressed washed rind cheeses

Not all washed rind cheeses ripen to a soft, sticky consistency. Some have gentle pressure applied once the curds are in their molds, extracting more moisture and producing a firmer cheese. Many pressed washed rind cheeses are produced in Alpine environments in large wheels with a lower rind-to-cheese ratio, so the surface bacteria play less of a role in ripening and flavoring the cheese. Such mild Alpine cheeses include Stelvio, largely produced at 1,600 to 6,500 feet above sea level; Murols and Saint-Nectaire (see page 207) from the mountains of Auvergne; and Swiss tilsiter (see page 221). Germany's small, firm handkäse is a strongly scented exception.

Serve: with hazelnuts or almonds and sourdough bread.
Drink: a clear fruit-based eau-de-vie or schnapps.

Jules Bérioux, inventor of Murols cheese, named it after his home village in the Auvergne, central France.

▌▌🐄 Murols

Invented in the 1930s by affineur Jules Bérioux, who distinguished the cheese of his French village, Murol, from the similar, better-known cheese from nearby Saint-Nectaire by cutting the center out of the young cheese, creating a distinctive shape and reducing the ripening time. The tradition is continued at Fromagerie du Grand Murols, part of the Dischamp Group.

Size: 1lb 5oz ring; Affinage: 2–4 weeks
Tasting notes: The dry, annatto-washed, orange–brown rind has little Brevibacterium, producing a mild aroma, and the pale, supple but firm interior has a mild, slightly sweet flavor. The plugs from the cheese's center are aged separately, developing a wrinkled blue–gray mold.

Pasteurized: Yes; Country: France (Auvergne)

▌▌🐄 Chaumes

Produced by Bongrain, one of France's largest cheese companies, this firm, orange-brown, flattened disk has a supple, mild, straw-colored interior dotted with eyes. The very mild aroma makes it popular with washed rind novices.

Pasteurized: Yes; Country: France (Aquitaine)

▌▌🐄 Stelvio (Stilfser) PDO

Named for the mountainous Stelvio-Stilfser National Park in Italy's Trentino-Alto Adige and matured for minimum 60 days on wooden boards, these 17½–22lb wheels of Alpine cheese have a yellow–brown rind and straw-yellow interior with irregular eyes and compact, supple texture.

Pasteurized: Either; Country: Italy (Trentino-Alto Adige)

▌🐄 Queso de l'Alt Urgell y la Cerdanya PDO

These 5½lb wheels have a thin, slightly moist, brown rind; pale, supple interior with tiny eyes scattered throughout; and a mild, slightly herbal flavor. They are produced in the Spanish Pyrenees.

Pasteurized: Yes; Country: Spain (Catalonia)

▬▬ 🐄 Odenwälder Frühstückskäse PDO

Frühstückskäse ("breakfast cheese"), or handkäse ("hand cheese"), small flat disks shaped by hand, are usually set by lactic fermentation. This rennet-set version, made by one dairy, has a thin, brownish-yellow rind; dense interior; strong flavor and aroma.

Pasteurized: Yes; Country: Germany (Hesse)

beer cheese

Pungent and firm washed rind cheeses are popular in the beer-drinking nations of Germany, Austria, Belgium, and the Czech Republic. Too strong for most wines, they work well with beer and are common on pub menus in those countries. German bierkäse (also called weisslacker) doesn't contain beer, but, pungent and salty, it's an ideal beer accompaniment; some people even dunk it in their beer before eating it. There are many regional variations, all similar to limburger. German immigrants brought this style of cheese to the USA (notably Wisconsin), where it has developed a strong following.

Serve: with pickled onions and dark bread.
Drink: a Czech pilsner or dark German beer.

Cheesemaker Joe Widmer with his 7–10 day old brick cheeses; Joe prefers the flavor at 4–5 months.

Limburger

The 12th-century Duchy of Limburg covered an area now divided between Belgium, the Netherlands, and Germany. Both Belgium and the Netherlands today have a province of Limburg. Limburger cheese originated in Trappist monasteries (see Trappist cheeses, page 118) in what is now northeastern Belgium. Today it is produced in all three countries, predominantly Germany.

Size: Typically 7oz loaves, may be larger; Affinage: About 2 weeks

Tasting notes: The sticky, pink-orange, ridged rind has a pungent aroma, while the firm, pale yellow interior is milder than the aroma suggests, with a spicy, slightly sweet, almost meaty flavor. It softens with age, when many consider it past its best.

Pasteurized: Either; Country: Germany, Belgium, Netherlands

Schloss Käse

The aroma of Austrian schloss käse isn't as strong as limburger, on which it's modeled, but the smooth, creamy, pale yellow interior is still savory and slightly nutty and the orange rind may have some patches of white mold.

Pasteurized: Yes; Country: Austria

American Limburger

Myron Olson, from the Chalet Cheese Co-op in Wisconsin, is America's only Master Limburger Cheesemaker. He produces a cheese with a creamy brown rind, milder than its European cousins but still with a distinct aroma and creamy savory interior.

Pasteurized: Yes; Country: USA (Wisconsin)

Remoudou PDO

This larger, stronger version of Belgian Herve (see page 123) was traditionally made with the rich milk taken in a surreptitious second milking (*remoud*) after the milk taxes had been paid. It's now enriched with added cream. German romadur is milder.

Pasteurized: Either; Country: Belgium (Liège)

Brick Cheese

With a sticky orange rind and sliceable, supple, mild, fruity-sweet interior that becomes more pungent with age, this American classic, modeled on limburger, was created in the 1870s. It is still produced the traditional way by Wisconsin's Widmer's Cheese Cellars.

Pasteurized: Yes; Country: USA (Wisconsin)

munster-géromé

Around 660 CE, Irish Benedictine monks settled in France's Vosges
Mountains, in modern-day Alsace, and a village, Munster (from the
Latin for "monastery"), grew up around their abbey. The monks taught the
peasants to preserve milk by making cheese, a skill that spread throughout the area, including the
village of Gérardmer in what is now Lorraine. Munster's original AOC appellation was revised in
1978 to include Gérômé, the identical cheese from Gérardmer. Only milk from Vosgienne cows is
used and the cheeses are typically aged for 2–3 months, rubbed with brine every few days to help
develop their deep red skins.

Serve: traditionally with potatoes boiled in their skins and a sprinkling of caraway seeds.
Drink: Alsatian pinot gris.

Munster is drained in cheese molds before being aged and regularly rubbed with a light brine.

Munster PDO

This is a cheese that fans adore and detractors hate, though once they get past the pungent rind, which can be removed before eating, the interior is surprisingly mild (it becomes more tangy as it matures). Petit-Munster, a smaller version aged for a minimum of 2 weeks, weighs about 4oz and is ³/₄–2¹/₂in in diameter.

Size: Minimum 15oz, 2³/₄–7¹/₂in disks; Affinage: Minimum 3 weeks

Tasting notes: A creamy, supple, pale yellow interior with the texture of melted chocolate and a slightly sweet, milky flavor is hidden beneath a salty, stronger-flavored, moist, orange–red rind with a pungent aroma.

Pasteurized: Either; Country: France (Alsace)

Münster

Similar to Alsatian Munster, this cheese, also called münster käse, is produced in the town of Münster in western Germany. With Munster-Géromé being granted PDO status by the European Union, Germany has agreed to stop using the name by 2019.

Pasteurized: Either; Country: Germany (North Rhine-Westphalia)

Fleur de Sureau

Elderflower petals added to the curds give this Munster-like cheese a slightly tart, anise flavor. *Sureau* (French for "elder") is common in Alsatian cooking, as it was planted to attract good spirits and for its medicinal properties. Also called holunderkas.

Pasteurized: Yes; Country: France (Alcace)

Muenster

Loaf-shaped American muenster, very mild and pale, often rubbed with orange vegetable dye to create the authentic color, bears little resemblance to the French version. Bass Lake Cheese Factory produces a buttery version called Muenster Del Ray, closer to German münster.

Pasteurized: Yes; Country: USA

Ardrahan

This Irish farmhouse cheese has a honey-colored, smooth, semi-firm interior with buttery, toasty flavors beneath a pungent, moist, pinky-beige rind. The milk comes from Friesian cows bred on the farm in County Cork where the cheese is produced.

Pasteurized: Yes; Country: Ireland (Cork)

pavés & carrés

Pavé (referring to France's rough square paving stones) and *carré* (literally "square") are terms used almost interchangeably in France for big squares of cheese, generally from the north, especially Normandy, but also farther south. Not all have washed rinds, though many do, often with a dusting of white mold. Most don't ripen to an oozy consistency, but soften to a supple stickiness while still holding their shape. The rinds were often traditionally brushed with a small damp brush (*croûte-brosée*) rather than washed with cloths, or dipped in the washing solution (*croûte-lavée*), though this distinction has largely vanished. See also Pavé d'Affinois (page 105).

Serve: with dried fruit (such as prunes or dates) and nuts (such as walnuts or almonds).
Drink: pommeau, a popular Normandy apéritif of hard apple cider and Calvados.

Calvados, the apple brandy of Normandy, is also a good match with aged Pave d'Auge.

▌▌🐄 Pavé d'Auge

Produced for centuries in Pays d'Auge, a traditional area of Normandy famous for its cheeses, these look like a larger, thicker version of Pont-l'Évêque, the most significant *croûte-brosée* cheese (see page 137). Pavés are sometimes named for specific locales or producers, such as Pavé du Plessis from Fromagerie du Plessis in Upper Normandy.

Size: 1½–1¾lb squares, 2–2½in high; Affinage: 2–3 months
Tasting notes: The mild, supple, pale yellow interior with scattered eyes and a slightly sweet, nutty, rich, creamy taste, due to its relatively high fat content (50%), becomes earthier with age. The russet-orange rind is wrinkled and dusted in white mold.

Pasteurized: Either; Country: France (Lower Normandy)

▌▌🐄 Curé Nantais

Supposedly introduced to Nantes in Loire (*Nantais* means "of Nantes") by a priest (*curé*), this thick, 7oz square has a smooth, moist, orange rind; supple, golden interior; and strong aroma. Also now in larger wheels and small muscadet wine-washed wheels.

Pasteurized: No; Country: France (Loire)

▬ 🐄 Red Hawk

These small, thick triple-cream disks (see page 102) from Cowgirl Creamery have been been compared to Époisses (see page 137) and Munster (see page 131), with a pale orange, white mold-dusted rind; supple, creamy yellow interior; pungent musky aroma; and balanced, meaty flavor.

Pasteurized: Yes; Country: USA (California)

▌▌🐄 Carré de l'Est Lavée

These small, brine (or eau-de-vie) -washed squares (literally "squares of the east washed") from northeastern France develop a sticky, orange rind and meltingly soft, slightly salty, bacony interior. Unwashed versions develop a bloomy white rind and buttery flavor.

Pasteurized: Yes; Country: France (Alsace, Champagne-Ardenne, Lorraine)

▨ 🐐 Le Petit Prince

This 7oz block of goat's milk cheese from South Australia is firm and mellow when young, the thin red rind dusted in white. With age the rind becomes slightly grainy and the pale, creamy interior softens, developing richer, stronger flavors.

Pasteurized: Yes; Country: Australia (South Australia)

vacherin

Vacherin Mont d'Or—disks of soft washed rind cheese held in shape by a strip of spruce sapwood (inner layer of bark)—has been made during winter around Mont d'Or in the Jura Mountains, the border between Switzerland and France, since at least the 19th century. Switzerland was assigned rights to the name in 1951 (see page 272) and France later protected the names Mont d'Or and Vacherin du Haut Doubs with AOC (later PDO) status. Two French vacherins, d'Abondance and des Bauges, are similar to Mont d'Or, while Swiss Vacherin Fribourgeois (see page 229) is a semi-hard, washed rind cheese used in fondue.

Serve: at room temperature with chunks of bread.
Drink: fruity white wine such as Alsatian gewürztraminer.

Disks of Vacherin Mont d'Or are packed into individual wooden boxes.

🇨🇭 🐄 Vacherin Mont d'Or AOC

During summer, cows graze in Alpine pastures and large wheels of cheese such as Gruyère and Beaufort (see page 215) are made in cooperative dairies. In snowy winter, when the cows return to the farms' stables and it's difficult to reach the dairies, these smaller, shorter-aged cheeses are made for family use. Sold packed in individual wooden boxes.

Size: 14oz–5½lb rounds; Affinage: 4 weeks
Tasting notes: The undulating, brownish-pink, white mold-dusted rind is best cut around the top and folded back, so the creamy, pale yellow, spicy, salty, almost liquid interior can be spooned out. It has a faintly resinous aroma from the spruce girdle.
Pasteurized: No (thermized); Country: Switzerland (Vaud)

🐄 Mont d'Or (Vacherin du Haut-Doubs) PDO

The wrinkled orange rind beneath a downy coating of white mold is encircled in the traditional spruce girdle. Ripened on spruce planks for at least 3 months and packed in spruce boxes, the aroma is distinctly resinous.

Pasteurized: No; Country: France (Franche-Comté)

🐄 Tourrée de l'Aubier

Another French *faux* vacherin, l'Aubier (meaning "sapwood") is soft and creamy with a sweet, mild flavor; spicy aroma; and white mold-dusted rind. Originally wrapped in a spruce girdle, it's now scented by a spruce insert in the box's base.

Pasteurized: Yes; Country: France (Lorraine)

🐄 L'Edel de Cléron

This pasteurized version of French vacherin, encircled with a spruce bark strip and sometimes called *faux* vacherin ("imitation" vacherin), is widely exported. It has a mild, faintly tangy flavor; smooth, creamy texture; and mild aroma.

Pasteurized: Yes; Country: France (Franche-Comté)

🇨🇦 🐄 Vacherin Chaput

The damp, orange, white mold-patched rind of this unpasteurized Québécois cheese is encircled in a spruce strip. The pale, soft interior, not quite as unctuous and oozing as the original, has vacherin's typical fermented milk aroma and sweet, creamy flavor.

Pasteurized: No; Country: Canada (Quebec)

cheeses in wooden boxes

Normandy's lush pastures have long produced rich dairy products. In the Middle Ages local peasants paid taxes in butter and cheese, and angelot (or augelot) cheese, which appears in texts of the time, may be the ancestor of Pont-l'Évêque and Livarot, mentioned by name by the 17th century. Around 1890 someone developed the idea of transporting such fragile cheese, including Normandy's camembert (see page 96), in thin wooden boxes. This innovation, variously attributed to cheese merchant Lepetite, engineer Ridel, and exporter Rousset, meant such cheeses, including Mont d'Or (see page 135) and Époisses, could be safely shipped great distances, and their fame spread.

Serve: with slices of pear or apple and walnuts.
Drink: hard apple cider or a fruit beer.

Wooden boxes are still used to protect fragile cheeses.

■ ▌🐄 Pont-l'Évêque PDO

Named for a small town in Lower Normandy, this ancient cheese is still sometimes produced with the traditional brushed rind (see page 132), producing a drier, paler rind than the washed rind versions. There are three variations on the standard size: *demi* (5–7oz), *petit* (6–9oz), and *grand* (2½–3½lb).

Size: 10½–14oz squares, 4–4½in wide; Affinage: Minimum 15 days
Tasting notes: The ridged, often white mold-dusted rind grows sticky and russet-orange with age. The smooth, fine-textured, cream-colored interior (pale yellow in summer) has a strong aroma but a mild, faintly sweet, rich, nutty flavor, becoming stronger and more savory when fully ripe.

Pasteurized: Either; Country: France (Lower and Upper Normandy)

■ ▌🐄 Livarot PDO

An ancient cheese from Normandy, Livarot's rusty orange rind is encircled in five strips of reed or paper (called *laîches*, meaning "sedges"), earning it the nickname "The Colonel." It has a powerful aroma and a dense, sticky, spicy, nutty interior.

**Pasteurized: Either; Country: France
(Lower Normandy)**

■ ▌🐄 Soumaintrain

These small disks washed in marc de Bourgogne (a liquor distilled from leftover grapeskins) have a rich, salty, sweet, Époisses-like flavor and pungent aroma. There's also an unwashed version, which develops a white mold over the orange rind.

Pasteurized: Either; Country: France (Burgundy)

■ ▌🐄 Époisses PDO

Revived in the 1950s, this 15th-century cheese from Burgundy and Champagne has a wrinkled, sticky, pungent, orange rind washed in wine or marc de Bourgogne. The pale, smooth, salty, sweet, milky interior becomes luscious and oozy when ripe.

Pasteurized: Either; Country: France (Burgundy, Champagne-Ardenne)

■ ▌🐄 Galette des Monts du Lyonnais

The smooth, runny interior and soft, gentle, milky flavor of this cheese from Lyon make it ideal for people uncertain about the more pungent washed rinds. It's so runny, it's usually eaten with a spoon.

Pasteurized: No; Country: France (Rhône-Alpes)

irish artisan cheeses

Famous for green pastures and generous rainfall, Ireland has more cattle than people (6 million cattle, 4.3 million people in 2008). The cows roam the lush pastures, providing rich milk perfect for cheesemaking.

In the last few decades, the Irish tradition of farmhouse cheesemaking has been reinvigorated by a few dedicated artisans, and in 2008 around 50 farms produced more than 150 different cheeses. Cork, in the very south, with almost 100% humidity (ideal for washed rind cheeses), was the cradle for this renaissance and home to Milleens, Gubbeen, Durrus, Bill Hogan's Desmond and Gabriel (see page 217), and Imokilly Regato (see page 233). See also Lavistown (page 195).

Serve: soda bread and smoked meats, such as those from Gubbeen's smokehouse.
Drink: a dark beer such as Guinness.

The lush Beara Peninsula, southwestern Ireland, is the birthplace of modern Irish artisan cheese.

▌▐ 🐄 Milleens

Veronica Steele has lived on the remote Beara Peninsula with husband Norman since the late 1960s. She developed this washed rind cheese—the first modern Irish artisan cheese—in 1976, and helped start the Irish artisan cheese movement by inspiring other local farmers to become cheesemakers and by founding the Irish Cheesemakers' Association. Her son, Quinlan, is now the cheesemaker.

Size: 8oz and 3lb wheels; Affinage: Minimum 16 days
Tasting notes: Beneath the wrinkled orange-pink rind, the firm, supple, pale interior is soft, creamy, and flowing when fully mature. It has a mushroomy aroma and sweet milky flavor with hints of salty butterscotch and an herbal tang developing with age.

Pasteurized: Yes; Country: Ireland (Cork)

▌▐ 🐄 Durrus

Inspired by Veronica Steele (above), Jeffa Gill has produced this washed rind cheese since the late 1970s, using raw milk from a local farm. Rich, buttery, fruity, and semi-soft, it becomes softer and more pungent with age but never overpowering.

Pasteurized: No; Country: Ireland (Cork)

▌▐ 🐐 Ardsallagh Hard Goats Cheese

Jane Murphy began making goat cheese for her children, who were intolerant of cow's milk. In 1999 she started Ardsallagh Farm in Cork, producing this mild, semi-hard cheese, which becomes slightly crumbly with age. Ardsallagh also produces fresh goat cheese.

Pasteurized: Yes; Country: Ireland (Cork)

▌▐ 🐄 Gubbeen

Raised in Spain, Giana Ferguson grew up producing cheese. In 1980, after marrying Tom and moving to his farm in Cork, she developed Gubbeen, with its wrinkled, pinkish-orange, washed rind and its creamy, firm, pale interior. There's also a smoked version.

Pasteurized: Yes; Country: Ireland (Cork)

▌▐ 🐄 Cashel Blue

The first modern Irish artisan blue-veined cheese, developed in the mid 1980s by Jane Grubb on Beechmount Farm in County Tipperary, this natural-rinded, creamy, moist, semi-soft cheese with rich blue-gray streaks becomes softer, creamier, and sweetly salty when fully mature.

Pasteurized: Yes; Country: Ireland (Tipperary)

morbier—ashed cheeses

Ash from burned vine clippings was once used to protect fresh, young goat cheeses while they formed a rind and, in the case of Aisy Cendré, to store young cheeses through summer to feed the extra mouths during harvest in autumn. In southern Italy cheeses are coated in ash from the bonfires celebrating the feast of St. Anthony, on July 13, to protect them while they age in natural caves. Traditionally, when French Morbier was made, soot from the base of the cheesemaker's cauldron was scattered over fresh curds to prevent a skin from forming and keep insects out. See also ashed white mold cheeses (page 100).

Serve: traditionally melted and scraped onto bread or over potatoes, like raclette (see page 218).
Drink: soft red wine such as Burgundy or other pinot noir.

Alpine goats at the local farm where Cypress Grove Chèvre sources milk to make Humboldt Fog.

■ ■ 🐄 Morbier PDO

Named after a small village in eastern France, Morbier was originally produced with surplus curds from making large wheels of Comté (see page 215). The layer of soot protected curds left over from the morning's cheesemaking, which were topped with more leftovers in the evening. Today's versions are molded, then halved, and a layer of vegetable ash (or more commonly, food coloring) inserted.

Size: 11–17lb disk, 12–16in diameter; Affinage: Minimum 45 days, often 2–4 months

Tasting notes: Flat, bulging disks with firm, pale gray to orange rinds; pale, springy, semi-hard interiors with a horizontal black line through the middle; scattered eyes; nutty, yeasty, mildly fruity flavors; and pungent aroma. Pasteurized Le Caviste de Scey is exported.

Pasteurized: No; Country: France (Franche-Comté)

■ ■ 🐄 Aisy Cendré

A young Époisses, soumaintrain (see page 137) or similar Burgundian cheese, is buried in ashes for a month or so. When young it has a chalky center (creamier toward the grayish-brown rind), which softens with age. The ash is removed before eating.

Pasteurized: No; Country: France (Burgundy)

■ ■ 🐑 Cinerino di Fossa

This southern Italian sheep's milk cheese is not washed, but coated in fine gray ash from myrtle bonfires before aging in nearby natural pits (*fossa*). The semi-hard interior has scattered small eyes, a rich "sheepy" taste, and aroma of myrtle, becoming creamier near the rind with age.

Pasteurized: No; Country: Italy (Campania)

🇦🇺 🐄 Pompeii

A thin layer of ash is added to the fresh curds when this Morbier-like cheese from South Australia's Woodside Cheese Wrights is molded. It's then washed to develop a rusty red rind; semi-hard, pliable texture; and tangy, herbal flavor.

Pasteurized: Yes; Country: Australia (South Australia)

🇺🇸 🐐 Humboldt Fog

The white mold-dusted rinds of these squat cylinders of goat cheese from California's Cypress Grove Chèvre aren't washed, but coated with ash. The moist, firm interior has a central vein of Morbier-like vegetable ash and a creamy, earthy flavor.

Pasteurized: Yes; Country: USA (California)

semi-soft cheeses

There's no perfect system for categorizing the world's diverse array of cheeses. They can be grouped by the type of milk used (cow, goat, sheep, and so on), by the way they're aged (under a bloomy rind, with surface bacteria encouraged by washing the rind, cloth-wrapped, and so on), or by their texture (soft, fresh cheeses through to very hard, grating cheeses), to name just a few variables. And as a number of different elements contribute to the character of every cheese, all will fit into more than one category. This next group of cheeses is a bit of a diverse bunch, brought together by their semi-soft texture. Some such as the snack cheeses (see page 158) are very mild, while others such as the cheese spreads (see page 154) can be very pungent. Processed cheeses (see page 156) have a lot in common with both of those groups: they're mild and popular as snacks, and they originally came about as a way to use up excess cheese, which is also why the pungent cheese spreads were originally made.

This group includes cheeses made from cow's milk, goat's milk, and sheep's milk; some have thin, soft rinds, while others are rindless. Some develop a bloomy rind (see page 88) or at least patches of white or blue-gray mold, while bacteria such as *Brevibacterium linens*, responsible for the distinctive orange color and strong aroma of washed rind cheeses (see page 114), may grow on the rind of some. Many, such as the robiolas (see page 146), can be aged for different periods of time, starting with a simple, fresh, milky taste when young and developing tangier, more complex flavors with age once bacteria and molds have time to develop and influence their flavor and texture. They rarely become strongly flavored, though those made from goat's or sheep's milk will develop stronger, sharper flavors than the cow's milk versions.

The cheesemaking techniques used also vary significantly, though high moisture content is essential to obtain the distinctive soft texture. This means the curds will generally be drained without pressure, or only lightly pressed, so that plenty of moisture remains in them. And in the case of processed cheeses and cheese spreads (often made from harder, drier cheeses), moisture is added back, often in the form of milk.

Semi-soft cheeses of all descriptions are appreciated for their texture, ranging from soft and spreadable to supple and smooth, and most have mild buttery flavors. They account for a large percentage of cheeses sold worldwide and are a great introduction for people just starting to explore the complex world of cheese. They make great snacks on their own, are often popular on sandwiches and in salads, and melt well into dishes such as polenta. Many have additional ingredients added, from the truffled and leaf-wrapped robiolas, to the highly seasoned liptauer (see page 155) and the many flavor variations of processed cheeses.

German halbfester schnittkäse ("semi-soft cheese") is sometimes flavored with spices.

robiolas

These small, soft, often mixed-milk, Italian cheeses have many variations, including leaf-wrapped (chestnut, cabbage, fig, and grape) and flavored with pine needles or truffles. Rinds may be thin and pale or, if aged, velvety and white- or red-tinged; the name likely comes from *rubium*, Latin for "red." All are made by gently draining the barely cut curds under their own weight without pressing, producing a mild, approachable, soft-textured cheese that's only briefly aged (usually 3 days to 3 weeks). Those produced in Piedmont are usually disk-shaped, while Lombardy's are typically square, like small Taleggios (see page 125). Small robiolas are sometimes called robiolina.

Serve: with thin slices of walnut or raisin bread.
Drink: Asti spumante from the same region as Robiola di Roccaverano.

An Italian cheesemaker milks her goats at Roccaverano.

Robiola di Roccaverano PDO

Made in the region around the hillside town of Roccaverano in the northwestern Italian region of Piedmont, this cheese dates back at least 2,000 years. Sometimes still made the traditional way from 100% goat's milk (often labeled *classica*), many are now made with up to 85% cow's milk blended with goat's, or goat's and sheep's, milk.

Size: 7–14oz; Affinage: Minimum 3 days

Tasting notes: A thin, pale rind with brownish-red patches covers a firm, white to cream interior (goat's milk produces whiter cheeses). Becoming soft, silky, and stronger with age, the sweetness is balanced by a slight tang and saltiness with faintly nutty, herbal flavors.

Pasteurized: Either; Country: Italy (Piedmont)

Murazzano PDO

A thin, white to pale gold-colored rind covers a firm, pale, fine-grained interior, sometimes with a scattering of eyes. The delicate, slightly savory flavor strengthens with age. Traditionally 100% sheep's milk, they may now contain up to 40% cow's milk.

Pasteurized: No; Country: Italy (Piedmont)

Robiola Mondovi

This small, 100% cow's milk robiola has a pale, fragile, soft, sweet, buttery interior and a thin rind with just a hint of white bloom. Largely unknown outside Piedmont, they're also called robiola di ceva.

Pasteurized: Either; Country: Italy (Piedmont)

Robiola d'Alba

Hailing from the Piedmont town of Alba, famous for truffles, these semi-soft, off-white disks are often flecked with black truffles, giving the cheese a darker appearance and distinctive aroma. They taste of sweet milk with a mild pleasant tang.

Pasteurized: Yes; Country: Italy (Piedmont)

Robiola di Capra in Foglia di Verza

Goat cheese is often wrapped in savoy cabbage leaves (*foglia di verza*) in Piedmont to accelerate ripening, producing an almost meltingly soft, piquant, intensely "goaty" white cheese with a slightly acidic aftertaste.

Pasteurized: No; Country: Italy (Piedmont)

stracchino

"Stracchino" covers a large family of cheeses, including Taleggio (see page 125). Stracchino was originally made in autumn from the milk of cows weary after their long walk back from the summer Alpine pastures; *stracca* means "tired" in the dialect of Lombardy, the home of stracchino tipico, "typical" stracchino. Made from unpasteurized milk, drained without pressing, usually in square molds, and ripened on straw matting, most are now factory-made, but those from Nesso, near Como, eaten after just a few days ripening, and the longer-aged version from the Scalve Valley near Schilpario (see right) are good examples of the traditional styles.

Serve: on sandwiches or with salads.
Drink: a crisp Italian white wine such as Frascati.

Cows roam the upland plains of Lombardy near Lake Como.

▋▋🐄 Stracchino della Valle dei Campelli

Stracchino produced from the milk of cows grazing in the summer Alpine pasture of the upper Scalve Valley, an upland plain in northeastern Lombardy, is traditionally aged among rhododendron flowers. Huts in the neighboring Valle Camonica are also used to store the cheeses while they mature, covered with these flowers.

Size: 6½–11lb disks or squares; Affinage: 2–3 weeks

Tasting notes: The rhododendrons add more complex sweet flavors and aromas to the cheese, while the ridged rind develops a pinky-white bloom. The white interior has a meltingly soft texture with occasional irregular eyes.

Pasteurized: No; Country: Italy (Lombardy)

▋▋🐄 Crescenza

This mild, rindless cheese produced in Lombardy, Piedmont, and Veneto has a delicate milky aroma and flavor. Now largely factory-produced, the moist, smooth, firm white body melts in the mouth like cream cheese.

Pasteurized: Yes; Country: Italy (Lombardy, Piedmont, Veneto)

🇺🇸 🐄 BelGioioso Crescenza-Stracchino

This fresh, rindless cheese with a soft, creamy, spreadable texture and mild, milky flavor with a faint tartness is produced in Wisconsin by fourth-generation Italian-American cheesemaker Errico Auricchio.

Pasteurized: Yes; Country: USA (Wisconsin)

▋▋🐄 Quartirolo Lombardo PDO

Eaten within 5–30 days (*fresco*), Quartirolo is almost rindless with a faint pink tinge and soft, crumbly, slightly sour body. Aged beyond 30 days (*maturo*), it develops a reddish rind (similar to Taleggio in appearance) and a faint bitterness.

Pasteurized: Either; Country: Italy (Lombardy)

🇺🇸 🐄 Franklin's Teleme

This American classic, invented by cheesemaker Franklin Peluso's grandfather, has a slightly chewy, rice-flour-dusted rind, and tastes smooth and creamy like a crescenza, becoming more earthy and nutty and softening with age.

Pasteurized: Yes; Country: USA (California)

soft cow's milk cheeses

Northern Spain, from the Atlantic Ocean along the Bay of Biscay to the
Pyrenees bordering France, is a 621 mile-long, 62 mile-wide green belt
with a cool, wet climate, mountain pastures, and lush valleys perfect
for cattle grazing. The mountainous terrain meant that communities in these regions of Galicia,
Asturias, and Cantabria were traditionally quite isolated, each producing their own distinctive
cheese. Nine such cheeses currently have PDO status under EU law, including the most recently
accredited, Cebreiro, and arzua ulloa's application is underway. Opposite are three semi-soft
cheeses from this group. San Simón, Liébana (see page 263), Afuega'l Pitu (see page 267), Cabrales,
Gamoneu, and Picón (see page 175) are discussed elsewhere.

Serve: with crusty bread.
Drink: pale cream sherry; the slight sweetness and faint bitterness echo the flavor of these cheeses.

Queso Nata de Cantabria is made in the Spanish region of Cantabria.

Queso Nata de Cantabria PDO

Nata, meaning "cream," is a perfect descriptor for this rich cheese from the Bay of Biscay, previously called simply queso de cantabria. Originally made by Trappist monks in the Cóbreces Cistercian Monastery and modeled on Port-du-Salut (see page 120), it is now made virtually throughout Cantabria, one of the lushest regions of northern Spain.

Size: 1–6½lb wheels or blocks; Affinage: Minimum 15 days

Tasting notes: A thin, smooth, deep yellow rind covers a smooth, semi-soft, pale yellow interior with a buttery aroma. The flavor of sweet milk is balanced by a pleasant lactic tang; it almost melts on the tongue.

Pasteurized: Yes; Country: Spain (Cantabria)

Arzua Ulloa

These golden wheels from Galicia have a thin, waxy rind. The pale yellow, thick, almost runny interior has a few scattered eyes and a buttery, slightly salty flavor with a distinct tang. A PDO application has been filed.

Pasteurized: Yes; Country: Spain (Galicia)

Casatella Trevigiana PDO

Similar in texture and flavor to the above cheeses, this fresh, white, rindless cheese from Treviso in Italy's Veneto region tastes sweetly milky with a slight tang. It's semi-soft and creamy, occasionally with small eyes, and can be slightly crumbly.

Pasteurized: Yes; Country: Italy (Veneto)

Queso Tetilla PDO

Tetilla, meaning "teat," describes the shape of this distinctive, squat, cone-shaped, yellow cheese with a soft, smooth texture, scattering of eyes, and milky, buttery, slightly salty, tangy flavor. It is Galicia's most popular cheese.

Pasteurized: Either; Country: Spain (Galicia)

Rigotte

This family of French cheeses from Rhône-Alpes is usually eaten semi-soft with a thin rind and sweetly lactic milky flavor. They may have a bloomy white, mottled, or annatto-colored orange rind; others are occasionally made from goat's milk.

Pasteurized: Either; Country: France (Rhône-Alpes)

soft sheep's milk cheeses

Extremadura, bordering Portugal in southwestern Spain, is a treeless
steppe-like plain with long, hot, dry summers; short, mild, wet
winters; and excellent grazing. Seasonal flocks have grazed here since
earliest times and drovers' routes were already recognized by 1273.
Native breeds of sheep developed on both sides of the border, giving distinctive
qualities to local cheeses: the Serra da Arrábida breed for Portugal's Queijo de Azeitão and the
famous Merino, along with Entrefino, for Spain's Torta del Casar. Many cheeses from this area,
including the four on this page protected by PDO status, are set with cardoon thistle extract (see
page 236). See also Queijo Serpa (page 111).

Serve: traditionally by cutting off the top and scooping out the center with chunks of bread.
Drink: amontillado sherry for its rich nuttiness.

Locals shop at a traditional cheese market in Celorico de Beira, Portugal.

Torta del Casar PDO

Torta is a name given to Spanish cheeses (such as this one from Extremadura) that have an almost liquid center when fully ripe. The first written mention of this cheese, named for the town of Casar de Cáceres, was in 1791, though records of flocks of sheep grazing in the region date as far back as 1291.

Size: 1–2½lb wheels, 4–7in wide; Affinage: 60 days

Tasting notes: The thin, yellow to ocher crust tends to split, revealing a soft, spreadable, off-white center with smooth, slightly oily texture. It has a sheepy aroma and mild tangy flavor; the cardoon thistles used to set it give a slight bitterness.

Pasteurized: No; Country: Spain (Extremadura)

Queijo Serra da Estrela PDO

Made by Portuguese shepherds' wives for 800 years, these small, high rounds have thin, smooth, pinky-beige rinds; soft, smooth, off-white interiors; and buttery, salty, tangy flavors. *Velho* ("aged") versions are smaller, darker, and drier, with a sharper taste and aroma.

Pasteurized: No; Country: Portugal (Beira)

Queso de la Serena PDO

These 1½–4½lb disks from Spain's Extremadura have a firm, rough, brown rind and rich, buttery, off-white, slightly tart interior. Slightly milder than the smaller Torta del Casar, they're just as thick and satiny, with a strong, fruity-sweet aroma.

Pasteurized: Either; Country: Spain (Extremadura)

Queijo de Azeitão PDO

This small plump disk, introduced to the Serra da Arrábida area (south of Lisbon) by makers of Queijo Serra in 1830, has a rich, buttery, spoonable, off-white interior with bittersweet flavor, beneath a thick, waxy yellow–orange rind.

Pasteurized: No; Country: Portugal (Lisbon)

Foin d'Odeur

The moist, washed rind of this rustic-looking Canadian cheese from Quebec is decorated with thin strips of sweet grass (*foin d'odeur*). It has a yeasty aroma and semi-soft, chalky interior, almost liquid when fully ripe, with a sour, bittersweet flavor.

Pasteurized: Yes; Country: Canada (Quebec)

cheese spreads

In times when nothing was wasted, ingenious ways were found to make stale bits of cheese more appetizing; some of these homemade products are still enjoyed, usually for their pungent flavor. Grated or mashed bits of cheese are mixed with a little liquid to restart fermentation, which is often stopped with alcohol later, and seasonings are sometimes added. In France, fromage fort, literally "strong cheese," is the general name for such cheese spreads, while in Italy they're called bruss. An old proverb says that only love is stronger than bruss. Goat's milk cachat, from France and Italy, is often stronger still.

Serve: on toasted bread (remember, a little can go a long way).
Drink: marc, eau-de-vie, or grappa with the strongest versions.

Cancoillotte is a smooth cheese paste popular for breakfast and snacks.

▬ 🐑 🐑 Liptauer

In Hungary, brinza (see bryndza, page 62) a fresh sheep's milk cheese, was traditionally ripened, then mashed with paprika and salt. Cooks then added butter and their own seasonings to make a spread called körözött, known as šmirkás in Slovakia and liptauer in English. Today any fresh white cheese, often made from cow's milk, is used as the base.

Size: Various; Affinage: None

Tasting notes: This creamy spread varies from white to dark orange, depending on added flavorings, which can include more than 20 ingredients such as anchovies, beer, capers, caraway, chives, mustard, onion, and more paprika. Taste varies, though it's often quite hot and spicy.

Pasteurized: No; Country: Hungary, Slovakia

▌▌🐄 🐐 🐑 Bruss

In northern Italy leftover cheese is mixed with a little fresh milk and left in glass or earthenware containers to re-ferment. Alcohol, such as grappa, is later added, creating a firm, smooth, spreadable white paste. Also spelled bross or brus.

Pasteurized: Either; Country: Italy (Piedmont)

▌▌🐄 Cancoillotte

Metton, a granular yellow cheese, is melted in water or milk with salt and butter, producing a pale, mild, slightly salty, smooth, semi-liquid paste popular for breakfast or snacks. Also known as kachkéis in French Lorraine and Luxembourg.

Pasteurized: Yes; Country: France (Franche-Comté)

▌▌🐄 🐐 Fromage Fort du Lyonnais

This specialty from Lyon, often made from pungent washed rind cheeses such as Époisses (see page 137) and Maroilles (see page 119), is re-fermented in a stoneware jar, producing a pungent mustard-colored spread.

Pasteurized: No; Country: France (Rhône-Alpes)

▬ 🐐 🐑 🐄 Naboulsi

Soft, Feta-like akawi (see page 61) is boiled in brine to produce a firmer, longer lasting cheese, which is seasoned with spices, such as nigella, mahlab, and mastic, and stored in fresh brine. Popular in Lebanon, Syria, Palestine, and Jordan.

Pasteurized: Either; Country: Lebanon, Syria, Palestine, Jordan

processed cheeses

Processed cheese, made by heating and mixing cheese with other dairy products, such as milk, cream, butter, or whey, then pasteurizing at a very high temperature, was invented in Switzerland around 1908 to utilize excess cheese. The first factory opened in 1917 in France, and J.L. Kraft applied for an American patent for a similar method around the same time, launching processed cheese slices on the American market in 1950 (see page 9). The major advantage is long shelf life, though the bland flavor often suits children and cheese novices; salt, emulsifiers, food coloring, and flavorings such as herbs or pepper, are often added.

Serve: as a lunchbox snack.
Drink: fruit juice or a glass of milk.

Processed cheese, invented to utilize surplus cheese, is produced in large factories all over the world.

▮▮ 🐄 🐐 La Vache Qui Rit

In 1921 the trademark for La Vache Qui Rit (translated directly as "the cow that laughs" and marketed as Laughing Cow in English-speaking countries) was registered by Léon Bel (founder of what is now the multinational Bel Group) and the red-faced laughing cow with the cheese-box earrings began its journey to becoming a household name. Traditionally sold as foil-wrapped triangles packed in a circular cardboard box.

Size: Various; Affinage: None, but long shelf life

Tasting notes: These tiny wedges of soft, slightly sweet, mild cheese with a buttery texture are popular lunchbox snacks. There is now also a range of Laughing Cow cheese products including spreads made from chèvre and blue-veined cheese, introducing more sophisticated tastes.

Pasteurized: Yes; Country: France

✚ 🐄 Tiger

Swiss company Emmi produces small foil-wrapped triangles in round cardboard boxes under both the Gerber and Tiger brands. Similar to the Laughing Cow, they come in a range of flavors including herbs, smoked, ham, and mixed boxes.

Pasteurized: Yes; Country: Switzerland (Berne)

▮▮ 🐄 Kiri
(Children's Cheese Spread)

Developed specifically for children in 1966 by Bel Group, who created the Laughing Cow and Bonbel, this sweet, white, creamy cheese, traditionally packed in small foil-wrapped squares, has now expanded into dips, trays, and other variations.

Pasteurized: Yes; Country: France

▮▮ 🐄 🐐 Baby Bel & Bonbel

Developed in 1931, these small French, red-waxed disks of pale, semi-soft cheese are today recognized around the world. They have expanded to yellow-waxed emmental and green-waxed chèvre; both Baby Bel and Bonbel are produced by the Bel Group.

Pasteurized: Yes; Country: France

▬▬ 🐄 String Cheese (Pizza Cheese)

Thin strands of bland, pale yellow, stretched-curd cheese are folded over and over in layers. Sold as snack-sized sticks that children love to pull apart into thin chewy strands or in bulk for melting onto pizzas.

Pasteurized: Yes; Country: USA

snack cheeses

Italian poet Dante Alighieri coined the phrase *bel paese*, "beautiful country,"
to describe Italy; 600 years later it became the name of a mild, semi-soft
cheese. Such commercially produced, firm yet supple, mild cheeses account
for a large percentage of world cheese production and are popular for snacks
in many countries. On the beaches of Brazil, queijo coalho, a light, rather salty cheese with an
almost "squeaky" texture, is browned on sticks in hand-held charcoal ovens and sold by wandering
vendors, often with a sprinkling of oregano and garlic-flavored sauce. Hushållsost, one of Sweden's
most popular cheeses, is known throughout Scandinavia.

Serve: with crackers and pickles or fruit paste, such as guava.
Drink: a lager or pilsner beer.

Chanco cheese is sold at the Angelmo market, Puerto Montt, Chile.

 Bel Paese

Meaning "beautiful country," this cheese, created in 1906 by Egidio Galbani, is named for a book by geologist Antonio Stoppani (though Dante coined the phrase). It's produced in Italy and under license in the USA, with a map of Italy on the Italian cheese and one of the Americas on the US-produced product.

Size: 4½–6lb wheels; Affinage: From about 4 weeks

Tasting notes: A thin, pale yellow-waxed rind covers a firm, supple, cream-colored interior with small eyes; mild, buttery, slightly tangy flavor; and milky aroma. The range now includes a crescenza-mozzarella blend spread (see pages 76 and 149), and foil-wrapped triangular or circular portions of spreadable cheese.

Pasteurized: Yes; Country: Italy, USA

Butterkäse

Buttery in taste and color, this yellow to orange-rinded, supple German and Austrian cheese was introduced to the USA by immigrants; Roth Käse in Wisconsin makes a good version. Also called damenkäse, as the mild flavor appealed to the ladies.

Pasteurized: Yes; Country: Germany, Austria, USA

Chanco Cheese

Originally from Chanco in central Chile, this semi-hard, yellow cheese scattered with eyes is now produced all over south-central Chile and accounts for about half the country's cheese consumption. It has a mild, slightly sour and salty flavor.

Pasteurized: Yes; Country: Chile (traditionally Maule)

Queijo Minas

Originally made by farmers in the Brazilian state of Minas Gerais, this cheese is now mainly factory-produced, with production spreading to São Paulo and Rio de Janeiro. Soft-rinded wheels have a white, semi-hard, open-textured interior with a slightly sour taste.

Pasteurized: No; Country: Brazil (Minas Gerais)

Hushållsost TSG

One of Sweden's most popular cheeses, these pale, smooth, supple cylinders with small scattered eyes have a mild, creamy, lemony flavor. It was originally farm-produced and is sold as "farmer's cheese" in the USA. Oltermanni and Pohjanpoika are popular Finnish brands.

Pasteurized: Yes; Country: Sweden

blue-veined cheeses

Like bloomy rind cheeses (see page 88), blue-veined cheeses, which are also known as blue mold cheeses, are ripened by the action of oxygen-loving molds. In this case the molds grow inside the cheese, rather than on the surface. The channels along which the molds grow are sometimes natural channels and cracks, as the curds have been loosely packed, but they are most often introduced by the cheesemaker, who spikes the cheese with long, thin, metal needles (like knitting needles) to encourage the mold to grow from the center of the cheese out toward the rind.

Made since at least Roman times, many classic blue-veined cheeses, such as French Roquefort (see page 168) and Italy's most famous blue cheese, Gorgonzola (see page 172), have similar stories regarding their origin, usually of cheese being left in a cool dark place, a cellar, or cave, and later discovered attacked by mold. These early cheeses would have had blue-veining growing under their rinds and along any cracks from the surface toward the center. Many of the wild molds that caused this original blueing wouldn't have tasted good, or even been safe to eat. No doubt these first blue-veined cheeses were eaten out of hunger rather than desire or curiosity. But slowly, by a process of trial and error, some were found to have a pleasant flavor and texture, and so those strains of mold would have been cultivated, first by placing more cheeses in the same spot and later by placing bread in the cellars or caves and allowing the molds to grow on the bread. Then fine crumbs of the moldy bread would be mixed into the milk when a fresh batch of cheese was being made.

Almost all blue-veined cheeses today are made using laboratory-grown molds related to *Penicillium roqueforti*, the mold discovered in the famous caves of Roquefort. These molds need oxygen and moisture to grow, so the curds for most blue-veined cheeses are only loosely packed, leaving plenty of moisture in them along with pockets of oxygen to encourage the mold to grow. The mold doesn't generally start to grow, however, until more oxygen is introduced by spiking the cheese. If you look at a cross section of a wheel of blue-veined cheese, you can often see the channels made by the needles; most blue-veined cheeses are sold cut in half, so that the cheesemaker can check that the veining has occurred evenly.

English Stilton (see page 176) and French Roquefort are probably the best-known, most widely copied blue-veined cheeses worldwide. The techniques used to produce them are quite different, however. The French spike their cheeses almost as soon as they're made to encourage mold growth, then, when enough mold has grown, wrap them so that the oxygen supply is cut off, halting the growth of the mold, and leave the cheeses to finish their maturing. Stilton producers, on the other hand, drain the curds for up to a week, then seal

Stilton develops its characteristic blue veining after the cheese has matured.

the surface of the cheese and leave it to mature for 5–6 weeks, spiking it to allow blue-vein growth only after it's matured.

As they grow, the molds give off ammonia and other by-products, which contribute a distinctive flavor and aroma. Most are also quite salty and tangy, as a relatively high salt and high acid environment discourages the growth of undesirable molds and yeasts, while the desirable blue mold strains don't mind high salt and acid levels. This makes them very savory cheeses that marry well with slightly sweet flavors, such as dessert wines, fruit, and chutneys.

As with most cheese types, there's a wide range of flavors and textures among blue-veined cheeses. People who are hesitant about eating a blue cheese often enjoy bloomy rind cheeses with just a few pockets of blue mold throughout their interior (see blue white molds, page 164) working their way up through some of the creamier, slightly sweeter, scraped-rind cheeses such as King Island Roaring Forties (see page 169), to the more strongly blued and spicy, natural-rinded Stilton.

blue–white mold cheeses

These hybrids are a great introduction to blue-veined cheese. White and blue mold spores are generally added to the milk when the cheese is made. Once the white mold forms, sealing the surface of the cheese, the blue mold has limited access to the oxygen necessary for growth. Thus, rather than veins, these cheeses often just have flecks of blue and a milder flavor, the white mold producing a soft, creamy texture. Most of these cheeses are relatively new, Bresse Bleu leading the way in the 1950s, followed by Blue Castello (1960s), Cambozola (1970s), Montbriac (1990s), and MouCo Blü (2000s).

Serve: with crusty baguette.
Drink: slightly sweet wines such as a French Monbazillac moelleux or late-picked riesling.

Blue cheeses aging in a cheesemaker's cellar in Auvergne, France.

▌▌🐄 Bresse Bleu

Italian Gorgonzola (see page 173) became unavailable in France during World War II, so the dairies of Bresse (also famous for its chickens) produced an alternative called Saint Gorlon. Gorgonzola imports were re-established after the war and in 1951 the Bresse cooperative turned its hand to a milder blue cheese. The brand is now owned by dairy giant Bongrain.

Size: 1oz–1lb cylinders; Affinage: About 3 weeks

Tasting notes: The white mold coating ages to reveal patches of beige rind. The soft cream-colored interior dotted with blue–gray mold has occasional pockets of white mold and a buttery, melt-in-the-mouth richness with a sweet, slightly spicy tang and mushroomy aroma.

Pasteurized: Yes; Country: France (Rhône-Alpes)

▌▌🐄 Montbriac RocheBaron

A thin, ash-coated rind dusted with white mold covers a moist, smooth, off-white interior flecked with blue and a scattering of eyes. These mild, creamy, slightly tangy disks, from France's Auvergne region, become runny when fully ripe.

Pasteurized: Yes; Country: France (Auvergne)

▬ 🐄 Cambozola

A thin white mold rind covers a pale-yellow, creamy interior dotted with blue–green mold. This double-cream cheese (see page 104), named for the ancient Bavarian settlement of Cambodunum plus Gorgonzola (see page 172) is one of the mildest blue cheeses.

Pasteurized: Yes; Country: Germany (Bavaria)

▬ 🐄 Blue Castello

This Danish industrial, rindless, double-cream cheese (see page 104) has pockets of blue–gray mold scattered through its white interior. Inoculated with both white and blue *Penicillium* spores, it has a mildly spicy blue cheese flavor and soft, spreadable texture.

Pasteurized: Yes; Country: Denmark

▬ 🐄 MouCo Blü

This small bloomy-rinded wheel from Colorado has delicate blue veins streaked through its soft pale yellow interior. Developed with assistance from Master Cheesemaker Franz Halbreiter (father of MouCo co-owner Birgit Halbreiter), who also helped develop Cambozola.

Pasteurized: Yes; Country: USA (Colorado)

mild french blues

Large wheels of blue-veined cheese produced in the French mountains are among the mildest blues. In the 14th century, monks from the ancient region of Dauphiné, where Bleu de Sassenage is made, brought their cheesemaking skills to the Jura Mountains, creating two virtually identical cheeses: Bleu de Gex and Bleu de Septmoncel. They were initially grouped together under a PDO called Bleu du Haut-Jura, which has been recently modified to Bleu de Gex Haut-Jura and Bleu de Septmoncel. Fourme d'Ambert and Fourme de Montbrison, another pair of similar cheeses from the Massif Central, were initially grouped under one PDO, but have now applied for separate appellations, reflecting their separate, though similar origins.

Serve: melted over grilled chicken breasts.
Drink: a sweet French wine such as one from Rivesaltes, Barsac, or Banyuls.

Steak is another popular match for blue cheese.

Fourme d'Ambert PDO

Fourme, an old word for "cheese" still common in Auvergne, comes from the molds or "forms" used to shape cheeses. Fourme d'Ambert was being produced around the town of Ambert, on the western side of Monts du Forez, at least as early as the 9th century, when it was being used to pay taxes.

Size: 4½lb cylinders; Affinage: Minimum 4 weeks
Tasting notes: One of the mildest blue-veined cheeses, its dry, gray to brown-orange natural rind covers a firm, creamy, pale yellow interior marbled with blue veins. The mild, earthy, buttery flavor has hints of nuts and a mushroomy aroma.
Pasteurized: Either; Country: France (Rhône-Alpes, Auvergne)

Fourme de Montbrison PDO

Made in Montbrison (on the eastern side of Monts du Forez) and virtually identical to Fourme d'Ambert, these large, cylindrical blue-veined cheeses may have been made in this area in pre-Roman times.

Pasteurized: Either; Country: France (Rhône-Alpes, Auvergne)

Bleu du Vercors-Sassenage PDO

This traditional mild blue cheese produced in large wheels in the Savoy Alps' Vercors Massif is also named for Sassenage on the plains below, where the cheese was sold and used to pay taxes to landlords in the 14th century.

Pasteurized: Either; Country: France (Rhône-Alpes)

Saint Agur

Created in 1986 by Bongrain, this moist, white, double-cream cheese (see page 104) with blue-green veins and the distinctive octagonal shape has proved popular around the world. It has a slightly spicy flavor but is still a beginner's blue.

Pasteurized: Yes; Country: France (Auvergne)

Bleu de Gex Haut-Jura & Bleu de Septmoncel PDO

White mold dusting the smooth, thin rind should be wiped off before eating the mild, ivory-colored interior marbled with green-blue veins. This PDO covers two similar cheeses from neighboring towns, Gex and Septmoncel, in the Jura Mountains.

Pasteurized: No; Country: France (Rhône-Alpes, France-Comté)

roquefort

Praised by Pliny the Elder in 79 CE and granted France's first AOC in 1925, one of the oldest known cheeses is named for the village of Roquefort-sur-Soulzon in southern France's limestone mountains. Now made from December to July by just seven companies, all Roquefort is aged in the moist, cool caves of these mountains, which contain over 600 strains of naturally occurring *Penicillium roqueforti* mold. Traditionally loaves of bread were put into the caves to "harvest" the mold, then dried and ground to a powder used to inoculate the cheese; today the mold is laboratory-grown from strains sourced in the caves.

Serve: cut with a warm knife, alongside dark bread and unsalted butter.
Drink: a sweet botrytized dessert wine such as Sauternes.

Fresh Roquefort matures in moist cool limestone caves in Roquefort, France.

▮▮ 🐑 Roquefort PDO

Legend says that a shepherd, distracted by a pretty shepherdess, left his meal of fresh sheep's cheese and bread in a cave; weeks later, when he rediscovered it, it had turned blue. Eating it, he found it to be delicious. Roquefort is only produced seasonally, because sheep don't produce milk year-round.

Size: 5½–6½lb cylinders; Affinage: Minimum 90 days
Tasting notes: With a moist, rindless surface and soft, moist, crumbly, ivory-colored interior with well-distributed green–blue mold, Roquefort has a lingering, pleasant flavor and aroma of sheep's milk, slightly sweet and distinctly salty. Spreadable at room temperature.
Pasteurized: No; Country: France (Midi-Pyrénées, Languedoc-Roussillon)

▮▮ 🐄 Bleu des Causses PDO

These 5–6½lb disks of usually unpasteurized cow's milk cheese are matured in the Peyrelade Caves in the Gorge du Tarn near the famous Roquefort caves. Often called "poor man's Roquefort" and previously Bleu d'Aveyron.

Pasteurized: Either; Country: France (Midi-Pyrénées)

▦ 🐄 King Island Roaring Forties

This blue-waxed disk of cow's milk cheese, loosely modeled on Roquefort, has a buttery texture and sweet, mildly salty, nutty, yellow interior marbled with blue. It's named for the winds that sweep through Bass Strait between Tasmania and mainland Australia.

Pasteurized: Yes; Country: Australia (Tasmania)

≡ 🐄 San Ignacio Blue

This industrial Argentinian cheese is made using French technology, thanks to a partnership with French Laiteries Hubert Triballat. The moist, pale rind covers a creamy, slightly crumbly, white interior with blue–green veining and a mild, buttery, tangy flavor.

Pasteurized: Yes; Country: Argentina (Santa Fe)

▥ 🐑 Lanark Blue

Cheesemaker Humphrey Errington is quite a pioneer, reviving sheep's milk cheese in Scotland and winning a long, bitter battle with the authorities to make this much loved Roquefort-style cheese from unpasteurized milk.

Pasteurized: No; Country: UK (Scotland–Lanarkshire)

other bleus

Bleu (meaning blue) is a common prefix for French blue-veined cheeses, especially those made from cow's milk, usually followed by a town's or region's name. When production of Bleu de Laqueuille (from the village of Laqueuille) spread to the whole of the surrounding region of Auvergne, it became Bleu d'Auvergne. Meanwhile Bleu de Laqueuille is still made by a cooperative in Laqueuille. Blue goat's milk cheeses, specifically from the Savoy Alps, are often collectively called *persillés*, meaning "marbled." Typically made from 100% goat's milk or a mixture of milks, they can occasionally be 100% cow's milk cheeses.

Serve: in creamy salad dressings or crumbled into a salad of bitter greens and nuts.
Drink: Alsace's famous sweet wine, Sélection de Grains Nobles.

Lyonnais maître-affineur Alain Martinet ages and sells Bleu de Termignon.

▌▌🐄 Bleu d'Auvergne PDO

Legend says that in 1854 Antoine Roussel, from the village of Laqueuille, discovered a small local cheese that had come into contact with a loaf of moldy bread. Today a similar cheese is produced throughout Auvergne and in parts of several neighboring regions. It's also made in 2lb, 1lb, and 12oz disks.

Size: Traditionally 4½–6½lb disks; Affinage: Minimum 2–4 weeks depending on size

Tasting notes: This creamy, Roquefort-like cheese has very fine veins spread evenly through the interior, a piquant aroma, and tart, salty, buttery flavor with herbal notes. With age the moist natural rind, dotted with blue and gray mold, reddens and becomes sticky.

Pasteurized: Either; Country: France (Auvergne, Midi-Pyrénées, Limousin, Languedoc-Roussillon)

▌▌🐄 Bleu de Termignon

Cows from the mountain village of Termignon, in the French region of Rhône-Alpes, ingest natural mold among the flowers and herbs of their Alpine pastures, producing intermittent natural blue veining through this cheese with hard brown rind and crumbly interior.

Pasteurized: No; Country: France (Rhône-Alpes)

▌▌🐐 Persillé

The natural blue mold used in these small cylindrical cheeses from Rhône-Alpes only appears after about three months, so they're often well-aged with dry brown rinds and firm, white, crumbly interiors, or eaten young before the blue mold appears.

Pasteurized: No; Country: France (Rhône-Alpes)

▌▌🐄 Bleu de Laqueuille

The dry, gray, natural rind of this cylindrical cheese from Auvergne is often patched with white or green mold. The soft, off-white interior has pockets of blue–green mold and a creamy, spicy, slightly salty, tangy flavor.

Pasteurized: Yes; Country: France (Auvergne)

▌♦▌🐄 Bleu Bénédictin

The rind of these 4½lb wheels produced at Quebec's Abbaye Saint-Benoit-du-Lac has patches of greenish-gray and white mold. The slightly crumbly interior is creamier near the center with abundant blue veins, mushroomy aroma, and creamy, slightly salty flavor.

Pasteurized: Yes; Country: Canada (Quebec)

gorgonzola

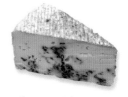

Accounts of Gorgonzola's origin involve young wheels of stracchino (see page 148) accidentally left behind in the cellar of the inn in the village of Gorgonzola, a resting place for cattle on their way back from the summer Alpine pastures, after the cowherds spent a night celebrating their return from the mountains. Discovered months later, the wheels were blue but delicious. Traditional Gorgonzola is made with curds from two separate milkings; the evening curds that rest overnight develop some acid and don't blend evenly with the fresh warm curds from the morning milking, leaving air pockets to encourage the desired blue mold growth.

Serve: *dolce* melted into butter and cream over pasta; *piccante* with bread and walnuts.
Drink: vin santo, the amber-colored dessert wine of Tuscany.

After the whey is removed, Gorgonzola is shaped and aged at low temperatures.

Gorgonzola PDO

Gorgonzola *piccante* ("spicy"), sometimes called *naturale* or *stagionato* ("aged"), is made the traditional way, with curds from two separate milkings and aged a minimum three months. The more commonly seen *dolce* ("sweet"), developed in the 1930s, is made from a single milking. No cheese, however, is actually produced in Gorgonzola, which has now become an outlying suburb of Milan.

Size: 22–26½lb; Affinage: Minimum 2 months (*dolce*)
Tasting notes: Piccante is firm (slightly chalky when young), dense, strong, spicy, moist, and buttery with balanced sharp sweetness and complex blue-mold flavors. Dolce is higher in fat, younger, softer, moister, and slightly sweeter with less blue mold.
Pasteurized: Either; Country: Italy (Lombardy, Piedmont)

Mascarpone Reale

Italy's rich cream cheese, mascarpone (see page 53), and spicy, salty Gorgonzola complement one another beautifully. The two are often thoroughly blended to make mascarpone reale, or layered and sold as torta di mascarpone e gorgonzola.

Pasteurized: Yes; Country: Italy (Lombardy)

Gippsland Blue

Developed from a Gorgonzola recipe by pioneering cheesemakers Richard Thomas and Laurie Jensen, this was Australia's first farmhouse blue. It has a firm, natural gray rind; sweet, yet tangy, buttery flavors; a gentle spiciness; and moist, luscious texture.

Pasteurized: Yes; Country: Australia (Victoria)

Mycella

Named for the *Penicillium mycelium* mold that forms the fine, greenish-blue streaks through its pale creamy interior, this slightly crumbly cheese, sometimes called "Danish Gorgonzola," has a mild, buttery flavor ideal for blue-cheese novices.

Pasteurized: Yes; Country: Denmark

Castelmagno PDO

The blue mold in these predominantly cow's milk cylinders from Piedmont comes from the caves in which they're aged, so veining is erratic. Today they're often preferred while the interior is still white, before veining develops. This cheese may contain some goat's or sheep's milk.

Pasteurized: No; Country: Italy (Piedmont)

spanish blues

All Spanish blue-veined cheeses come from the north, where mixed herds of cows, goats, and sheep are common in the mountain pastures of the Picos de Europa, and where cool, damp, limestone caves provide an ideal environment for blue mold. Unlike most blue cheeses, Cabrales, Gamoneu, and Picón Bejes-Tresviso aren't inoculated with *Penicillium roqueforti* or spiked; their blue veining comes from naturally occurring molds in the caves. Cabrales no longer has its traditional wrapping of plane tree leaves, but Valdeón, which is inoculated with blue mold and no longer cave-ripened, now has this leaf wrapping, as does Picón Bejes-Tresviso.

Serve: melted over a big juicy steak.
Drink: a sweet *sidra* (hard cider), a popular local drink in northern Spain.

Picón Bejes-Tresviso cheese is sold wrapped in Sycamore leaves in Esperanza Market, in Santander, Spain.

Cabrales PDO

About 40 artisan and farmhouse producers make Spain's most famous blue cheese from pure cow's, goat's, or sheep's milk or a mixture of two or three types from their mixed herds. The color of this cave-ripened cheese from Asturias varies from white to pale yellow, depending on the type of milk (cow's milk produces a yellower cheese).

Size: 1½–9lb cylinders, 2¾–6in high; Affinage: Minimum 2 months
Tasting notes: A soft, thin, moist, gray rind with reddish-yellow patches covers a compact, almost imperceptibly grainy interior with streaks of blue–green. The slightly spicy flavor is more pronounced in sheep's or goat's milk versions, as is the piquant, nutty aroma.
Pasteurized: Yes; Country: Spain (Asturias)

Gamoneu (Gamonedo) PDO

Lightly smoked to form a thin rind, then cave-aged for at least 2 months so light greenish-blue streaks form near the edges of the pale, crumbly interior, this cheese has slightly smoky, piquant, and buttery flavors and a nutty aftertaste.

Pasteurized: No; Country: Spain (Asturias)

Picón Bejes-Tresviso PDO

Mainly ripened in the villages of Bejes and Tresviso and made from a single milk, or a mixture of two or three types, this spicy, soft, scraped-rind cheese is compact with green–blue patches and veins.

Pasteurized: No; Country: Spain (Cantabria)

Estrella la Peral

The only one of these Spanish blues produced near the coast, this rich, buttery, slightly piquant and salty cheese, with stripes of blue–green through its yellow interior, is made by a fourth-generation family dairy in San Jorge de la Peral.

Pasteurized: Yes; Country: Spain (Asturias)

Queso de Valdeón (Picos de Europa) PGI

Sometimes called "fake Cabrales" and named for the Valdeón Valley in Castile-León, where cheese was made in pre-Roman times, this leaf-wrapped, cheese has an intense, salty, spicy, slightly sharp flavor with an underlying sweetness.

Pasteurized: Either; Country: Spain (Castile-León)

stilton

Soft, blue-veined, sheep's milk cheeses were once made all over England.
Monks from Kirby Bellars Priory likely introduced cheesemaking to
Leicestershire in the 1300s. In the early 1700s the housekeeper of
Leicestershire's Quenby Hall, Elizabeth Scarborough, made "Lady Beaumont's
cheese" from an old household recipe. Perhaps she passed it on to a local woman,
Frances Pawlett, who perfected it and organized local farmers to produce it, selling it to
the Bell Inn in Stilton, an important stagecoach stop on the London–Edinburgh road. Thus the
fame of the cheese "from Stilton" spread, though it has never actually been produced in Stilton.

Serve: with crackers and mango chutney, a reminder of Britain's colonial past.
Drink: port, but alongside, not poured over the cheese as some traditions dictate.

Stichelton, sold in Neal's Yard Dairy (London), can't be called Stilton because it's made with raw milk.

🇬🇧 🐄 Blue Stilton Cheese PDO

Stilton's origins are hazy, though records suggest all the people mentioned opposite may have played a role in its development. The first British cheese with strict guidelines agreed upon by all producers, Stilton is today produced by just six dairies in Nottinghamshire, Derbyshire, and Leicestershire, though milk sometimes comes from farther afield. Sometimes produced from raw milk until 1989, only pasteurized milk is now permitted.

Size: Cylinders, about 16½lb; Affinage: Minimum 6 weeks
Tasting notes: The slightly wrinkled natural rind covers a creamy, off-white to pale yellow interior with blue-green mold radiating from the center and a firm, moist, creamy texture. "Mature" and "Vintage" Blue Stiltons have a fruity, slightly minerally flavor and velvety texture.
Pasteurized: Yes; Country: UK (England—Nottinghamshire, Derbyshire, Leicestershire)

🇬🇧 🐄 Stilton Truckle PDO

These small cylinders may have first been produced to use curd left over from making a batch of regular-sized Stilton. Popular as Christmas gifts, they can be milder (and dry out quicker) than large Stiltons.

Pasteurized: Yes; Country: UK (England—Nottinghamshire, Derbyshire, Leicestershire)

🇬🇧 🐄 White Stilton Cheese PDO

Made in the same way as Blue Stilton, without the inclusion of *Penicillium* spores and aged for only a week, this firm, moist, white, open-textured cheese has a tangy flavor and smooth, moist, white exterior.

Pasteurized: Yes; Country: UK (England—Nottinghamshire, Derbyshire, Leicestershire)

🇬🇧 🐄 Stilton Pot PDO

Crumbled into small pots, pressed, and sealed with wax, Stilton is partially preserved and stops maturing until the seal is broken, though it still requires refrigeration. Pots have a firmer texture and sharper flavor.

Pasteurized: Yes; Country: UK (England—Nottinghamshire, Derbyshire, Leicestershire)

🇬🇧 🐄 Stichelton

Developed from a Stilton recipe by Joe Schneider on Wellbeck Estate in Nottinghamshire in 2006, this raw milk cheese can't be called "Stilton," though some say it's a reminder of how Stilton used to taste.

Pasteurized: No; Country: UK (England—Nottinghamshire)

stilton-style blues

When Stilton-maker Andy Williams from Hartington Dairy returned to his native Inverness in Scotland in the 1970s to establish Castle Stuart Dairy and produce the Stilton-style Blue Stuart, he found sales were slow because the cheese was in direct competition with genuine Stilton. His friend, Dennis Biggins of Shropshire cheese factory Westry Roberts, suggested dying it with annatto after the style of blue cheshire. The annatto-dyed cheese of Cheshire (see page 189), which often developed natural blue molding, was traditionally produced in neighboring Shropshire, North Wales, Worcestershire, and Herefordshire. As Biggins handled the distribution from his Shropshire-based company, the new cheese was called shropshire blue.

Serve: with a fruit paste such as quince or fig.
Drink: a full-bodied sweet wine such as a Portuguese verdelho or bual Madeira.

Madeira is a delicious beverage to accompany Stilton-style blues.

🇬🇧 🐄 Shropshire Blue

When Castle Stuart Dairy closed in the 1980s, Dennis Biggins approached Stilton-producer Colston Bassett to make shropshire blue for him, while London purveyor John Adamson, who'd been buying through Biggins, approached another Stilton producer, Long Clawson Dairy. Rather than eating into Stilton sales as initially feared, shropshire blue stole market share from imported blues and now every Stilton maker also produces shropshire blue.

Size: 17½lb cylinders, 10in high; Affinage: About 3 months
Tasting notes: The natural orange-brown rind is mold-dotted and the striking deep orange interior contrasts beautifully with the gray-green veining. Closer-textured, fudgier, and moister than Stilton, with a milder, less "meaty," slightly more tangy, salty flavor with a hint of rich, buttery, burnt caramel.
Pasteurized: Yes; Country: UK (England—Nottinghamshire, Derbyshire, Leicestershire)

🇬🇧 🐄 Barkham Blue

Named for the town in Berkshire where Two Hoots Cheese produces these award-winning, 2½lb, curved disks with mottled rind, moist golden interior, dark blue-green veining, buttery texture, and rich, relatively mild flavor.

Pasteurized: Yes; Country: UK (England—Berkshire)

🇬🇧 🐄 Exmoor Blue Cheese PGI

This semi-hard yellow cheese with sweet, buttery, spicy (but not overwhelming) blue flavors is made on Willett Farm in Somerset from locally sourced milk. After spiking, the cheese is sprayed with *Penicillium candidum* to form a white mold rind.

Pasteurized: No; Country: UK (England—Somerset)

🇬🇧 🐄 Oxford Blue

This moist, semi-soft cheese, created in 1995 by Baron Robert Pouget and Stilton-maker Steve Peace, is a smaller (5½lb), milder, creamier, less salty alternative to Stilton. Spiked shortly after pressing (French-style), it's aged in Oxfordshire and also available in 14oz truckles.

Pasteurized: Yes; Country: UK (England—Oxfordshire, Wales—Cardiganshire)

🇺🇸 🐄 Berkshire Blue

Developed in Somerset, England, and made under license by Michael Miller in the Berkshires of New England, this buttery blue cheese has a thin mottled rind; pale yellow, well-veined interior; and sweet, not too salty, flavor.

Pasteurized: No; Country: USA (Massachusetts)

british territorial blues

It's tempting to think that British blue cheese begins and ends with Stilton (see page 176), but that isn't so. In Dorset, in southwestern England, Blue Vinny (or Vinney) was produced for centuries from skim milk left over from cream or butter making; its name came from *vinew*, an old English word for "mold." Like so many traditional cheeses, it was virtually extinct by the end of World War I. Yorkshire, in the northeast, also had a long tradition of blue cheesemaking that almost became extinct; Judy Bell, from Shepherd's Purse, was at the vanguard of the reintroduction of blue cheesemaking in this area.

Serve: with halved small black figs.
Drink: an Australian fortified muscat.

Black figs are a delicious accompaniment to blue cheese.

Dorset Blue Cheese PGI

Seeing second-rate Stilton sold as "blue vinney" post-World War I encouraged Michael Davies of Woodbridge Farm to revive a traditional recipe. Sold as "Dorset Blue Vinny" (without the "e"), to distinguish it from Stilton versions still sold as "blue vinney," unlike Stilton it's made from skim milk, though matured for several weeks before piercing in the Stilton-style.

Size: 13lb cylinder; Affinage: 12–20 weeks
Tasting notes: The rough, dry, mold-coated rind covers a pale interior with irregular blue-green veining and peppery flavors. Milk powder is added to the hand-skimmed milk to produce a slightly creamier cheese than the traditional hard, dry Blue Vinny of past centuries.

Pasteurized: No; Country: UK (England—Dorset)

Harbourne Blue

Dark-blue veining runs through an almost white, crumbly interior with salty, slightly sweet flavors. Produced by Ticklemore Cheese in Devon from local milk with significant seasonal variation, the more strongly flavored versions are not for the fainthearted.

Pasteurized: Yes; Country: UK (England—Devon)

Yorkshire Blue

This soft, creamy cheese from Shepherd's Purse in North Yorkshire is spiked early (Roquefort-style) rather than weeks after production (Stilton-style). It is buttery, sweet, and slightly salty, and milder and softer than both Stilton and Roquefort.

Pasteurized: Yes; Country: UK (England—North Yorkshire)

Buxton Blue PDO

Made by Stilton-producer Long Clawson Dairy as a firmer, milder alternative to Stilton, the interior of this hard, blue-veined cheese is dyed red with annatto. Unlike Stilton, it's pierced as soon as it's unmolded.

Pasteurized: Yes; Country: UK (England—Leicestershire)

Strathdon Blue

A rusty-gray natural rind covers a creamy, buttery interior with sweet, milky, salty, savory flavors. Fully ripe, the texture of this Scottish cheese is soft and yielding, more like a French blue than a Stilton.

Pasteurized: Yes; Country: UK (Scotland—Ross-shire)

semi-hard & hard cheeses

These are the cheeses most people from northern Europe and New World countries think of when they say "cheese": firm yellow stuff with a relatively mild aroma and flavor. Cheddar (see page 186), colby (see page 198), gouda (see page 202), emmental (see page 210), and parmesan (see page 250) all appear in this category. Most are ancient cheeses, now often mass-produced but also still made by dedicated artisan and farmhouse producers.

These cheeses are aged for longer than other cheeses, starting out semi-hard, often quite smooth and supple, becoming harder and often quite granular with age; making it impossible to subdivide them into semi-hard and hard groups because most are both at different ages in their lifetime. Different cheesemaking techniques also determine a cheese's texture.

Granular grating cheeses, such as parmesan, are often made from very finely cut curds, while the curds for smooth-textured cheeses aren't cut as finely, retaining more moisture, giving an elastic, pliable texture. Most cheeses are at least 50% water; removing some of this extends their life. This can be done by heating, finely cutting, and pressing the curds, and by evaporation as the cheese ages.

Curds are heated in whey or water, causing contraction, which expels whey. Curds for washed-curd cheeses are heated in water, washing off some of the lactose that feeds bacteria, reducing their activity, and creating mild, nonacidic cheeses such as jack (see page 200) and edam (see page 202). The firmer stretched-curd cheeses (see page 72), like provolone (see page 82), are also semi-hard, washed-curd cheeses. Their curds are washed in very hot water, melting them into a cohesive mass that can be stretched to develop an elastic texture. "Semi-cooked" cheeses are cooked at a lower temperature, while "cooked" cheeses are cooked for longer at a higher temperature, causing greater contraction, expelling more moisture, resulting in harder cheese. When curds are cooked at a high temperature, the lactose in them cooks, producing toasty, nutty, caramelized flavors.

Whether the curds are cooked or not, they're always pressed. The more pressure used, the more whey expelled and the firmer the cheese. Some are lightly pressed, just by the weight of stacking several cheeses atop one another (see Asiago d'Allevo, page 209), while the cheeses of Auvergne (see page 206) are double-pressed to expel even more moisture. The curds for traditional cheddars are cut into slabs, stacked atop one another and turned for several hours; a process called "cheddaring." They're then finely milled, put into hoops and pressed again. Most so-called "cheddars" aren't made by cheddaring but are stirred-curd cheeses: the curds are cooked and stirred in their whey, extracting as much moisture as possible, then drained and pressed without being milled, producing a moister, slightly sweeter cheese with a more open texture and shorter life.

Traditional pecorino cheese is sometimes stored in a wooden container to mature.

As a cheese ages, moisture evaporates through its rind. All of these cheeses are salted to draw out moisture and encourage a rind to develop. These rinds take different forms. "Cloth-wrapped" or "bandaged" cheeses are wrapped in cheesecloth to protect them while their rind develops. Some develop a hard natural rind of dried-out cheese on which surface molds grow, others are rubbed with oil to discourage mold growth, creating a smooth, shiny rind. Some are sealed in plastic film that breaks down as the cheese matures and its own natural rind develops, but some are coated in impermeable wax, which is more decorative than functional as it prevents the cheese from expelling moisture and gases, affecting both texture and flavor. Some, such as raclette (see page 218) and tilsiter (see page 221), have washed rinds (see page 115); semi-hard washed rind cheeses, such as Trappist cheeses (see page 118), could just as easily be included in this chapter.

In order to age and become hard without becoming unpleasantly dry, most of these cheeses are made in large thick wheels that can be stacked and stored for years while retaining some moisture; Emmentaler (see page 211), the largest, is made in wheels weighing up to 265lb.

cheddar

Over half the cheese consumed in English-speaking countries is called "cheddar," but squeeze tubes, shelf-stable blocks, and plastic-wrapped slices are a far cry from the authentic cloth-wrapped farmhouse cheese from the rich pasturelands of southwestern England. The Somerset village of Cheddar gave its name to "cheddaring," the unique process by which traditional cheddars are made, stacking blocks of curd atop one another to drain. Standardized commercially in the 1800s, this process may date as far back as Roman times and certainly to the 15th century, when local cheese was likely aged in the caves of Somerset's Cheddar Gorge.

Serve: melted on toast.
Drink: hard cider (another specialty of southwestern England) or buttery chardonnay.

Grilled cheese on toast is a popular snack using cheddar cheese.

🇬🇧 🐄 West Country Farmhouse Cheddar PDO

Traditional farmhouse cheddar from the counties of Dorset, Somerset, Devon, and Cornwall, nearly extinct by the end of World War II, is enjoying a resurgence under the "West Country Farmhouse Cheddar" appellation. Cylinders are wrapped in lard or oil-dipped muslin to help form a hard rind, allowing the cheese to breathe but preventing mold penetration.

Size: Traditionally about 62lb; Affinage: Minimum 9 months

Tasting notes: The firm, light-golden interior is moist, open, and a little granular (slightly crumbly if aged) and may have occasional crunchy white lactate crystals. An earthy aroma leads to a rich, nutty flavor with a long finish.

Pasteurized: Either; Country: UK (England—Dorset, Somerset, Devon, Cornwall)

🇬🇧 🐄 Denhay's Dorset Drum

This firm, creamy, cloth-wrapped truckle, a smaller cheese traditionally made with curds left over after making large cheddar wheels, is matured for about 6 months (it dries out if aged longer), so it is not covered by the PDO.

Pasteurized: Either; Country: UK (England—Dorset)

🇺🇸 🐄 Cabot Clothbound Cheddar

Vermont's Cabot Creamery makes just 15 wheels of cloth-wrapped cheddar each month, then sends them to be matured in the cellars of neighboring Jasper Hill Farm (see Aspenhurst, page 193). Their 12-month-old has a crumbly, ivory-colored interior with buttery, caramel flavors.

Pasteurized: Yes; Country: USA (Vermont)

🇬🇧 🐄 Quickes Oak Smoked Cheddar

Pieces of traditional, 12- to 15-month-old Devonshire cheddar, made with milk from the farm's own herd, are lightly smoked over oak, infusing the light old-gold-colored interior with rich, smoky aromas and flavor. Smoked cheddar is not PDO-accredited.

Pasteurized: Yes; Country: UK (England—Devon)

🇦🇺 🐄 Healey's Pyengana Cheddar

Australia's oldest specialist cheese, dating to the 1900s, this Tasmanian farmhouse, cloth-wrapped, stirred-curd cheese is made by fourth-generation cheesemaker Jon Healey. Aged for a minimum of 14 months, it has a fine texture and the subtle flavor of herbs and honey.

Pasteurized: Yes; Country: Australia (Tasmania)

british territorial classics

Semi-hard British cow's milk cheeses are traditionally named for their native counties. Cheshire, Britain's oldest named cheese, is often dyed orange with annatto. When blue–green mold seeps under the rind, it's called "blue fade" on white cheese and "green fade" on orange cheese. Leicester, traditionally dyed deep orange–red, became white during World War I, so post-war the name became "red leicester" to differentiate it from pale wartime versions. Gloucester, produced since at least the 1500s, died out during World War II but was revived in 1978; "single" was usually made from skim milk on buttermaking days, and "double" on days when full-cream milk was available.

Serve: with crisp slices of apple or pear.
Drink: a soft red wine like merlot or a Rhône blend.

Annatto, from the seeds of a South American tree, is used to dye the curd for red leicester orange.

🇬🇧 🐄 Lancashire

Made since at least the 1800s, and derived from the cheese of neighboring Cheshire, traditional "creamy" and "tasty" lancashire cheeses are produced by mixing curds from two or three days' milkings. "Crumbly" lancashire, developed in the 1960s to compete with young cheeses like cheshire, wensleydale, and caerphilly (see page 194), uses a single curd. PDO appellation applies to cheeses labeled Beacon Fell Traditional Lancashire Cheese (see page 273).

Size: 44lb and 20lb cylinders; Affinage: Traditionally minimum 8 weeks

Tasting notes: "Creamy" lancashire (aged 8–12 weeks), smooth and slightly crumbly with a lemony tang and buttery aroma and flavor, becomes drier and slightly peppery as it ages to "tasty" (12 weeks+). "Crumbly," at 3–4 weeks, is milder, moister, and less complex.

Pasteurized: Either; Country: UK (England—Lancashire)

🇬🇧 🐄 Red Leicester

Authentic farmhouse versions are traditionally 22–44lb, cloth-wrapped wheels, with smooth, semi-hard, flaky interiors (resembling dark double gloucester) and mild, sweet-savory, nutty, citrusy flavors. Sparkenhoe is currently the only red leicester produced in Leicestershire.

Pasteurized: Either; Country: UK (England—traditionally Leicestershire)

🇬🇧 🐄 Sage Derby

A sage-flecked center is usually sandwiched between smooth, flaky, pale yellow derby cheese, giving the mild, buttery, nutty flavor a distinct herbal tang. Imposters are made with white curd marbled with spinach-dyed curd.

Pasteurized: Yes; Country: UK (England—traditionally Derbyshire)

🇬🇧 🐄 Cheshire

Appleby's, in neighboring Shropshire, produces the only traditional farmhouse cheshire currently made; it's semi-hard, moist, and crumbly, with a savory, slightly salty tang and long aftertaste when mature. It is sometimes called "chester" after the port from which it was exported.

Pasteurized: Either; Country: UK (England—traditionally Cheshire)

🇬🇧 🐄 Double & Single Gloucester

Single Gloucester PDO, produced on farms with rare Gloucester cattle, has a smooth, creamy, slightly crumbly texture and mild, lactic, buttery flavor. Similar double gloucester is larger, longer-aged, richer, and denser; it may be dyed yellow–orange.

Pasteurized: Either; Country: UK (England—Gloucestershire)

revived traditional british cheeses

Centralized food production in Britain during World War II sounded the death knell for many traditional farmhouse cheeses. From 1939 available milk was transported to factories and made into industrial versions of hard cheeses such as cheddar (see page 186) and undyed leicester, while production of softer gloucester, lancashire (see page 189), staffordshire (see page 197), caerphilly, and wensleydale (see page 195) virtually ceased. By 1945, when the war ended, Cheshire farmhouse cheese production had dropped from 405 farms to 44 and in Wensleydale from 176 to just nine. Thankfully the 1970s and 1980s saw a resurgence in interest in "real" food and the revival of traditional recipes by farmhouse cheesemakers.

Serve: melted into a white sauce to pour over steamed broccoli or cauliflower.
Drink: a Bordeaux or New World blend of cabernet sauvignon, cabernet franc, and merlot.

Ribblesdale Original Sheep Cheese is made in North Yorkshire's Ribble Valley.

Swaledale Cheese PDO & Swaledale Ewes Cheese PDO

The valleys (or dales) of Yorkshire have a long cheesemaking history—Teesdale, Swaledale, and Wensleydale being the best known. In 1986 the late David Reed became the sole producer of traditional Swaledale Cheese, later developing a sheep's milk version, harking back to the 16th century when sheep were the main dairy animals in the region. His family continues the business.

Size: 7³/₄oz–5¹/₂lb cylinders; Affinage: 3–4 weeks

Tasting notes: Made from a centuries-old recipe, these handmade cheeses have pale, moist, creamy, crumbly interiors with mild, slightly tangy flavors and either a natural greenish-gray rind or clear wax coating. The Ewes Cheese is firmer, paler, and tangier than the cow's milk cheese.

Pasteurized: Yes; Country: UK (England—North Yorkshire)

Curworthy

Drum-shaped with waxed or natural gray rind, Curworthy is produced in Devon by Rachel Stephens with milk from her own herd. Based on a 17th-century recipe, it has a creamy, supple interior with a rounded, melted butter taste.

Pasteurized: Yes; Country: UK (England—Devon)

Cotherstone

A likely descendant of wensleydale, first mentioned in the early 20th century, this moist, crumbly, melt-in-the-mouth cheese, with a yeasty, pleasantly acidic flavor, was revived by Joan and Alwyn Cross from an old Dales' recipe.

Pasteurized: No; Country: UK (England—Durham)

Dunlop

Developed in Dunlop, Ayrshire, in the 1600s and virtually forgotten by the end of World War II, this dense, semi-hard Scottish cheese was revived in 1988 by Anne Dorwald, using traditional Ayrshire milk. It is mild, nutty, buttery, and slightly sweet.

Pasteurized: Either; Country: UK (Scotland)

Ribblesdale Original Sheep Cheese

This crumbly wensleydale-like cheese, with mild, creamy, tangy flavors, recalls the days when wensleydale was a sheep's milk cheese. It is made in North Yorkshire's Ribble Valley by Iona Hill, niece of its developer, the late Iain Hill.

Pasteurized: Yes; Country: UK (England—North Yorkshire)

classic british-style cheeses

Many British dairy farmers have turned to cheesemaking over the past 20 years, some reviving traditional recipes (see page 191), others building on Britain's tradition of semi-hard cow's milk cheeses to create their own distinctive products. Simon Jones created Lincolnshire Poacher in 1992, named for his native Lincolnshire, an area not traditionally known for cheesemaking. By the end of the 1990s, as milk prices fell, many more dairy farmers became cheesemakers. British cheesemaking skills were also exported around the world via immigration, and good examples of classic British-style cheeses are found today as far afield as Australia and the USA.

Serve: as part of a ploughman's lunch with bread, relish, and pickled onions.
Drink: one of South America's excellent wines such as Chilean chardonnay or Uruguayan reza.

British-style cheeses are delicious in a traditional "ploughman's lunch" with bread, relish, and a little salad.

Lincolnshire Poacher

Ulceby Grange Farm has been in the Jones family since 1917 but only began dairying in 1970. After agricultural college, with help from cheesemaker Dougal Campbell and brother Tim, Simon Jones decided to turn the milk from the farm's Holstein herd into this cheese, which has won consecutive golds at the British Cheese Awards and Best Export Cheese in 2006.

Size: 44lb wheels; Affinage: Minimum 12 months

Tasting notes: This cheddar-like cheese has a hard, golden to gray–brown rind with patches of white mold and a smooth, firm, pale yellow center, with occasional eyes. It becomes flaky and crumbly with age. Sweet, rich, and creamy with fruity, nutty, spicy notes.

Pasteurized: No; Country: UK (England—Lincolnshire)

Spenwood

This thick, 4½lb wheel from Berkshire has a white mold-dusted natural brown rind and cream-colored interior. Moist and mild at six months, it becomes harder and flakier (ideal for grating) with a balanced sweet nuttiness as it ages.

Pasteurized: No; Country: UK (England—Berkshire)

Ashgrove Double Gloucester

English-trained Australian cheesemaker Jane Bennett produces a range of British-style cheeses on her family's Tasmanian dairy farm. Her double gloucester is annatto-dyed and aged for six months, producing a smooth, firm, pale orange cheese with a mild buttery flavor.

Pasteurized: Yes; Country: Australia (Tasmania)

Hereford Hop

Charles Martell, producer of Stinking Bishop (see page 123) created this Single Gloucester-style cheese in 1990. The dense yellow interior has a sweet, buttery flavor; the flaky yellow-brown coating of toasted hops adds a yeasty crunch.

Pasteurized: Yes; Country: UK (England—Gloucestershire)

Aspenhurst

This cloth-wrapped, undyed leicester-style cheese is made in very small quantities by Vermont's Jasper Hill Farm. It is named after a neighborhood on nearby Caspian Lake. Matured 12–18 months, it has citrusy, almost pineapple notes and occasional lactate crystals.

Pasteurized: No; Country: USA (Vermont)

caerphilly

This lightly pressed traditional Welsh cheese is typically aged for just a few weeks to a few months, so is moister than most other British cheeses. First made in Caerphilly (Castle Town) near Cardiff in 1831, it's soaked overnight in brine baths to help the rind form. It was supposedly popular with Welsh miners who needed to replenish their salts after a hard day's work. As popularity grew, Welsh cheesemakers couldn't meet demand and production spread to southwest England, where most of it is now made, providing Somerset cheddar-makers with much needed cash flow while their harder, longer-aged cheddar matures.

Serve: mixed with mustard and beer and melted on bread as Welsh rarebit.
Drink: a slightly sweet Alsatian riesling or perry (pear cider).

Caerphilly Castle was built in the fourteenth century, long before the eponymous cheese was first made.

Caws Cenarth Caerffili

In 1987, when EU milk quotas made the sale of liquid milk unviable, Gwynfor and Thelma Adams began cheesemaking on their Welsh family farm, thereby leading the revival of Welsh farmhouse caerffili (the Welsh spelling). Now the oldest farmhouse producer of caerphilly, Caws Cenarth has won Best Farmhouse Caerffili at the Royal Welsh Show a record number of times.

Size: 10lb, 6½lb, 15oz wheels; Affinage: 3–6 weeks

Tasting notes: These pale yellow wheels of organic cheese have a thin, smooth, dull rind and loose-textured, velvety interior with eyes and fissures. The relatively short aging gives them a fresh lemony tang and creamy aftertaste. Also flavored with garlic and herbs.

Pasteurized: Yes; Country: UK (Wales–Carmarthenshire)

Duckett's Caerphilly

Produced by Westcombe Dairy in Somerset since 2008, this award-winning farmhouse caerphilly is aged for 4–6 weeks; the firm, open-textured, creamy, pale yellow interior softening around the edges and the lemony acidity mellowing to a buttery, faintly salty flavor.

Pasteurized: Either; Country: UK (England–Somerset)

Yorkshire Wensleydale

The best known of the Yorkshire Dales cheeses, white wensleydale, traditionally eaten with apple pie and fruitcake, is pale, crumbly, and moist with a slightly honeyed, tangy flavor, similar to young caerphilly. A PDO application has been filed.

Pasteurized: Either; Country: UK (England–North Yorkshire)

Llangloffan

Created by Leon Downey in Wales in the 1970s and named after his Pembrokeshire village, this caerphilly-like cheese, with a buttery, melt-in-the-mouth texture and slightly grassy flavor, is now made by Carmarthenshire Cheese Company.

Pasteurized: No; Country: UK (Wales–Carmarthenshire)

Lavistown

One of Ireland's first contemporary farmhouse cheeses, this partially skimmed milk cheese is made today by Knockdrinna Farmhouse Cheese's Helen Finnegan. Named 2008 British Cheese Awards Best Irish Cheese, its semi-soft, crumbly texture and buttermilk flavor resemble caerphilly.

Pasteurized: Yes; Country: Ireland (Kilkenny)

flavored cheddar-style cheeses

While added flavorings are often used to disguise bland, second-rate cheese, Britain has a long history of flavored cheeses, such as sage derby (see page 189). White Stilton blended with fruits such as apricots even carries the Stilton PDO logo. Long Clawson Dairy produced its first flavored cheese, Windsor Red, in 1969, followed closely by Huntsman (Blue Stilton sandwiched between two layers of double gloucester) and Cotswold (double gloucester with minced chives and onion). Swaledale Cheese Company (see page 191) produces chive, garlic, and apple-mint flavored cheeses, as well as one soaked in Old Peculier ale.

Serve: with sourdough bread and a few cornichons or sliced sweet pickles.
Drink: a traditional British ale; the best match for these strongly flavored cheeses.

The beer in Cahills Porter Cheese gives it a slight bitterness without overwhelming the cheddar taste.

Staffordshire Organic

Monks brought cheesemaking to Staffordshire in the 1400s, but traditional farmhouse Staffordshire cheese, similar to the better-known cheese from neighboring Cheshire (see page 189), didn't survive World War II. Betty and David Deaville have revived the county name with an organic, cheddar-style cheese (plain and flavored), while John Knox from the Staffordshire Cheese Company produces a more cheshire-style PDO-accredited Staffordshire.

Size: 3lb, 20lb, 40lb cylinders; Affinage: 3–12+ months
Tasting notes: This moist, sweetly buttery cheese has a mild tang and smooth, fine-grained texture. Herbs (wild garlic, chives, apple mint, and more) grown on the farm by Betty are used for flavored versions. There's also a lightly oak-smoked version.
Pasteurized: No; Country: UK (England—Staffordshire)

Windsor Red

Stilton-maker Long Clawson Dairy produces this pale yellow cheddar, which was traditionally mixed with elderberry wine. Now, however, a blend of port and brandy is used to create the same striking red-and-cream marbled effect.

Pasteurized: Yes; Country: UK (England)

Cahills Porter Cheese

This brown-waxed truckle of Irish cheddar marbled with Guinness (a "porter" beer) looks like a dark nut-studded fruitcake with cream-colored chunks through a dark brown body. The beer gives a slight pleasant bitterness to the firm, smooth interior.

Pasteurized: Yes; Country: Ireland (Limerick)

Y Fenni (Red Dragon)

This blend of cheddar, whole-grain mustard, and Welsh ale is coated in yellow wax and named for the town where it's made (Abergavenny in English). The red-waxed export version is named for the dragon on the Welsh flag.

Pasteurized: Yes; Country: UK (Wales—Monmouthshire)

Five Counties

Layers of double gloucester, red leicester, cheshire, derby (see page 189), and Somerset cheddar (see page 187) give this cheese its name and striped appearance. Saxon Shires is virtually identical, while Singleton's very similar Stripey Jack contains a second layer of cheddar instead of derby.

Pasteurized: Yes; Country: UK (England)

colby

Joseph Steinwand invented this American classic in 1855 in his father's cheese factory near Colby, Wisconsin. It's often compared to cheddar (see page 186), but it is actually closer to gouda or edam (see page 202), because the curds are washed thoroughly to remove excess whey and lactose, reducing the acidity and producing a milder, sweeter flavor and more supple texture. It has a softer, more open texture than the Dutch cheeses, however. Often rindless and waxed, most are bland, factory-produced cheeses, though some specialist cheesemakers, such as Widmer's Cheese Cellars and those opposite, produce distinctive artisanal versions.

Serve: in a classic baked macaroni cheese.
Drink: a mild red wine such as Beaujolais or gamay.

Orb Weaver Cave Aged Farmhouse Cheese is an artisanal colby-style cheese.

Carr Valley Colby

Fourth-generation Master Cheesemaker Sid Cook purchased Carr Valley Cheese Company in 1976 and has developed an extensive range of cheeses using cow's, goat's, and sheep's milk. He's particularly well-known for his cheddar-style and other hard cow's milk cheeses, and his colby won first place in its class at the 2006 American Cheese Society Awards.

Size: 12lb wheels, 40lb blocks; Affinage: 1–4 months

Tasting notes: Annatto-dyed (as most colby is) to a rich orange–yellow color, these cloth-wrapped wheels have an open, elastic texture; fresh lactic aroma; and mild, vaguely sweet flavor that develops a pleasant tang and bite with age.

Pasteurized: Yes; Country: USA (Wisconsin)

Crowley

America's oldest continually operating cheese factory still produces an artisan colby-style cheese in waxed cloth-wrapped wheels or waxed blocks. Depending on age, it's semi-hard to hard and mild to extra-sharp in flavor. Flavored versions include sage, chile, and smoked.

Pasteurized: No; Country: USA (Vermont)

Colby Jack

Developed by the Peterson family in Wisconsin (at what is now Arena Cheese) in the 1970s, originally by marbling orange colby and white monterey jack (see page 200) together, colby jack is now often made by dividing a cheese vat, coloring one side, then removing the divider.

Pasteurized: Yes; Country: USA

Orb Weaver Cave Aged Farmhouse Cheese

These 10lb wheels of colby-style cheese from Vermont are handmade from November to May. Beneath a beige natural rind, the buttery, slightly tangy, moist interior is pale to dark yellow depending on the season, with a springy texture.

Pasteurized: No; Country: USA (Vermont)

Henning's Colby

This family owned creamery has produced semi-hard cheeses since 1914. Their mild, moist colby, produced with milk from local Wisconsin farms, was awarded Best of Class in the 2004 and 2007 US Championship Cheese Contest.

Pasteurized: Yes; Country: USA (Wisconsin)

jack cheese

The development of jack cheese is generally attributed to Monterey businessman David Jacks, who started producing and distributing it in the 1890s, perhaps based on a Spanish cheese introduced to California via Mexico by Franciscan monks in the 1700s. It was initially called monterey jack for its county of origin and producer, but as other counties began making it they added their names, and versions such as sonoma jack were born. Now made across the USA, it's often simply called jack cheese. Similar to colby (see page 198) in that the curds are washed, it's generally softer due to slightly higher moisture content.

Serve: in tacos, enchiladas, or burritos, or over tortilla chips for nachos.
Drink: California's favorite varietal, chardonnay; a great match for California's native cheese.

California's taste for Tex-Mex food makes jack cheese melted over nachos a popular choice.

Vella Dry Monterey Jack

San Franciscan cheese wholesaler DeBernardi is credited with creating dry jack when he salted surplus wheels of monterey jack to preserve them and aged them for longer than normal. This harder, drier cheese found a market during World War I when imports of parmesan stopped. Vella Cheese produces three ages of dry jack: 7–10 months, 10–24 months (Special Select), and 2+ years (Golden Bear).

Size: 7³⁄₄lb wheels; Affinage: 7–48 months

Tasting notes: The thin, dark brown rind of this handmade cheese is coated with vegetable oil, pepper, and cocoa. The golden yellow interior starts off firm and sweet, becoming hard (almost brittle), rich, fruity, and nutty with age, like good parmesan (see page 250).

Pasteurized: Yes; Country: USA (California)

Hanford Jack

These 20lb rindless wheels of fresh jack cheese are aged for just 14 days, time enough for the off-white interior to become soft and creamy with a mild, buttery flavor. Fresh jack resembles a creamier, springier edam or gouda (see page 202).

Pasteurized: Yes; Country: USA (California)

Co-Jack

This is the registered trademark for the colby jack (see page 199) now produced by Minnesota farmer-owned cooperative Land O' Lakes. It was first registered by the Peterson family, developers of colby jack, but has changed hands several times since then.

Pasteurized: Yes; Country: USA (Minnesota)

Flavored Jack

Mild, young, fresh jack cheese lends itself well to being mixed with different seasonings. Chiles, garlic, and various herbs and spices are all popular, as are combinations of Mediterranean or South American-style flavors.

Pasteurized: Yes; Country: USA (California)

Jack Goat Cheese

Meyenberg Goat Milk Products produces a stark white, goat's milk, fresh jack cheese with a mild, slightly tangy flavor and semi-soft creamy texture. Their smoked version has a golden rind and white interior; their flavored varieties include jalapeño, garlic and chive, and mushroom.

Pasteurized: Yes; Country: USA (California)

gouda & edam

The flat pasturelands of the Netherlands have long been associated with
dairying. Dutch cheese was exported to Paris as early as 1184, and cheeses
from the towns of Edam and Gouda achieved particular fame. These very similar
washed-curd cheeses (see page 184) vary in size and shape as well as having slightly different
fat contents. They have been widely copied around the world, prompting the cheesemakers of
northern Holland to protect their cheeses with PDO status, and a later application to grant PGI
status to all Dutch-produced edam and gouda, while traditional raw milk cheeses have been
granted TSG status (see page 273).

Serve: on dark bread as *broodje kaas* ("cheese sandwich"), a classic Dutch lunch.
Drink: a glass of buttermilk (the classic accompaniment).

A historic cheese market in Edam keeps tradition alive during the summer months.

Boerenkaas TSG

Until the late 1800s, all Dutch cheese was farm-produced, using raw milk from the farms' own herds. With industrial production transporting milk greater distances, came the need for pasteurization to guarantee food safety, and the individual character of farmhouse cheeses was largely lost. Today Dutch farmhouse raw milk gouda- and edam-style cheeses use the term *Boerenkaas* to differentiate them from industrially produced, pasteurized versions.

Size: From 7oz to 220lb; Affinage: Minimum 13 days on farm

Tasting notes: Mild and supple due to the washed curds; taste, texture, and color vary somewhat with the type of milk used (cow, goat, sheep), becoming firmer and drier with age. Flavoring with cumin and other spices or herbs is common.

Pasteurized: No; Country: Netherlands

Noord-Hollandse Gouda PDO

These 5½–66lb cylinders or blocks range from mild to strong depending on age, which ranges from 4 weeks to 18 months. Less salty than other gouda, and made from whole milk, they have a buttery aroma and very malleable, soft, melt-in-the-mouth texture.

Pasteurized: Yes; Country: Netherlands (Noord-Holland)

Gouda Holland

A firm, smooth, dry rind develops on these 5½–44lb blocks or traditional flattened cylinders. The mild, slightly soft, ivory interior may have scattered eyes. It darkens, becoming firmer and more piquant as it ages up to a year. A PGI application has been filed.

Pasteurized: Yes; Country: Netherlands

Noord-Hollandse Edammer PDO

These slightly flattened 3¾–4lb balls are less salty than other edams. Made from partially skimmed milk (skimmed evening milk mixed with whole morning milk), edam is softer, more malleable, and has a slightly lower fat content than gouda.

Pasteurized: Yes; Country: Netherlands (Noord-Holland)

Edam Holland

Blocks or traditional balls of this cheese develop a firm, smooth, dry rind. Aged for the minimum 28 days (21 for baby edam), it's mild and soft but sliceable with a few small eyes, becoming firmer and stronger with age.

Pasteurized: Yes; Country: Netherlands

gouda-style cheeses

Traditional cheeses have spread to new countries largely through immigration. Patrice Savage-Onstwedder learned cheesemaking in Holland before she and husband John moved to Wales, where they founded Teifi Farmhouse Cheese, today best known for the washed-rind, gouda-style Celtic Promise. The Willems, immigrant Dutch restaurateurs, developed gouda-style Coolea in Ireland. Dutch cheesemakers, the Rympas, started Karikaas in New Zealand in 1984 and won acclaim for their Dutch-style cheeses for 20 years. Back in 1922, a different group of immigrants, Canadian Mennonites, relocated to the Mexican state of Chihuahua as dairy farmers and cheesemakers, where many remain today.

Serve: grated into an omelet with a few chopped herbs.
Drink: a California zinfandel; red or white depending on your preference.

A cheese omelet is a simple way to enjoy mild gouda-style cheeses.

Winchester Sharp Aged Gouda

Dutch immigrants Jules and Corrie Wesselink arrived in California in 1951 and ran several dairy farms before starting the Winchester Cheese Company and turning to cheesemaking in the 1990s. Today daughter Valerie and son-in-law David produce Boerenkaas-style gouda (see page 203) with raw milk on the family farm. They also make mild, medium, super-aged, smoked, and cumin-flavored versions.

Size: 10–12lb wheels; Affinage: 6–8 months

Tasting notes: A hard, waxy, pale yellow rind covers a dark golden yellow interior with a crumbly, flaky texture similar to aged parmesan (see page 250) and a rich, sharp flavor with nutty butterscotch notes and slight caramel aroma.

Pasteurized: No; Country: USA (California)

That Dutchman's Farm Farmstead Gouda

Dutch emigrants, Maja and Willem van den Hoek make gouda and age it from 2 to 24 months on That Dutchman's Farm in Nova Scotia. Their 4-month-old "mild gouda" won the semi-hard category in the 2006 Canadian Cheese Grand Prix.

Pasteurized: No (thermized); Country: Canada

Karikaas Gouda

Founding cheesemakers Rients and Karen Rympa sold their New Zealand dairy in 2004 after training the new owners, who use milk from one local farm to produce award-winning plain and flavored gouda, edam, maasdam (see page 213), and leyden, (see Boeren-Leidse met Sleutels, page 265).

Pasteurized: Yes; Country: New Zealand (Canterbury)

Teifi

Large wheels and smaller drums of this Welsh, golden-rinded, organic, gouda-style cheese are mild and fruity when young, becoming almost flaky with a lingering spiciness over time. Plain, flavored (cumin, nettles, laverbread), and oak-smoked versions are produced.

Pasteurized: No; Country: UK (Wales—Ceredigion)

Chihuahua

Also called menonita, this pale cheese comes in a range of shapes. Creamy and elastic, it has a mild, buttery, slightly salty flavor, similar to gouda or young cheddar. It is now made throughout Mexico and in the USA.

Pasteurized: Either; Country: Mexico (traditionally Chihuahua)

auvergne cheeses

Abundant rainfall, rich volcanic soil, and mountain pastures have
made the Auvergne in south-central France popular for grazing and
dairy products throughout history; its cheeses were mentioned by Pliny
the Elder 2,000 years ago. Medieval monasteries taught local peasants how to make the
cheeses from which today's modern, uncooked, pressed cow's milk cheeses have evolved. Produced
in stone huts (called *burons*) in remote mountain locations, they needed to be well preserved to
travel long distances to market, so a distinctive technique of double pressing developed. The very
similar, large, cylindrical Cantal, Salers, and Laguiole differ only slightly in size, region, and affinage.

Serve: in a cheese and onion quiche.
Drink: a Côtes d'Auvergne wine, usually made from gamay or chardonnay.

Named after the Province of Cantal, Fourme de Cantal is mentioned in writing as early as 100 CE.

▮▮🐄 Cantal (Fourme de Cantal) PDO

All aged Auvergne cheeses are made by a special double-pressing method: the curds are cut and pressed several times to form a slab-like "tome," which is left to drain and ripen overnight before being ground, salted, and pressed into its final molds and matured. Cantal, the best known of these cheeses, is made year-round and named for the province where it was traditionally produced.

Size: Thick wheels, 77–99lb; Affinage: Minimum 30 days

Tasting notes: A balanced saltiness enhances the rich, nutty flavor of the pale gold-colored cheese, which is sweet when young and quite robust when aged, with a rough golden-orange rind. A smaller version called Petit (22lb) is also made.

Pasteurized: Either; Country: France (Auvergne, Midi-Pyrénées, Limousin)

▮▮🐄 Salers PDO

Farm-produced from April to November with milk from cows grazing mountain pastures. The 77–110lb cylinders, aged minimum 3 months, have thick, hard, brown rinds; firm, moist, golden interiors with meaty aroma; strong, sweet, nutty, salty, almost herbal flavors; and rich, oily mouth-feel.

Pasteurized: No; Country: France (Auvergne, Midi-Pyrénées, Limousin)

▮▮🐄 Saint-Nectaire PDO

These flat, 3¾lb, pressed, washed-rind (see page 114) wheels have a purple–gray rind flecked with white and orange mold. The semi-firm, supple, tangy interior has a nutty, slightly metallic taste. When ripe, they develop a mushroomy aroma.

Pasteurized: Either; Country: France (Auvergne)

▮▮🐄 Laguiole PDO

Originally made only in summer, now year-round, with milk produced above 2,600 feet, these 55–110lb cylinders, aged for a minimum of 4 months, have thick, beige rinds, and yellow interiors that become amber–brown with age, developing tangy, fruity flavors and a moist, crumbly texture.

Pasteurized: No; Country: France (Auvergne, Midi-Pyrénées, Languedoc-Roussillon)

▮▮🐄 Aligot (Tome Fraîche)

Ivory-colored, elastic, unsalted, pressed "tome" curds are used in a regional specialty of potatoes mashed with garlic and the cheese. It may have developed from a dish fed to pilgrims heading to Santiago de Compostela.

Pasteurized: Either; Country: France (Auvergne)

asiago

Asiago is named after the Asiago Plateau in the Veneto region of northern Italy; cheese was traditionally produced in this mountainous area from sheep's milk. In the old dialect, Asiago is still called *pegorin*, the generic name for sheep's cheese, though today cows have replaced the sheep. As people migrated, production spread into adjacent foothills and the neighboring region of Trentino-Alto Adige. The similar Montasio, also once a sheep's milk cheese, is named for the mountains of the Giulian Alps in the region of Friuli-Venezia Giulia, where the herds traditionally grazed during summer.

Serve: mixed with red pepper, arugula, and eggs for an Italian frittata.
Drink: a Trentino wine such as Bianco dei Sorni or Rosso dei Sorni.

Asiago is made in the mountainous regions of Veneto and Trentino-Alto Adige in Italy.

Asiago d'Allevo PDO

Allevo literally means "raised," and this traditional Asiago is made in mountainous areas from semi-skimmed milk. It's cooked twice and pressed under the weight of only three or four cheeses stacked atop one another. Aged for at least 3 months it's called *mezzano*, becoming *vecchio* after 10 months and *stravecchio* after 15 months. Aged Asiago d'Allevo from the province of Trento is called vezzena.

Size: 17½–26½lb, thick wheels; Affinage: Minimum 3 months
Tasting notes: A thin, springy, brown rind covers a mild, slightly sweet, smooth, semi-hard, off-white interior with occasional irregular eyes. As it ages it becomes darker, much harder, and grainy, with a fuller, sharper, richer flavor and is used for grating.
Pasteurized: No; Country: Italy (Veneto, Trentino-Alto Adige)

Asiago Pressato PDO

Made generally by large dairies from whole milk in the foothills beneath the d'Allevo production zone, these 24¼–33lb, slightly bulging wheels have a pale, thin, springy rind. The off-white interior has many eyes and a mild, delicately milky flavor.

Pasteurized: Yes; Country: Italy (Veneto, Trentino-Alto Adige)

Montasio PDO

Originally a mountain cheese, now also made in the lowlands. Virtually rindless when young and developing a pale yellow, elastic rind with age, the supple, mild interior has a few eyes, becoming hard and flaky with deeper nutty flavors over time.

Pasteurized: Either; Country: Italy (Friuli-Venezia Giulia, Veneto)

Piave

This natural-rind cylindrical cheese from the Veneto is similar to Asiago, with a full, rounded, nutty, slightly sweet flavor and some crunchy lactate crystals when fully mature. Named for the River Piave and sold at various ages from 1 to 12 months. A PDO application has been filed.

Pasteurized: Yes; Country: Italy (Veneto)

Ragya Yak Cheese

On the Qinghai–Tibetan Plateau where nomadic herders bring their animals for summer pasture, local monk Jigme Gyaltsen heads a project to produce a hard mountain cheese, similar to aged pecorino (see page 246), from local yak's milk. Proceeds fund the local school.

Pasteurized: No (thermized); Country: China (Tibet)

emmental

Not all cheese made in Switzerland has holes, but Emmentaler gave Swiss cheese its holey reputation. The name "Emmentaler" ("of the Emmental") is protected by AOC appellation within Switzerland, though cheeses called emmental are currently produced around the world. Emmental was introduced to France by immigrant Swiss cheesemakers in the 1200s, and two versions produced in the mountains of eastern France have PGI appellations. Swiss cowhands also immigrated in the early 19th century to southern Germany, where they found similar conditions to those of the Emmental and introduced their famous cheese.

Serve: melted onto slices of baguette floating in a bowl of French onion soup.
Drink: a crisp white Swiss wine such as fendant, made from chasselas grapes.

Emmental is often melted onto slices of baguette in French onion soup.

➕ 🐄 Emmentaler AOC

Produced in the valley of the Emme River since the 1200s, wheels of fresh cheese are placed in warm maturing rooms so heat-loving propionic bacteria added to the milk can ferment and give off bubbles of carbon dioxide, producing the cheese's characteristic eyes. *Réserve* is aged a minimum 8 months; "cave-aged" at least 12 months (with at least 6 in a natural cave).

Size: 165–265lb bulging wheels; Affinage: Minimum 4 months
Tasting notes; The dry natural rind darkens from yellow to speckled dark brown with age. The ivory- to light yellow-colored interior with cherry-sized holes has a smooth, sliceable texture that becomes crumbly with age, the initial mild, nutty flavor becoming rich and spicy.

Pasteurized: No; Country: Switzerland (Bern)

▮▮ 🐄 Emmental Français Est-Central PGI

Made since the 1200s in eastern France in the Vosges and Jura Mountains (also in the Savoy Alps), these 154lb wheels are aged for at least 10 weeks. They have a soft texture and fruity flavor.

Pasteurized: No; Country: France (Lorraine, Champagne, Burgundy, Franche-Comté, Rhône-Alpes)

▬ 🐄 Allgäuer Emmentaler PDO

In the early 1820s, Swiss cowherds migrated across the border to Bavaria, taking their cheesemaking skills with them. These 132lb, natural-rinded wheels or 88lb blocks are very similar to Swiss Emmentaler and produced to similar strict standards.

Pasteurized: No; Country: Germany (Bavaria, Baden-Württemberg)

▮▮ 🐄 Emmental de Savoie PGI

Produced in the Savoy Alps since the early 1800s, these 132lb wheels are very similar to Emmental Français Est-Central except that wild rather than cultivated bacteria are used to ferment the milk and they are aged at slightly different temperatures.

Pasteurized: No (may be thermized); Country: France (Rhône-Alpes)

▬ 🐄 Allgäuer Bergkäse PDO

As well as introducing emmental, the migrant Swiss herders also influenced the production of similar existing mountain cheeses such as these natural-rinded, 33–110lb wheels with scattered pea-sized eyes, aged for a minimum of 4 months.

Pasteurized: No; Country: Germany (Bavaria, Baden-Württemberg)

emmental-style cheeses

Emmental's traditional inheritance system, whereby the youngest (and presumably fittest) son had the right to buy his brothers' shares in the family farm, left many cowhands with money but no land. Some emigrated, taking their cheesemaking skills with them, and Emmentaler (see page 211), with its distinctive holes, became one of the most widely copied cheeses worldwide ("swiss cheese" becoming a generic name for any holey cheese). *Propionibacter shermani* bacteria, which produce carbon dioxide, are responsible for the holes (the cheese's "eyes") as well as the distinctive flavor. The larger the eyes, generally the stronger the flavor, because the bacteria have been more active.

Serve: with ham on a rye bread sandwich.
Drink: vin jaune from the French Jura Mountains or a nutty amontillado sherry.

Southern Norway is the traditional home of Jarlsberg, the most widely known emmental-style cheese.

Jarlsberg

In the 1830s, Swiss cheesemakers migrated to the county of Jarlsberg and Larvik in southern Norway, introducing their classic "holey" cheeses. In 1956 work done by graduate student Per Sakshaug and Professor Ystgaard at the Norwegian University of Life Sciences led to the development of Jarlsberg, using a strain of the same bacteria, *Propionibacter shermani*, that gives emmental its holes.

Size: 22lb wheels, 22–44lb blocks; Affinage: 3–12 months

Tasting notes: The thin, yellow-brown rind may be covered in yellow wax. The smooth, supple, pale yellow interior with large scattered eyes is slightly sweeter and less nutty than emmental, but still has the distinctive, slightly sweet earthiness from the propionic bacteria.

Pasteurized: Yes; Country: Norway

Samsø

Developed in the 1800s and, in 1952, named after the Danish island of Samsø (which had a reputation for Swiss-style cheese), samsø cheese is softer and paler than emmental with fewer eyes and a mild, tangy, slightly sweet, nutty flavor, intensifying with age.

Pasteurized: Yes; Country: Denmark

Maasdam

Created in the 1980s as a Dutch alternative to imported emmental, maasdam is higher in moisture and therefore softer, with a sweet, buttery flavor and slightly fruity aftertaste. Leerdammer is the Bel Group's trademarked version of maasdam.

Pasteurized: Yes; Country: Netherlands

Grevé

This emmental-style Swedish cheese, developed in the early 1960s, has a smooth, shiny, pale, natural rind and dense, supple, pale yellow interior with scattered large eyes. It has a creamy mouth-feel and a mild, sweetly nutty flavor. Also called grevéost.

Pasteurized: Yes; Country: Sweden

Edelweiss Creamery Emmentaler

Master Wisconsin Cheesemaker Bruce Workman uses a Swiss copper cheese cauldron to turn milk from five local family farms into 176lb wheels of raw-milk emmental. Aged 17–24 months, they have a mild, slightly sweet, nutty flavor.

Pasteurized: No; Country: USA (Wisconsin)

gruyère

The name "gruyère" derives from a French word meaning "forest" or "forester/woodsman," perhaps referring to the wood needed to fuel the huge cheese cauldrons and the cheese the woodsmen received in payment for it. Large, hard, brine-scrubbed cheeses, like Comté and Beaufort (referred to collectively as gruyère cheeses) have been produced in France and Switzerland since the 11th century, traditionally with pooled milk from cows grazing on summer and autumn pastures brought down to the valleys' cooperative dairies. Gruyère produced in both France and Switzerland has AOC status. L'Étivaz AOC, from the Swiss canton of Vaud, is made like an old-fashioned traditional Gruyère.

Serve: in a Swiss fondue with Emmentaler (see page 211) and white wine.
Drink: with fondue a white wine (preferably Swiss) or beer; never water or red wine.

Dairies in several cantons of western Switzerland produce Gruyère cheese.

🇨🇭 🐄 Gruyère AOC

Associated with the Fribourg town of Gruyère, this Swiss cheese is made in several French-speaking cantons. Gruyère Réserve is matured for minimum 10 months, and Gruyère Alpage is made in the high pastures of the Alps and Jura Mountains in summer. Negotiations are underway to have Swiss Gruyère's AOC status recognized within the EU, though France has also applied to register the name.

Size: Slightly bulging, 55–88lb wheels; Affinage: Minimum 5 months
Tasting notes: Beneath a pale-brown, moist, natural rind, the dense, smooth, supple interior becomes slightly crumbly with age. Color varies seasonally (cream to pale yellow), and it may have small scattered eyes and cracks. The creamy, nutty, fruity flavor is slightly salty.
Pasteurized: No; Country: Switzerland (Fribourg, Vaud, Neuchâtel, Jura, Bern)

🇫🇷 🐄 Comté PDO

France's most popular cheese, these broad, flat wheels from the Jura Mountains have moist, brown rinds; firm, dense, supple, cream-yellow interiors with a few small eyes; and balanced, tangy, nutty, salty flavors with a slightly caramel aftertaste.

Pasteurized: No; Country: France (Franche-Comté, Rhône-Alpes, Burgundy, Champagne-Ardenne, Lorraine)

🇫🇷 🐄 Abondance PDO

These 15½–26½lb wheels are named for the cattle introduced by the Abondance Monastery in the 11th century. Like a small Beaufort, they have a complex, balanced, tangy, salty, sweet flavor. The rind develops a gray layer beneath its surface.

Pasteurized: No; Country: France (Rhône-Alpes)

🇫🇷 🐄 Beaufort PDO

Hard, brown-orange, 44–154lb wheels, with concave sides, from France's Savoy Alps. The interior has a buttery aroma and balanced, tangy, salty flavor. Winter cheese is almost white, while summer cheese (d'été) is pale yellow; d'Alpage is made in Alpine chalets.

Pasteurized: No; Country: France (Rhône-Alpes)

🇬🇷 🐄 🐄 🦌 Graviera Naxou PDO

Mild, nutty graviera (hard Greek cheeses named for Gruyère) from the isle of Naxos contains at least 80% cow's milk. Graviera Agrafon PDO (from Agrafa Mountains) and Graviera Kritis PDO (from Crete), made from sheep's and/or goat's milk, are much sharper.

Pasteurized: Either; Country: Greece (Naxos)

gruyère-style cheeses

Swiss-style cheeses have been imitated the world over, often by large factories producing bland cheese with holes, but also by artisan producers. John and Janine Putnam of Thistle Hill Farm, lawyers-turned-dairy-farmers, visited the Alps in 1999 to investigate cheesemaking. Tarentaise, modeled on Beaufort d'Alpage (see page 215), was the result. Herrgårdsost ("manor house cheese"), developed for Count Eric Ruuth by a Swiss cheesemaker in the late 1800s, was so-named because the count declared it good enough to be served at his manor house. Swiss emigrant cheesemaker Frank Marchand went to Australia in the 1970s and in 1985 started Heidi Farm, now owned by National Foods (owners of King Island Dairies).

Serve: in a toasted sandwich with ham for a classic croque monsieur.
Drink: a medium, fruity red such as barbera or spicy white such as Alsatian gewürztraminer.

Gruyère-style cheeses are delicious in a toasted sandwich with ham for a classic croque monsieur.

▌▌🐄 Gabriel

Produced by Bill Hogan and Sean Ferry, of West Cork Natural Cheeses, who learned cheesemaking in the late 1980s in the Swiss Alps, Gabriel (named after nearby Mount Gabriel) is made only from June to September, with milk from local farms whose cows graze the natural pastures of the lush southern tip of Ireland.

Size: 15½lb wheels; Affinage: 10–36 months

Tasting notes: The smooth, thick rind is golden-brown. The hard, smooth, yellow interior becomes more granular with age until it resembles parmesan (see page 250) and turns deep golden. The complex flavor has a salty, fruity tang and gentle spiciness.

Pasteurized: No; Country: Ireland (Cork)

▨🐄 Heidi Farm Gruyere

These thick, 66lb, orange–brown-rinded wheels are Australia's largest cheese. The firm, supple interior has tiny, crunchy, lactate crystals and a sweet, fruity, nutty, buttery flavor. Regularly awarded medals as Australia's best cooked hard cheese.

Pasteurized: Yes; Country: Australia (Tasmania)

▦🐄 Herrgård

These hard, 26½lb waxed-rind wheels of Swedish cheese have a softer, suppler interior than Gruyère, smaller eyes, a buttery aroma, and mild, slightly tangy, nutty flavor. "Mild" is 3 months old, "mature" at least 8 months. Also called herrgårdsost.

Pasteurized: Yes; Country: Sweden

▥🐄 Tarentaise

Named for the Tarentaise Valley in the Savoy Alps, where Beaufort and Abondance (see page 215) are made, this dense, smooth Vermont cheese, handmade in a copper cauldron from organic milk, is complex, with subtle nutty, buttery, caramel flavors, and brown–orange rind.

Pasteurized: No; Country: USA (Vermont)

▨🐄 Klein River South African Gruyere

The dense, supple texture and fruity, nutty flavor of the 6-month-old cheese becomes granular, slightly crunchy, and strong by 10–12 months, and won gold at the 2007 World Cheese Awards.

Pasteurized: Yes; Country: South Africa (Western Cape)

raclette

Similar to Gruyère (see page 214), though smaller, raclette has been produced since the Middle Ages when cowherds heated their cheese in front of an open fire, scraping the melted layer onto a piece of bread; the name comes from the French *racler* ("to scrape"). The popular Swiss dish also called "raclette" is rarely made in front of open fires anymore; sometimes a grill like a small electric bar-heater is used with the cut face of the half wheel held to the heat until it melts; more commonly small tabletop grills are used to melt slices of raclette in individual pans.

Serve: melted and scraped onto bread or over potatoes with pickled onions and cornichons.
Drink: a white wine with good acid such as chasselas from Switzerland or the Savoy Alps.

Raclette is traditionally heated then scraped onto a plate or over bread or potatoes.

🇨🇭 🐄 Raclette du Valais AOC

Although much of Switzerland's raclette production comes from other cantons, raclette has long been associated with the canton of Valais in southwestern Switzerland, where it's still made in small batches by traditional producers and typically ripened for 4–6 months.

Size: 12–16½lb wheels or blocks; Affinage: Minimum 2 months

Tasting notes: Beneath the orange-brown washed rind, the dense, supple interior is ivory to pale yellow with scattered eyes and a mellow, creamy, nutty flavor, becoming more aromatic, earthy, and tangy with age. Melted, it doesn't turn oily, and the flavor intensifies.

Pasteurized: No; Country: Switzerland (Valais)

🇫🇷 🐄 French Raclette

Traditionally produced in the Savoy Alps, though now made throughout France, in 10–15½lb wheels or blocks, the thin yellow-brown rind covers a semi-hard, supple, ivory to pale yellow interior with small scattered eyes and a mild, milky flavor.

Pasteurized: Either; Country: France (traditionally Rhône-Alpes)

🇨🇭 🐄 Appenzeller

The yellow-brown rind of these Swiss, 15½lb wheels is washed with an herbal brine. The supple, ivory to pale yellow interior has a few small eyes and a balanced sweet, smoky flavor; it develops occasional crunchy lactate crystals with age.

Pasteurized: No; Country: Switzerland (Appenzell, Saint Gallen)

🇦🇺 🐄 Fromart Raclette

These moist, orange-yellow wheels from Swiss cheesemaker Christian Nobel, in the foothills of Queensland's Glass House Mountains, have a dense, supple interior with a savory, yeasty, almost meaty flavor and a hint of sweetness. The aroma becomes stronger with age.

Pasteurized: Yes; Country: Australia (Queensland)

🇿🇦 🐄 Witzenberger

Kimilili Farm in South Africa's Witzenberg Ranges makes these 11–15½lb wheels modeled on Appenzeller. Aged for at least 6 months, the dense interior has tangy, nutty flavors and strong aromas. Silver medal winner at 2008 World Cheese Awards.

Pasteurized: No; Country: South Africa (Western Cape)

tilsit

Tilsiter cheese was developed by Swiss cheesemakers living in Tilsit, in what was then East Prussia (now Russia). It was brought to Switzerland's eastern cantons of Thurgau, St. Gallen, and Zurich in 1893 by immigrating Swiss-Prussian cheesemakers. The remaining German-speaking population were expelled in 1945 when Soviet forces occupied Tilsit and renamed it Sovetsk. In 2007, after a Swiss cheese importer announced plans to import Russian tilsiter, Otto Wartmann, whose great-great-uncle was one of the original Swiss-Prussian immigrants, had his Thurgau farm officially renamed "Tilsit," creating a locality of Tilsit for the first time in more than 60 years.

Serve: sliced with cold cuts and bread as an appetizer.
Drink: müller-thurgau white wine.

A monument in Sovetsk, the former Tilsit, is a reminder of its Soviet history.

🇨🇭 🐄 Swiss Tilsiter

Several variations are produced: pasteurized (green label) and the softer cream-enriched yellow label are both aged 30–75 days; raw milk (red label), aged 2½–4 months, and the slightly longer-aged organic (Bio) version; Surchoix, made with raw milk and aged 4–6 months; and Alpine (or Alpen Tilsiter), aged 4–6 months and washed with a blend of Alpine herbs and müller-thurgau white wine.

Size: 9–10lb wheels; Affinage: Minimum 30 days
Tasting notes: Beneath the reddish-brown rind, the interior is ivory-colored when young, becoming pale yellow with age. It has a few scattered eyes and a supple texture (the cream-enriched version is very soft). Over time it becomes firmer and the mild, tangy flavor develops nutty notes.

Pasteurized: Either; Country: Switzerland (Saint Gallen, Thurgau, Zurich)

▬ 🐄 German Tilsiter

Introduced by Prussian emigrants and now a north-German classic, this typically brick-shaped, 4½–11lb cheese has a thin, dry, pale yellow rind; slightly spicy aroma; and smooth, supple interior with tiny, scattered eyes and a buttery, fruity, slightly spicy flavor.

Pasteurized: Either; Country: Germany (north)

🇨🇭 🐄 Küssnachter

From Schwyz in north-central Switzerland, these wine-washed wheels have a buttery texture when young. Well-aged variations, such as Hoch Ybrig, aged by affineur Rolf Beeler, develop nutty, tangy, slightly salty, toffee flavors and crunchy little lactate crystals.

Pasteurized: No; Country: Switzerland (Schwyz)

🇩🇰 🐄 Havarti

Named after Denmark's Havarti Farm where it was developed in the 1800s, semi-hard, supple, buttery havarti is like a mild German tilsiter. Richer, softer "cream havarti" is now also produced; both are often flavored with dill, caraway, and other seasonings.

Pasteurized: Yes; Country: Denmark

🇩🇰 🐄 Gräddost

Created in the mid-20th century, these rindless drums, similar to havarti, are sometimes called "butter cheese," though *grädde* is Swedish for "cream." They have a firm, supple, pale yellow interior with a mild, creamy, tangy flavor and numerous scattered eyes.

Pasteurized: Yes; Country: Sweden

cheeses for the girolle

Created at the 12th-century Abbey of Bellelay in the Jura Mountains of northwestern Switzerland and originally called Bellelay, Tête de Moine is traditionally served by scraping rosettes off the top of the cheese. In 1982 a device called a girolle was invented for this purpose. Speared through a metal spike set into a wooden base, the cheese is scraped by a sharp blade on a swivel arm centered on the spike. Despite Swiss insistence that a girolle can be used only for Tête de Moine, it works well on other cheeses of a similar size and texture.

Serve: cold, so the rosettes form properly, alongside cold meats and bread.
Drink: dry white wine such as French Chablis.

Wheels of Tête de Moine age on wooden shelves.

🇨🇭 🐄 Tête de Moine AOC

The name Tête de Moine ("monk's head") may refer to the annual fee of one cheese for each monk ("per head") paid by local farmers for the right to produce the cheese to the monks' recipe. Or perhaps it refers to the way the cut cheese, with its pale top and darker brown sides, resembles a monk's traditional bald-top haircut (or *tonsure*).

Size: 1½–2lb drums; Affinage: 3–4 months

Tasting notes: Beneath the firm, slightly moist, reddish-brown rind, the color of the dense, semi-hard interior varies from ivory to pale yellow, with winter cheeses being paler. It may have a few small eyes and cracks, with buttery, nutty, earthy, tangy flavors.

Pasteurized: No; Country: Switzerland (Bern)

🇦🇺 🐄 Bruny Island Cheese Co. Tom

These 3lb drums from Tasmania are modeled on a Tomme de Savoie (see page 225), with a natural gray rind and pale yellow, mild, buttery, nutty interior. The side rind may be removed or left on before placing Tom on the girolle.

Pasteurized: Yes; Country: Australia (Tasmania)

🇺🇸 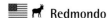 Redmondo

These 4½lb drums from Oregon's Juniper Grove Farm have a very firm, slightly granular texture. Aged for at least 9 months, their fruity, nutty flavors work well shaved into thin rosettes. Halve and remove side rind before placing on girolle.

Pasteurized: No; Country: USA (Oregon)

🇪🇸 🐑 Oveja al Romero

This semi-hard cheese from northwestern and central Spain is aged about 3–12 months. The natural rind is covered with blue–gray molds and rosemary, imparting a sweet, spicy, herbaceous flavor. Remove most of the side rind before placing on the girolle.

Pasteurized: Either; Country: Spain (Castile-León, Castile-La Mancha)

🇫🇷 🐄 Tomme de Thônes

These slightly bulging 2lb 3oz drums from the village of Thônes in the Savoy Alps have the distinctive Tomme de Savoie white mold-dusted, gray rind, which is best removed before scraping the interior into rosettes on the girolle.

Pasteurized: No; Country: France (Rhône-Alpes)

tomme

Tomme means "Alpine cheese" in the dialect of the Savoy Alps in eastern France, where these cheeses are most common. Small (typically 2–4½lb or less) tommes were traditionally made for domestic consumption from the milk of one herd so that the larger, more valuable cheeses such as Beaufort (see page 215), often made with milk pooled from several herds at the local cooperative, could be sold. Tome des Bauges PDO is a Tomme de Savoie from the Bauges Mountains. In neighboring Piedmont in northwestern Italy, the name toma is used for similar, often larger, cheeses, while tomme vaudoise is from nearby Switzerland.

Serve: grated over scalloped potatoes.
Drink: a Côtes du Rhône blend of grenache, shiraz, and mourvèdre.

Tomme is perfect grated over scalloped potatoes for a delicious potato gratin.

■ ■ 🐄 Tomme de Savoie PGI

Made by peasants since at least the 14th century to preserve summer milk, and still a mainstay of Savoyard cuisine, these small, uncooked, pressed cheeses are often made from skim milk. When there wasn't enough milk to make a large cheese, such as Beaufort, the cream was used for butter and the remaining milk for a small tomme.

Size: 2¹/₂–4¹/₂lb cylinders; Affinage: Minimum 6 weeks

Tasting notes: Beneath the hard, distinctive, gray rind spotted with red and yellow molds, the slightly sticky, semi-hard, pale yellow interior has scattered eyes, an earthy aroma, and mild flavor. It may be flavored with caraway, which grows wild in the Savoy Alps.

Pasteurized: No (may be thermized); Country: France (Rhône-Alpes)

■ ■ 🐐 Tomme de Chèvre

Goats are almost as popular as cows in the rough terrain of the Savoy Alps. Tommes made from their milk are slightly tangier than the cow's milk versions. Mi-chèvre are made from half cow's and half goat's milk.

Pasteurized: Either; Country: France

■ ■ 🐄 Toma Piemontese PDO

Toma, the Italian version of tomme, are produced mainly in the Alpine northwest corner of Italy, from either whole or semi-skimmed milk. Toma Piemontese, currently the only one with PDO status, covers a wide range of semi-hard Piedmont mountain cheeses.

Pasteurized: Either; Country: Italy (Piedmont)

■ ■ 🐄 🐐 🐑 Tomme des Pyrénées PGI

The guidelines for this cheese have recently changed to allow pasteurized, raw, goat's, and sheep's milk. Younger black-waxed wheels have a tangy flavor, which becomes more savory in the longer-matured, natural, golden-rinded cheeses.

Pasteurized: Either; Country: France (Pyrenees)

▤ 🐄 Thomasville Tomme

These semi-hard, 10lb wheels from Sweet Grass Dairy, in Thomasville, Georgia, are modeled on Tomme des Pyrénées. They have a rough, tan rind and slightly crumbly, golden-yellow interior with a mellow, buttery flavor and slightly tangy finish.

Pasteurized: No; Country: USA (Georgia)

bra & testun

Similar to Toma Piemontese (see page 225), Bra cheese is named for the market town of Bra in Piedmont in northwestern Italy, where the young cheeses from this section of the Alps were traditionally sold and consumed by the locals or matured in their cellars for later sale. Testun, another type of toma made from sheep's, goat's, or mixed milks, derives its name from Piedmontese dialect meaning "big, hard head." Like Bra, it can be eaten young (after about 2 months) or aged for 12 months or more when it becomes a good grating cheese. Testun al fieno is aged in hay.

Serve: with rye bread and Italian fruit chutney, such as apple or grape must.
Drink: Barolo, one of Italy's classic red wines, from the same region.

Cows in Piedmont, Italy, provide the milk for traditional Bra cheese.

▐▌🐄 🐐 🐑 Bra PDO

Two types of Bra are made, usually from partially skimmed cow's milk combined from morning and evening milkings, and sometimes with small amounts of goat's and/or sheep's milk added. *Tenero* ("tender"), aged for at least 2 months, is the youngest and softest; from 6 months onwards it becomes *duro* ("hard").

Size: 13–17½lb wheels; Affinage: 45 days–2 years

Tasting notes: Rinds vary with age from pale and thin to brown and hard. The pale, supple interior with a few small eyes and mild, grassy, milky flavors becomes dark yellow, harder, and crumbly as it matures, developing slightly sour, bitter flavors.

Pasteurized: Either; Country: Italy (Piedmont)

▐▌🐄 🐐 🐑 Bra d'Alpeggio

This artisan product is made from the milk of cows grazing the summer pastures (at least 3,000 feet above sea level) from June to October. Small amounts of sheep's and/or goat's milk may be added. Sold as *duro* or *tenero*.

Pasteurized: No; Country: Italy (Piedmont)

▐▌🐑 🐄 Testun di Pecora

Produced by Beppino Occelli, this sheep's milk testun (sometimes with small amounts of cow's milk added) has a thin, rough, beige rind and firm, pale interior that becomes marbled with darker streaks with age—when it's a good substitute for pecorino (see page 246).

Pasteurized: Yes; Country: Italy (Piedmont)

▐▌🐄 🐐 Testun al Barolo

Soaked in local Barolo wine and covered with crushed grape skins to produce a strong, fermented aroma. The interior near the rind is pinkish-purple and has a strong fruity flavor. Similar cheeses are called ubriaco, embriago, or ciuc, meaning "drunk."

Pasteurized: Yes; Country: Italy (Piedmont)

▐▌🐐 🐄 Testun di Capra

Also produced by Beppino Occelli, this goat's milk testun is aged on wooden boards for at least 4 months. It has a sharper, tangier flavor and whiter, flakier interior than the very similar sheep's milk version.

Pasteurized: Yes; Country: Italy (Piedmont)

alpine cheeses

In remote mountains, such as Europe's Alps, before refrigeration and modern transport, buttermaking and cheesemaking were ways to preserve milk. Large, cooked, well-pressed wheels, with as much whey as possible extracted, had a long shelf life and could survive the journey to distant markets. To collect enough milk for such large wheels, several milkings were often combined after cream had been skimmed off for butter. Lombardy's Formai de Mut dell'Alta Valle Brembana PDO, Swiss Bündner Bergkäse, and Sauerkäse AOC (also from Liechtenstein) and the cheeses below are mountain cheeses made year-round, though the versions made from summer Alpine milk are often considered superior (see page 230).

Serve: slices on a crisp bread roll with tomato, onion, olive paste, and grilled peppers.
Drink: an aged New World chardonnay with richness and complexity to match these cheeses.

Special frames have been developed for carrying cheese made in the Alps down to markets in the valleys.

▌▌🐄 Fontina PDO

Referred to by name in northwestern Italy's Valle d'Aosta since the 18th century, and likely much older, Fontina is a whole-milk cheese produced twice a day as soon as the cows are milked. Valle d'Aosta Fromadzo PDO is a similar cheese made with partially skimmed milk from at least two milkings and often containing a small amount of goat's milk.

Size: 17½–39lb flat wheels; Affinage: Average 3 months

Tasting notes: A firm, thin, reddish-brown rind covers the supple, yellow interior, which has a scattering of small eyes and a firm, buttery texture. The flavor is rich and buttery with slightly honeyed sweetness and hints of nuttiness.

Pasteurized: No; Country: Italy (Valle d'Aosta)

▌▌🐄 🐐 🐑 Raschera PDO

These semi-skimmed wheels and squares (more firmly pressed) from Piedmont may contain a little sheep's and/or goats' milk. Aged for 20–90 days, they have a springy texture with a buttermilk aroma and tangy, almondy flavor. Raschera d'Alpeggio is made above 3,000 feet.

Pasteurized: Either; Country: Italy (Piedmont)

▌▌🐄 Monte Veronese PDO

Skim milk Monte Veronese d'Allevo, the traditional cheese from the Veneto's Monti Lessini range, is an excellent grating cheese when aged for 6 months or more. Whole milk Monte Veronese is a more recent, shorter-aged cheese similar to Asiago Pressato (see page 209).

Pasteurized: No; Country: Italy (Veneto)

▌▌🐄 Spressa delle Guidicarie PDO

These 34–48lb wheels were traditionally made from two milkings after cream had been skimmed to make butter. They have a hard yellow–brown rind and supple, dense, pale, sweet, slightly bitter interior, becoming more savory with age.

Pasteurized: No; Country: Italy (Trentino-Alto Adige)

🇨🇭 🐄 Vacherin Fribourgeois AOC

These uncooked, lightly pressed wheels from western Switzerland, aged for 3–6 months, are similar to Fontina. Beneath the rough, washed-rind, the firm, supple interior has buttery, nutty, faintly tangy, caramelly flavors. Vacherin Fribourgeois d'Alpage is made from summer Alpine milk.

Pasteurized: No (some thermized); Country: Switzerland (Fribourg, Vaud, Jura)

seasonal alpine cheeses

Many countries have a tradition of transhumance (the temporary migration of livestock to high mountain pastures in summer and returning to their valley homes in winter). Mountain vegetation contributes to the milk's flavor and the cheeses produced are highly valued and distinguished from those made in the valleys year-round. The names and rules governing production vary from country to country; for example, in German-speaking countries bergkäse ("mountain cheese") is produced all year, but alpkäse ("Alpine cheese") is made only during summer Alpine grazing. Swiss Formaggio d'Alpe Ticinese AOC is produced only 3 months a year in the Italian-speaking canton of Ticino at 5,000–8,000 feet.

Serve: melted into soft polenta.
Drink: an Austrian riesling with its balanced fruit and acid.

Seasonal Alpine cheeses are delicious melted into soft polenta.

Tiroler Almkäse/Tiroler Alpkäse PDO

Alpkäse and Almkäse are regional names for the same cheese produced in western Austria during the 3–4 months of Alpine grazing. Washed in brine, often mixed with *Brevibacterium linens*, it can have a distinctive washed-rind aroma (see page 114). Similar Tiroler Bergkäse PDO is produced year-round with milk from cows fed on grass and hay, never silage (fermented fodder).

Size: 17½–132lb wheel; Affinage: 4.5–6 months

Tasting notes: The firm, brownish-yellow rind may have an orange tint. The interior has scattered medium-sized eyes; it starts off supple and pale, becoming firmer and darker. The mild, slightly sweet flavor becomes more tangy and more savory with age.

Pasteurized: No; Country: Austria (Tyrol)

Gailtaler Almkäse PDO

Produced since the 14th century, this southern Austrian cheese, also called Gailtaler Alpkäse, is made only from Alpine milk and may include up to 10% goat's milk. Golden, natural-rinded, 1–77lb wheels are usually aged for a minimum 7 weeks.

Pasteurized: No; Country: Austria (Carinthia)

Bitto PDO

Produced from June to September in Lombardy's Valtellina area and containing up to 10% goat's milk, these pale yellow wheels are often aged for a year or more, darkening and becoming intensely flavored. Valtellina Casera PDO is the nonseasonal version.

Pasteurized: No; Country: Italy (Lombardy)

Vorarlberger Alpkäse PDO

These large rough-rinded wheels (maximum 77lb) from western Austria are made with milk produced at 3,300–5,900 feet during summer. They age from pale, supple, and mild to darker, firm, and spicy after 6 months. Vorarlberger Bergkäse PDO is the nonseasonal version.

Pasteurized: No; Country: Austria (Vorarlberg)

Prättigauer

From Switzerland's easternmost canton, these 11lb wheels made from summer Alpine milk, have a pinkish-orange rind; dense, pale yellow, salty, tangy interior; and smoky aroma as the milk is heated in copper cauldrons over woodfires.

Pasteurized: No (maybe thermized); Country: Switzerland (Graubunden)

other seasonal cheeses

Cow's milk cheeses are usually only produced seasonally when they're made with Alpine milk (see page 230), while cheeses made from goat's or sheep's milk are often seasonal regardless of location, because these animals have much shorter lactation cycles and, when raised traditionally, don't produce milk year-round. For commercial reasons, many goat and sheep herds are now being raised in such a way that they produce milk year-round and cheeses that were once seasonal no longer are. However, versions produced in the traditional season are still widely regarded as superior to those produced out of season.

Serve: grated into the center of split baked potatoes.
Drink: Austrian grüner veltliner, juicy with crisp acid; a good all-round cheese wine.

Split baked potatoes are a good match for these seasonal cheeses.

▮▮🐑🐄 Casciotta d'Urbino PDO

From Marche in Italy's southeast, this largely sheep's milk cheese (with 30% cow's milk) dates from the 1300s. Produced December–September (the lambs getting the milk in October and November), the best are made in March–June, the sheep's traditional lactation period. *Cacio/caciotta* is a widely used Italian word for "cheese" (see caciocavallo, page 80); it's uncertain how this version developed its spelling (with an "s").

Size: Thick, bulging, 2lb wheels; Affinage: 15–30 days

Tasting notes: The beige-yellow rind is thin and springy; the moist, pale yellow interior is firm and crumbly with a few small eyes and a sweet, slightly tangy flavor; and the relatively short aging produces a fresh milky aroma and taste.

Pasteurized: Either; Country: Italy (Marche)

▮▮🦌 Casieddu

In Basilicata in southern Italy, where mixed herds of sheep and goats are common, this white cheese infused with calamint and wrapped in fern fronds is made from July to September when the sheep stop lactating and only goat's milk is available.

Pasteurized: Yes; Country: Italy (Basilicata)

▮▮🐄 Imokilly Regato PDO

Produced from February to October when the cows graze on the lush pastures of Cork in Ireland's south, these 9- to 12-month-old wheels have a firm, creamy yellow interior with rounded savory flavors and a rind embossed with a distinctive Celtic cord pattern.

Pasteurized: Yes; Country: Ireland (Cork)

🇺🇸🐄 Drunken Hooligan

These small wine-washed disks are made by Connecticut's Cato Corner Farm from September to April, when the cows' diet of hay gives a higher butterfat content ideal for washed rind cheeses. They have a strong aroma but mild, creamy interior.

Pasteurized: No; Country: USA (Connecticut)

🇨🇭🐄 Berner Alpkäse AOC

This seasonal Alpine cheese from central Switzerland's Bernese Oberland is produced daily during summer. The rind is washed in brine (sometimes with wine and spices) during its 6 months maturation. The best are aged an additional 12 months to become Berner Hobelkäse AOC.

Pasteurized: No; Country: Switzerland (Bern)

mixed milk cheeses

Small traditional farms have often kept a variety of animals, including goats, sheep, and cows, combining whatever milk was produced to make cheese. Such mixed herds are still common, especially in more remote areas, and many traditional cheeses do (or are permitted to) contain two or even three types of milk. These include Spanish los beyos, queso iberico (see page 255), Queso Majorero (see page 241), Quesucos de Liébana (see page 263), and Máhon-Menorca (see page 237); Portuguese Queijo de Castelo Branco, Queijo Mestiço de Tolosa (see page 237), and Queijos da Beira Baixa (see page 239); Italian Castelmagno (see page 173), Bra (see page 226) and robiola (see page 146), and Greek cottage cheeses (see page 48).

Serve: with crusty bread and membrillo, Spanish quince paste.
Drink: a Spanish *rosado* (rosé) made from *garnacha* (grenache).

Many cheeses are traditionally made with milk from mixed herds of goats and sheep.

Queso Servilleta

This Valencian cheese has a distinctive shape. Traditionally it was made by women and tied in a towel (*servilleta*) to drain; the knot made in the cloth caused an indent in the top of the cheese. Traditionally a goat's milk cheese, it is now made from either cow's or goat's milk or a blend of the two.

Size: 1–6½lb, thick, indented wheels; Affinage: Minimum 15 days

Tasting notes: Aged for at least 15 days, these thick disks with indented tops have a thin, smooth, golden rind and springy, yellow interior with occasional eyes. The flavor is slightly sweet-tart, lightly salty, and buttery.

Pasteurized: Yes; Country: Spain (Valencia)

Chevrette des Bauges

In France's Savoy Alps, cheeses made with goat's and cow's milk are called chevrette, as opposed to the pure cow's milk Chevrotin (see page 125). These 1–2lb disks from the Bauges Mountains have a rough, white–gray rind and firm, pale interior.

Pasteurized: No; Country: France (Rhône-Alpes)

Altenburger Ziegenkäse PDO

Although Ziegenkäse means "goat cheese" in German, up to 85% cow's milk is allowed in these 9oz disks. Aged for just a few weeks, the thin, white mold-dusted rind covers a creamy, mild, slightly tangy interior. Caraway may be added.

Pasteurized: Yes; Country: Germany (Thuringia, Saxony)

Matocq

These thick, 9lb wheels from southwestern France are made from pure cow's milk, pure sheep's milk (covered by Ossau-Iraty PDO, see page 244), or a mixture. They have a white mold-dusted, golden-orange rind and rich, nutty, semi-hard interior with a few eyes.

Pasteurized: Either; Country: France (Aquitaine)

Tronchón

Named for a small village in mountainous northeastern Spain where mixed goat and sheep herds are traditional, this smooth, buttery cheese smells of hay and butter. It's pressed in wooden molds, which create an indent top and bottom.

Pasteurized: Either; Country: Spain (Valencia, Catalonia, Aragon)

cheeses made with traditional vegetarian rennet

The first step in cheesemaking is curdling the milk into solid curds and liquid whey; this is usually done with an animal extract called rennet. So-called "vegetarian rennet," synthesized in a laboratory, is popular in cheeses today because many lacto-vegetarians (vegetarians who eat dairy products) won't eat cheese produced with traditional rennet. In Portugal and parts of neighboring Spain, however, a truly vegetarian rennet-alternative, extracted from the flower heads of cardoon thistles (*Cynara cardunculus*), has been used for hundreds of years. See also soft sheep's milk cheeses (page 152).

Serve: as an appetizer with sourdough bread, olives, and sardine pâté.
Drink: white port stands up well to the slight bitterness in these cheeses.

Alantejo is a very dry region of Portugal where grazing is best suited to sheep and goats.

Queijo de Évora PDO

Named for the fortified medieval town of Évora, east of Lisbon in the region of Alentejo, where the Mediterranean climate features hot, dry summers, and mixed farms with crops, cattle, and sheep are common on the broad plains. This cheese is produced from pure sheep's milk; the curds being slowly drained to produce a moist, semi-hard texture.

Size: 3¹/₂ and 6oz disks; Affinage: 6–12 months
Tasting notes: The pale, compact, semi-hard interior has only a few eyes, becoming hard and crumbly with long aging. The flavor is creamy, fruity, salty, and slightly tangy, and the pale beige-yellow rind has a crosshatch pattern from the draining rack.
Pasteurized: No; Country: Portugal (Alentejo)

Queijo de Nisa PDO

From the municipality of Nisa in northern Alentejo in Portugal, these wheels are aged for at least 45 days, producing a fine rind and pale, supple, semi-hard interior with small eyes and a buttery, earthy, nutty flavor and pronounced aroma.

Pasteurized: No; Country: Portugal (Alentejo)

Queijo Mestiço de Tolosa PGI

From Tolosa in Nisa, *mestiço* ("mixed") refers to the mixed sheep's and goat's milk used to make these semi-hard cheeses set with either thistle or animal rennet. The rind is washed with chile water, producing a distinctive color and flavor.

Pasteurized: No; Country: Portugal (Alentejo)

Queijo de Castelo Branco PDO

Slightly bulging, 1³/₄–3lb wheels similar to Queijo de Azeitão (see page 153), with a soft, smooth, slightly tangy interior and sharp aroma after the minimum 40 days, becoming harder and sharper with age. Part of the Queijos da Beira Baixa PDO (see page 239).

Pasteurized: No; Country: Portugal (Centro)

Máhon-Menorca PDO

These Spanish, 2–9lb squares from the island of Minorca are eaten after 3 weeks or rubbed with oil or paprika and aged for up to 10 months, becoming hard, crumbly, saltier, and tangier. May contain 5% sheep's milk.

Pasteurized: Either; Country: Spain (Minorca)

portuguese cheeses using animal rennet

Portuguese cheesemaking is distinctive for its use of cardoon thistle as a rennet-alternative; the traditional Portuguese cheeses opposite are unusual in that they're made with animal rennet. While Spanish cheeses occasionally use cardoon extract, tronchón (see page 235) is interesting because it's made in two variations, with either animal rennet or cardoon extract. Originating in northern Spain, where animal rennet is typically used, tronchón was introduced to warmer Portugal, where the herders traditionally took their flocks for winter. Here, cardoon extract is often used, producing a moister tronchón with the slightly bitter taste typical of cardoon (see page 236).

Serve: with slices of raw ham, such as jamon iberico.
Drink: Portuguese red wine, such as touriga, or fruity reds, such as gamay or merlot.

Traditional raw ham, such as Spanish jamon iberico, is a good accompaniment to these cheeses.

Queijos da Beira Baixa PDO

This appellation covers three cheeses from the Beira area of central Portugal. Queijo Amarelo da Beira Baixa, named for its yellow color (*amarelo*), and Queijo Picante da Beira Baixa, named for its spicy flavor (*picante*), are made with pure sheep's milk or mixed sheep's and goat's milk. Pure sheep's milk Queijo de Castelo Branco (see page 237) is set with cardoon thistle.

Size: 1½–1¾lb; Affinage: Minimum 40 days
Tasting notes: Amarelo ranges from semi-soft to semi-hard depending on age, with a buttery, slightly tangy flavor and yellow rind. Longer-aged Picante is semi-hard to hard with an off-white to grayish rind; pale interior; tangy, earthy, herbal flavors; and sharp aroma.

Pasteurized: No; Country: Portugal (Centro)

Queijo Rabaçal PDO

These semi-hard to hard plump disks from central Portugal are made from mixed sheep's and goat's milk. They have smooth, yellow rinds and off-white interiors, with a few irregular eyes and a strong, faintly buttery flavor.

Pasteurized: No; Country: Portugal (Centro)

Queijo São Jorge PDO

These 17½–26½lb wheels from the Azores island of São Jorge (Saint George), aged 3–5 months, have a hard, dark yellow rind, sometimes mottled with red, and a firm, crumbly, cheddar-like (see page 186) interior with a tangy, nutty, slightly spicy flavor.

Pasteurized: No; Country: Portugal (Azores)

Queijo Terrincho PDO

These small (1½–2½lb) thick wheels from northeastern Portugal have thin, smooth, yellow–orange rinds sometimes tied with straw topped with a wheat stalk. The pale, semi-hard interior with scattered eyes turns crumbly with age, developing salty, toasty, sharp, nutty flavors.

Pasteurized: No; Country: Portugal (Norte)

Queijo do Pico PDO

Produced on the Azores island of Ilha do Pico since at least the late 1700s, these 1½–1¾lb disks have a bulging yellow rind; semi-soft, moist, doughy, pale interior with a few irregular eyes; an intense aroma; and a salty, buttery flavor.

Pasteurized: No; Country: Portugal (Azores)

spanish goat cheeses

Goats are far more adaptable than cattle or sheep, happy to feed on scrubby vegetation and nimble enough to climb around rocky ground in search of food. They love the hot, dry climate of much of Spain, where they have been kept for milk and meat for hundreds of years. Sixteenth-century documents attest to the importance of cheese on the Canary Islands, while records from 1465 refer to Queso Ibores being sold at markets in Trujillo, where the *Calle de los Cabreros* ("street of the goatherds") identifies the route along which the goats were driven to market.

Serve: mixed with sliced boiled potato and beaten eggs, pan-fried into a Spanish tortilla.
Drink: cava, Spanish sparkling wine (the acidity works well with tangy goat cheese).

Goats thrive on the island of Fuerteventura where Queso Majorero is made.

Queso Majorero PDO

Up to 15% sheep's milk may be used if this semi-pressed cheese is intended for aging. It is considered "semi-aged" between 20 and 60 days and "aged" over 60 days. The name "majorero" refers to anything from the Canary Island of Fuerteventura, after *mahos*, the sandals of untanned goatskin traditionally worn by the shepherds.

Size: Thick, 2–13lb wheels; Affinage: Minimum 8 days

Tasting notes: The pale rind embossed with a plaited pattern—recalling the plaited palm leaves traditionally used to shape the curds—may be rubbed with paprika, oil, or roasted cornmeal. The pale, firm, creamy interior has toasty, slightly sweet, tangy flavors.

Pasteurized: Either; Country: Spain (Canary Islands)

Queso Palmero (Queso de la Palma) PDO

These flattened disks from small farms on La Palma in the Canary Islands are generally eaten fresh, though sometimes smoked, or coated with olive oil or roasted cornmeal, and aged. They have a smooth, elastic interior and fresh, fruity flavor.

Pasteurized: No; Country: Spain (Canary Islands)

Rondeño

Named for the rugged Ronda Mountains of Andalusia, these thick, 2–6½lb wheels have a hard, rough, golden rind and well-pressed, firm, yellow interior with scattered eyes; a rich, buttery flavor; and the pleasant aroma of goat's milk.

Pasteurized: Either; Country: Spain (Andalusia)

Queso Ibores PDO

These thick, 1½–2½lb wheels have a smooth, oil- or paprika-coated rind; pale, firm, moist interior that becomes crumbly with age; mild, sweet aroma; and strong, slightly tangy, salty flavor. Farm-made cheese matured for at least 100 days is labeled *artesano*.

Pasteurized: No; Country: Spain (Extremadura)

Queso de Murcia PDO

This mild, slightly salty, tangy cheese may be lightly pressed in molds lined with esparto grass and eaten fresh; pressed more firmly and matured for 2 months or more; or immersed in local red wine (*al vino*) and matured for 1–2 months.

Pasteurized: Yes; Country: Spain (Murcia)

manchego—spanish sheep cheeses

Spain's best-known cheese, Manchego, comes from La Mancha, a high plateau in central Spain, with fiercely cold winters and searing summers. Sheep and goats thrive on the scrubby rosemary and thyme there, giving their milk a distinctive flavor. Spain's tradition of sheep farming spans over 2,000 years. Originally sheep were kept for meat and wool, with shepherds making cheese for their own consumption, but as wool's global importance decreased, that of cheese increased. Many central Spanish sheep's cheeses, including Manchego, have a zigzag pattern on their sides, traditionally created by esparto grass molds, though today synthetic molds are common (see page 254).

Serve: as part of a tapas selection, with bread, olives, and jamon (Spanish raw ham).
Drink: dry manzanilla sherry; the salty, nutty flavors echo those in the cheese.

Deep-fried Queso Manchego is delicious served hot as an appetizer.

Queso Manchego PDO

Mild, soft cheeses aged for 2 months (30 days if under 3lb) are called *semi-curado*. After 3 months, they become harder, crumbly, and sharper (*curado*). After 1-2 years they become dry and splinter when cut. Only milk from Manchega sheep can be used to make Manchego; similar-looking cheeses made outside the area of La Mancha are "Manchego-style" but cannot use the PDO.

Size: 14oz–9lb; Affinage: 30 days–2 years

Tasting notes: The smooth, yellow to black rind is embossed top and bottom with ears of wheat. The pale, dense, slightly oily interior, typical of sheep's milk, has tiny, uneven eyes; a lingering, buttery, salty taste; and slightly nutty aftertaste.

Pasteurized: Either; Country: Spain (Castile-La Mancha)

Queso Zamorano PDO

Zamora, with a long tradition of semi-nomadic shepherds, is Spain's major sheep's milk producer. Its cheese is dense yet creamy with salty, buttery, nutty flavors. Traditional grass molds are no longer used; plastic molds with the traditional design engraved have replaced them.

Pasteurized: Either; Country: Spain (Castile-León)

Castellano

Castile-León is Spain's largest cheese producer. The brown rind of its classic cheese, castellano, carries the zigzag esparto grass pattern. Its dense, granular interior doesn't have any eyes and tastes slightly salty and tart, with a buttery aroma.

Pasteurized: Either; Country: Spain (Castile-León)

Roncal PDO

Production is tightly controlled by a cooperative of seven villages in Navarra, dating back to the Middle Ages. A longer aging period than similar cheeses (minimum 4 months) produces a hard, granular, buttery, savory, nutty-flavored cheese with mushroomy aromas.

Pasteurized: No; Country: Spain (Navarra)

La Mancha

This golden yellow Manchego-style cheese from Tasmania's Grandvewe organic sheep's milk dairy has a waxy, almost cheddar-like (see page 186) texture with crunchy, little lactate crystals and a salty, nutty, developed flavor (having aged for 12–24 months).

Pasteurized: Yes; Country: Australia (Tasmania)

ossau-iraty

This appellation covers the hard sheep's milk cheeses of two neighboring ancient provinces in southwestern France bordering Spain, now included in the modern département of Pyrénées-Atlantiques. Iraty is named after the Iraty Forest in the Basque country (Pays Basque), and Ossau for the Ossau Valley in Béarn. Cheesemaking in this region almost certainly dates to pre-Roman times, and likely much earlier, as traces of a Neolithic farming-herding system attest. Certainly Latin authors mentioned sheep's milk cheeses being sold in the markets of Toulouse. Local cheeses that aren't made according to PDO guidelines are called simply fromage de brebis ("sheep's cheese").

Serve: with thin slices of firm white bread, butter, and black cherry jam.
Drink: white Jurançon wine from southwestern France.

The milk of Black Faced Manech sheep in the French Pyrénées is used to make Ossau-Iraty cheese.

◼◼🐑 Ossau-Iraty PDO

Made with milk from local breeds (red- and black-faced Manech and Basco-Béarnaise), these thick wheels of lightly pressed cheese with orange–yellow or gray rinds are aged for different periods depending on their size. A number of individual cheeses, including Matocq (see page 235), are covered by this appellation. Some experts argue that Ossau and Iraty are distinctive enough to deserve separate appellations.

Size: 4½–6½lb and 9–15½lb drums; Affinage: Minimum 60 or 90 days

Tasting notes: Varying from valley to valley and maker to maker, generally these are thick wheels or drums with a thick, hard, orange–brown, natural rind; dense, faintly granular, slightly oily, pale yellow interior; and a rich, sweet, nutty flavor.

Pasteurized: Either; Country: France (Aquitaine)

◼◼🐑 Etorki

When the rules governing Roquefort (see page 168) production were tightened to exclude sheep's milk from Aquitaine, it was diverted into this factory-produced Ossau-Iraty-style cheese developed in the 1970s. It is made only from December to July when the Manech sheep are lactating.

Pasteurized: Yes; Country: France (Aquitaine)

◼◼🐑 Ardi-Gasna

The general name for sheep's milk cheese in Basque (*ardi* meaning "ewe" and *gasna* meaning "cheese"), these thick wheels are often made by shepherds in mountain huts during summer. Some, but not all, are covered by Ossau-Iraty PDO.

Pasteurized: No; Country: France (Aquitaine)

◼◼🐑 Abbaye de Belloc

These orange-rinded 9lb wheels, with fruity, nutty, caramelized flavors similar to Ossau-Iraty, are made by a local dairy for Aquitaine's Abbaye de Notre-Dame de Belloc to the abbey's recipe, then aged in the abbey's cellars. Not covered by the PDO.

Pasteurized: Yes; Country: France (Aquitaine)

▤ 🐑 Vermont Shepherd

These thick, bulging, 6½–9lb farm-produced wheels, similar to Ossau-Iraty, are made only from April to October when the sheep graze on fresh grass. The smooth, semi-hard, dense, creamy, pale interior, beneath a rough orange–brown rind, has rich, earthy, nutty, slightly sweet flavors.

Pasteurized: No; Country: USA (Vermont)

pecorino

Pecorino, from *pecora* (Italian for "sheep"), is the generic name for Italy's pale sheep's milk cheeses, made since ancient times and usually named for their region of origin. They are particularly common in the warmer south, especially rocky Sardinia and Sicily where much of the land isn't suitable for  crops or cattle and sheep farming is often the sole means of income. They're usually cooked, pressed cheeses, aged until hard enough for grating, but sometimes sold young before they develop a granular texture. Pecorino Toscano (from Tuscany and neighboring regions) is only semi-cooked. Oddly, in some countries, cheeses called "pecorino" are made from cow's milk.

Serve: with roughly mashed broad beans drizzled with extra-virgin olive oil.
Drink: Sardinian vermentino; its oiliness echoes the texture of these cheeses.

The Italian dish tagliatelle primavera is delicious served with a little pecorino sprinkled over the top.

▊▊🐏 Pecorino Sardo PDO

There are two versions of this semi-cooked cheese from the island of Sardinia: *dolce* ("mild") is aged for weeks, and *maturo* ("matured"), which is occasionally also smoked, is aged for months. Unusually for a sheep's milk cheese, it is set with calf's rennet. It is traditionally regarded as an alternative to Pecorino Romano, also made on the island.

Size: 3¾–9lb cylinders; Affinage: 20–60 days; 2–12 months

Tasting notes: Dolce is supple, mild, and slightly tangy. Firmer maturo, not as hard as Pecorino Romano and Fiore Sardo (see page 248), is slightly sweet until about 6 months of age, becoming granular with a stronger flavor thereafter, when it's best used for grating.

Pasteurized: No; Country: Italy (Sardinia)

▊▊🐏 Pecorino Romano PDO

This hard, cylindrical, cooked cheese evolved around Rome, but is now mostly made on Sardinia, where more land is available for sheep grazing. Lamb's rennet is used and the 44–77lb wheels are larger than other pecorinos.

Pasteurized: No; Country: Italy (Lazio, Sardinia, Tuscany)

▊▊🐏 Pecorino Siciliano PDO

Traditionally drained in baskets called *fascedde* (see basket molds, page 254) creating a distinctive patterned rind, and aged a minimum 4 months for PDO appellation, this mild cheese becomes harder and spicier with age. Sold fresh, soft, and white, before aging, it's called tuma.

Pasteurized: Either; Country: Italy (Sicily)

▊▊🐏 Pecorino Toscano PDO

These 2–6½lb cylinders from Tuscany, Umbria, and Lazio are only semi-cooked, and are therefore softer than most pecorino. Unusually for a sheep's milk cheese, calf's rennet is commonly used, producing a milder cheese than those from farther south.

Pasteurized: Either; Country: Italy (traditionally Tuscany)

▊▊🐏 Pecorino Pepato

Pecorino with black peppercorns (*pepato* in Italian) is particularly popular in Sicily, the pepper adding heat and crunch to the firm, savory cheese. Peppercorns are permitted in Pecorino Siciliano PDO, but similar cheeses are produced elsewhere, (see piacintinu, page 255).

Pasteurized: Either; Country: Italy

pecorino-style cheeses

Sardinia's oldest-known cheese, Fiore Sardo PDO, predates Roman times; these thick, bulging wheels of hard, uncooked sheep's milk cheese are named for the fact that vegetable extract was traditionally used instead of rennet to set the curds (*fiore* means "flower") though lamb's or kid's rennet is used today, (see cheeses made with traditional vegetarian rennet, page 236). Sheep are popular worldwide and pecorino-style cheeses (see page 246) are made in many countries. Britain has a long history of sheep farming, with sheep's cheese once more common than cow's, while New Zealand, where a pecorino-like cheese is produced in Nelson on the South Island, is famous for having more sheep than people.

Serve: melted over slices of tomato and onion on toast.
Drink: aged New World rieslings; their acidity and complexity match aged sheep's milk cheeses well.

Berkswell is made using milk from Friesland sheep.

🇬🇧 🐑 Berkswell

In the late 1980s, Stephen Fletcher added sheep to his farm in Berkswell, near Coventry in the British Midlands, initially just for milk. He developed Berkswell cheese when a local shop asked him to produce a sheep's milk cheese for them, and he still produces it using only milk from the farm's flock of Friesland sheep.

Size: Thick 5½–6½lb wheels; Affinage: 3–8 months

Tasting notes: The dense, firm but supple, yellow interior is reminiscent of Pecorino Toscano (see page 247), as are the nutty, caramel-like flavors that become more pronounced with age without becoming too strong. The thin, natural, orange-brown rind is marked from the basket mold.

Pasteurized: No; Country: UK (England—Warwickshire)

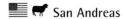 Lord of the Hundreds

These hard, slightly granular squares from southeast England have rich, sweet, nutty salty, slightly caramel flavors. Semi-hard at 4 months, they're more pecorino-like by 6 months, when they're good for grating. Dangate Gold is a smoked version.

Pasteurized: No; Country: UK (England—East Sussex)

🇺🇸 🐑 San Andreas

These smooth, golden, 3lb wheels from California's first sheep dairy, Bellwether Farms, are aged for just 2–4 months, producing a pale, smooth, supple cheese with scattered eyes and creamy, mildly tangy flavors. They also produce a pepato (see page 247).

Pasteurized: No; Country: USA (California)

 Neudorf Ewes Milk Cheese

These thick, 3lb wheels have a thin, natural, gray-brown rind and semi-hard, golden interior with sweet, nutty flavors, occasionally with naturally occurring patches of blue. Aged at least 8 months, it was 2008 New Zealand Cheese Awards Champion Sheep's Cheese.

Pasteurized: Yes; Country: New Zealand (Nelson)

🇺🇸 🐑 Stony Man

This cooked farmhouse cheese made by retired doctor Pat Elliot at Virginia's Everona Dairy is modeled on pecorino. It has a pale, dense, smooth interior with nutty, caramel flavors. Aged for 3–10 months, it becomes slightly granular and sweeter over time.

Pasteurized: No; Country: USA (Virginia)

parmesan

The name "parmesan" refers to hard grating cheeses worldwide, from the best Italian Parmigiano to the worst, pre-grated, rancid-smelling powders in supermarkets. Also called "grana," referring to its grainy texture, this style of cheese may date to around 1000 CE; it's traditionally made in 44–110lb wheels from partly skimmed raw cow's milk, the curds very finely cut and heated to release as much whey as possible. Matured for 1–3 years, their flavor sharpens and price increases with age. These cheeses were very important in medieval times, sometimes used as currency, as their low moisture content meant they kept well and could be easily transported.

Serve: grated over pasta or risotto or alone as a table cheese.
Drink: Barolo or other full-bodied, elegant, northern Italian wine.

An Italian cheesemaker burns the quality mark into a wheel of parmesan.

▌▌🐄 Parmigiano Reggiano PDO

The appellations of Parma and Reggio Emilia in northern Italy were joined to create this benchmark parmesan. Mostly family run farms make 4 to 12 wheels/day (150 gallons making one 77lb wheel). "Parmigiano Reggiano," the mark of the *consorzio* (producer's association), dairy, date, and grade 1–5 are stenciled on the rind. Always buy Parmigiano "broken" from a whole wheel with a parmesan knife.

Size: Minimum 53lb; Affinage: Minimum 14 months

Tasting notes: The flaky, pale, finely grained interior has a mild aroma and sweet, slightly nutty flavor. Fresco (14–18 months) is mildest; vecchio (2+ years) develops a sweet-salty crunch and is an ideal table cheese; while stravecchio (3+ years) is better for cooking.

Pasteurized: No; Country: Italy (Emilia Romagna)

▌▌🐄 Grana Padano PDO

The most common and respected grana, these 53–88lb wheels are stamped with "Grana Padano," the *consorzio*, dairy, and date. The pale yellow to golden, finely grained, flaky interior has fruity, mellow aromas and flavors. A good substitute for Parmigiano Reggiano.

Pasteurized: No; Country: Italy (Emilia-Romagna, Lombardy, Piedmont, Veneto)

🇲🇽 🐄 🐐 Queso Cotija

Nicknamed "Mexican parmesan," cotija, also called queso añejo ("aged cheese"), is traditionally made with raw milk and ripened 4–12 months. Its dry, granular, very salty interior means it's best used for cooking and seasoning.

Pasteurized: Either; Country: Mexico (Michoacán)

🇨🇭 🐄 Sbrinz AOC

Named for Brienz, from where it was transported to Italy, Switzerland's oldest cheese may be the model for Parmigiano Reggiano. Aged for 2 years or more, the finely grained interior darkens with age, becoming more crumbly and its fruity, nutty, spicy flavors deepening.

Pasteurized: No; Country: Switzerland (Lucerne, Schwyz, Obwalden, Nidwalden, Zug, Bern, Argau)

🇺🇸 🐄 Serena

Marisa Simoes of Three Sisters Farmstead Cheese produces these 17½lb wheels with raw milk from her family's California farm. Aged 12–18 months, they have a smooth, hard interior with sharp, nutty, slightly caramelized flavors, ideal for grating.

Pasteurized: No; Country: USA (California)

other hard grating cheeses

With its hot climate and often barren rocky terrain, Greece has a tradition of goat- and sheepherding because cows do not do well in such environments. The herds are often mixed, and both goat's and sheep's milk is used to make the softer, salted cheeses such as Feta (see page 58). Sheep's milk, however, is more suited than goat's to making larger, hard, aged cheeses for grating, though a little goat's milk may still be mixed in with the sheep's milk if it happens to be on hand. Sardo and reggianito are hard cow's milk grating cheeses from Argentina.

Serve: grated into béchamel sauce to top moussaka.
Drink: a Greek red wine such as xynomavro, or Argentinean malbec.

The Greek dish moussaka is most often made with kefalotyri or Kefalograviera.

🇬🇷 🐑 🐐 Kefalograviera PDO

This relatively new cheese from the mountains of northwestern Greece was developed in the 1960s using traditional methods. A cross between sharp, salty kefalotyri (see below) and mellower graviera (see page 215), it's made primarily from sheep's milk with up to 10% goat's milk. It is now popular throughout Greece.

Size: 12–22lb wheels; Affinage: Minimum 3 months

Tasting notes: This hard, pressed, cooked cheese has a thin, natural, dark yellow rind, which may be marked from the cloths used to drain the curds. The pale, smooth, firm interior has numerous small eyes and a salty, nutty, savory flavor.

Pasteurized: Yes; Country: Greece (Macedonia, Epirus, Sterea Ellada)

🇬🇷 🐑 🐐 Kefalotyri

An ancient cheese produced throughout Greece and Cyprus, these pressed natural-rinded wheels have a pale, firm, granular interior with scattered eyes. They become brittle and flaky with age. The salty, slightly sharp flavor makes it a popular grating cheese.

Pasteurized: Either; Country: Greece, Cyprus

🇬🇷 🐑 🐐 Ladotyri Mytilinis PDO

A hard, cooked, pressed cheese produced from sheep's milk, sometimes with added goat's milk, on the island of Lesvos (Mytilinis is Lesvos' capital). The ripened cheese is traditionally stored in olive oil (*lado*), though today it may also be waxed.

Pasteurized: Either; Country: Greece (Lesbos)

🇬🇷 🐄 San Michali PDO

Cow's milk cheeses are unusual in Greece; however, Venetian monks introduced dairy cows to the island of Syros in the 1500s, and this hard, natural-rinded, mild, buttery cheese has been made from their descendants' milk since the 1940s.

Pasteurized: Yes; Country: Greece (Syros)

🏵 🐐 Queijo de Cabra Transmontano PDO

This hard goat's milk cheese (*cabra* means "goat") from the remote region Trás-os-Montes ("beyond-the-mountains") in northeastern Portugal is aged for at least 2 months. It has a smooth, thin, golden rind and pale interior, which crumbles with age.

Pasteurized: No; Country: Portugal (Bragança, Vila Real)

basket mold cheeses

One of the earliest ways to drain fresh curds was in baskets woven from
local grasses (reeds and esparto) or other suitable plants (such as rushes).
Many cheese names recall this practice, including Flemish mandjeskaas (see
page 51) and Greek Kalathaki Limnou (see page 59), *mandjes* and *kalathaki* both meaning "basket."
The Italian word for "cheese," *formaggio*, and the French word, *fromage*, come from the Latin
word *forma*, meaning "form" or "container," referring to the baskets used to drain curds in early
cheesemaking. The outside of many cheeses, including ricotta (see page 54) and Manchego (see
page 242), are marked from either traditional woven baskets or modern plastic molds designed to
resemble them.

Serve: grated into bread or scone dough to make cheese scones or cheese rolls.
Drink: a Sicilian red wine blend featuring nero d'avola.

Fresh curds for ġbejna are drained in plastic baskets; in past times they were woven from grass or rushes.

Canestrato Pugliese PDO

This cheese from Italy's southwestern region of Puglia is named for the ancient practice of draining the curds and shaping the cheeses in woven baskets (*canestri*) made by local craftsmen. Canestrato cheeses are made elsewhere in southern Italy; Pecorino Siciliano (see page 247) is sometimes called canestrato siciliano, and canestrato crotonese (from the Calabrian province of Crotone) is often called pecorino crotonese.

Size: Typically 4½–26½lb wheels; Affinage: 10–15 days to 1+ year

Tasting notes: A hard, natural, yellow–brown, olive oil-rubbed rind, imprinted with basket marks, develops over time. Mild and sweet when young, the firm yellow interior, occasionally with tiny eyes, becomes crumbly, developing tangy, savory notes with age.

Pasteurized: No; Country: Italy (Puglia)

Pecorino di Filiano PDO

The rinds of these hard, 5½–11lb cylinders from mountainous Basilicata in Italy's south are rubbed with olive oil and vinegar. Aged, often in natural tufa caves, for a minimum 6 months, the pale, dense interior is mild, becoming slightly pungent with age.

Pasteurized: No; Country: Italy (Basilicata)

Fromage Corse

The name of this very regional cheese from the mountainous island of Corsica means simply "Corsican cheese." The rennet used is made by drying young goats' stomachs; the washed rind becomes mottled; and the moist interior has a strong flavor.

Pasteurized: Either; Country: France (Corsica)

Piacintinu di Enna

Similar to pepato (see page 247), golden-colored piacintino (*piacintinu* in Sicilian dialect) made around the town of Enna, contains saffron and black peppercorns. The 13–31lb wheels may be eaten fresh after just a few days or aged until hard and granular.

Pasteurized: Either; Country: Italy (Sicily)

Queso Iberico

The brown–gray rinds of these 4½–7¾lb cylinders from central Spain have a zigzag, esparto grass-basket pattern, similar to Manchego (see page 242). Made from a blend of cow's, goat's, and sheep's milk, they have a firm texture and mild, buttery flavor.

Pasteurized: Yes; Country: Spain (Central)

cheese mites

Bacteria and molds help shape the character of most cheeses, but the cheese mite, *Tyroglyphus casei*, plays a key role in just a few distinctive cheeses, most famously French mimolette. Undoubtedly eating mite-infested cheese began out of necessity when food was scarce, but today these products have a loyal following. A statue of a mite even stands in the German village of Würchwitz, where Milbenkäse ("mite cheese") has been produced for over 300 years. While cheese mites are often considered to have health-giving properties, the Italian tradition of using cheese-fly larvae, *Piophila casei*, to ferment cheeses is more contentious.

Serve: with dark bread and butter.
Drink: a dark European beer.

Dark rye bread is the perfect accompaniment to Milbenkäse.

Milbenkäse

Recently revived by local science teacher, Helmut Pöschel, who learned the technique from Liesbeth Brauer, the last of the village women to make this cheese, "mite cheese" is made by storing dried caraway-flavored quark (see page 47) in a wooden box with cheese mites. Rye flour is added to feed the mites, who also eat the cheese's crust, triggering fermentation.

Size: Small balls, cylinders, or wheels; Affinage: 3–12 months

Tasting notes: The rind changes from yellow to reddish-brown, to black in long-aged versions, and the firm interior, eaten with the mites still attached to the rind, tastes spicy and slightly bitter. Goat's and sheep's milk varieties have a stronger flavor.

Pasteurized: Either; Country: Germany (Saxony-Anhalt)

Mimolette Jeune

This annatto-dyed, cannon ball-shaped cheese from northern France resembles edam (see page 202), which it was likely invented to compete with. The name comes from *mi-molle*, meaning "semi-soft," as young (*jeune*) mimolette is semi-soft and mild with an intact thin brown rind.

Pasteurized: Yes; Country: France (Nord-Pas-de-Calais)

Marcetto

In Abruzzo in east-central Italy, pecorino (see page 246) infested with cheese-fly larvae is left to ferment for several months, producing a creamy, pinkish-brown paste sold in glass jars. It has a strong aroma and very tangy, spicy taste.

Pasteurized: Either; Country: Italy (Abruzzo)

Mimolette Vieille

Aged (*vieille*) for a year or more, mimolette's rind becomes infested with cheese mites and turns gray and crumbly. The interior turns orange-brown and the texture becomes hard, dense, and flaky with a fruity, hazelnut, caramel flavor.

Pasteurized: Yes; Country: France (Nord-Pas-de-Calais)

Casu Frazigu

In Sardinia, pecorino (see page 246) infested with cheese-fly larvae breaks down to a very soft consistency. Also called casu marzu ("rotten cheese"), it's banned from sale, but made for home consumption and listed as a "traditional food product" by the Italian government.

Pasteurized: Either; Country: Italy (Sardinia)

eastern european cheeses

Before 1989 Eastern Europe was largely closed to the Western world, its traditional cheeses virtually unknown internationally with the possible exception of white Feta-like cheeses such as Bulgarian sirene and Romanian telemea (see page 59). As the old "communist bloc" has opened up to the West, the dairy industry has been modernized and distinctive regional cheeses have started to find their way into the export market, initially supplying expat communities around the world, but also as new flavors for curious food-lovers. Often mountainous, much of this region is more suited to goats and sheep, though cow's milk cheeses are also popular. See also bryndza (page 62).

Serve: with fruit and nut bread or a fruit and nut relish such as Jewish haroseth.
Drink: slivovitz (plum brandy); popular all over Eastern Europe, it marries well with these rich cheeses.

Sheep in the Czech region of Bohemia provide the milk for Ovčí Arnika.

Ovčí Arnika

This traditional, hard, pressed, sheep's milk cheese is made at Salaš Ryžovna, near the town of Abertamy, a new sheep farm with restaurant and accommodations built to reinvigorate this area in the famous spa region of Karlovy Vary (previously Carlsbad) in the western Czech Republic. Produced only from May to September when the sheep can graze on natural pastures, including wild herbs such as arnica.

Size: 7oz and 4½lb wheels; Affinage: Typically 2–6 months

Tasting notes: The smooth, thin, natural, yellow–orange rind covers a semi-hard, ivory-colored interior with a distinctive savory flavor from the wild herbs consumed by the sheep. Abertam Balkan is a soft, brined, cow's milk cheese made by the same farm.

Pasteurized: Yes; Country: Czech Republic (Bohemia)

Paški Sir

These traditional 6½lb wheels of Croatian sheep's milk cheese are from the Adriatic island of Pag (the name means "Pag cheese"). They are sold young (5 months) or aged for a year or more, developing a hard, yellow–brown rind and granular interior, similar to aged pecorino (see page 246).

Pasteurized: Yes; Country: Croatia (Pag Island)

Balaton

This traditional hard cheese is named after Hungary's Lake Balaton. The thin, oily, natural rind covers a compact, semi-hard, pale yellow interior with scattered small eyes. It's popular throughout Hungary for its mild, slightly tangy flavor.

Pasteurized: Yes; Country: Hungary

Siraz

These flat disks of Serbian cheese are left outside to dry; rubbed with salt until a rind begins to develop; and then stored in brine for several weeks. The resulting firm, Feta-like (see page 58) cheese is salty and slightly tangy.

Pasteurized: No; Country: Serbia

 Jihočeská Niva

The rind of these 6lb wheels from southern Bohemia in the Czech Republic is washed off before the cheeses are dried and foil-wrapped. The pale interior, marbled with blue–green veins of *Penicillium roqueforti*, is crumbly, salty, tangy, and slightly spicy. A PGI application has been filed.

Pasteurized: Yes; Country: Czech Republic (Bohemia)

PGI cheeses

Several European Union schemes promote and protect names of regional foods (see page 270). While PDO (Protected Designation of Origin) is the strictest, PGI (Protected Geographical Indication) often allows production throughout an entire country (rather than specific region), using varied methods. Slovenský Oštiepok, for example, "may be steamed or unsteamed...smoked or unsmoked...sheep's milk, mixed sheep's and cow's milk or cow's milk." In 2010, a number of traditional cheeses, including Dutch gouda holland and edam holland (see page 202), were having their PGI status confirmed, and Polish Wielkopolski ser Smażony was among the latest to be accredited; no doubt more will apply in the future.

Serve: with crisp flatbreads and dried fruit such as dates or figs.
Drink: a shot of aquavit; Scandinavia's most popular liquor often works well with aged cheeses.

Danablu is sometimes served over herring on toast with mayonnaise.

Slovenský Oštiepok PGI

This traditional Slovakian sheep's milk cheese was once only produced by small-scale mountain sheep farms (*salaš*), sometimes with some cow's milk added, the curds stretched by hand (see page 72), and hung to dry in the rafters, where they absorbed smoke from the shepherd's fire. Commercial production of pasteurized cow's milk versions began in the 1960s, though traditional production continues.

Size: Egg-shaped, 11–18oz; Affinage: Typically 1–6 days

Tasting notes: The egg-like shape decorated with designs specific to individual areas defines this cheese with its smooth, shiny, yellow rind (golden-brown when smoked), and firm, white to yellow, mild, slightly salty, tangy interior, usually with smoky aromas and flavors.

Pasteurized: Either; Country: Slovakia

Danablu PGI

Created in Denmark by Marius Boel in the 1920s as an alternative to imported Roquefort (see page 168), this sharp cow's milk cheese is a popular export. The creamy, off-white interior contrasts with the blue–gray mold and has a salty bite.

**Pasteurized: Either (pasteurized/thermized)
Country: Denmark**

Olomoucké Tvarůžky

Semi-soft, ¾–1oz cylinders, rings, or sticks from Moravia in the Czech Republic, with a strong aroma and spicy flavor. Dating to the 15th century, they're also known as syrečky (Czech), olmützi quargel (Hungarian), and serki olomunieckie (Polish). A PGI application has been filed.

Pasteurized: Yes; Country: Czech Republic (Moravia)

Esrom PGI

Originating with the 12th-century monks of Denmark's Esrom Monastery, this supple, rectangular, Port Salut-style (see page 120) washed rind cheese has a thin, yellow–orange rind and a pale, mild, slightly tangy interior with soft, sliceable texture. The aroma strengthens with age.

Pasteurized: Yes; Country: Denmark

Svecia PGI

Produced in low-lying areas all over Sweden since about the 13th century and called Svecia (Latin for "Sweden") since the 1920s, these 26½lb waxed wheels have a semi-soft, yellow interior with small eyes and a rich, mildly tangy flavor.

Pasteurized: Yes; Country: Sweden

smoked cheeses

Smoking is an ancient way of preserving food, including cheese. Many ancient cheeses were smoked almost by accident, hung to dry in the rafters of cottages. The rising smoke from the fireplace coated the outside of the cheese, giving it a golden hue and pleasant smoky aroma and flavor, which was later deliberately copied. Many commercially produced "smoked" cheeses are treated with artificial flavorings, which should be declared in the ingredients list, so read the labels carefully and seek out cheeses naturally smoked over various aromatic woods. See also smoked ricotta (page 55), mozzarella affumicata (page 79), Metsovone, Slovenská Parenica (page 87), Gamoneu (page 175), Slovenský Oštiepok (page 261), and Quickes Oak Smoked Cheddar (page 187).

Serve: melted into a sauce to serve over pan-fried veal scallopine.
Drink: German Rauchbier, with smoky flavors from drying the barley over open fires.

A large herd of red cows and calves sun themselves on a green meadow in Poland.

Oscypek PDO

This ancient cheese was introduced to southern Poland in the 15th century by shepherds from Wallachia (in modern-day Romania). The name may come from *oszczypywać*, meaning "to pinch repeatedly," referring to the production process, or *oszczypek*, meaning "small javelin," referring to the shape. The regulations permit pasteurized milk and up to 40% cow's milk; however, raw milk is still mostly used.

Size: 1⅓–1¾lb spindle (double cone); Affinage: 1–2 weeks
Tasting notes: Produced from May to September during sheep's milk season and hand-shaped around a skewer to achieve the distinctive shape, then cold-smoked for 3–7 days over larch, ash, spruce, or alder, this cheese's pale interior is darker toward the shiny golden rind.

Pasteurized: Either; Country: Poland (Śląsk, Małopolska)

Basils Original Rauchkäse

These 2–4½lb bricks of Bavarian smoked cheese (Rauchkäse) were originally called Bruder Basil ("Brother Basil"). Cold-smoked over beech or oak, they have an orange-brown rind and buttery, smoky flavor. Also flavored with ham and chile.

Pasteurized: Yes; Country: Germany (Bavaria)

Quesucos de Liébana PDO

These primarily cow's milk 1lb *quesucos* ("small cheeses") from Liébana near Spain's northern coast (a region of mixed herds) may contain some sheep's or goat's milk. When smoked, the firm, compact, yellow interior becomes darker, drier, and more tart.

Pasteurized: Yes; Country: Spain (Cantabria)

Idiazábal PDO

These golden-rinded, 2–6½lb cylinders from northern Spain's Basque and Navarra regions are usually smoked over beechwood, hawthorn, or cherry wood. They have a firm, dry interior; sharp, slightly spicy flavor; and mild aroma.

Pasteurized: No; Country: Spain (Basque, Navarra)

San Simón da Costa PDO

These pointy, pear-shaped cheeses from northern Spain have a dense interior with a sharp, creamy flavor. Smoked over birchwood, they develop a somewhat oily, hard, golden-brown rind. They have a relatively short aging (minimum 45 days).

Pasteurized: Either; Country: Spain (Galicia)

cheeses flavored with caraway & cumin

Similar-looking cumin and caraway seeds are often confused in Europe, and both have long been included in cheese for their reputed digestive properties. Cumin (*Cuminum cyminum*), a native of Egypt cultivated in the eastern Mediterranean, was popular during the Middle Ages, while caraway (*Carum carvi*), a European native, largely replaced it after the Middle Ages. It's difficult at times to be sure which is being used today (though cumin is more pungent), as European names for caraway often refer to cumin, including Danish *kommen* (cumin is *spidskommen*), German *kummel* (cumin is *kreuzkümmel*), Swedish *kummin* (cumin is *spiskummin*), and French *cumin des prés*.

Serve: with slices of light rye bread.
Drink: New Zealand steinlager beer or kummel, a clear caraway-flavored liquor.

Wheels of Boeren-Leidse met Sleutels are stamped for identification.

▬ 🐄 Boeren-Leidse met Sleutels PDO

This Dutch farmer's (*boeren*) cheese has been made around the town of Leiden, between the ports of Amsterdam and Rotterdam, for over 300 years. Being a partially skimmed milk cheese, it was durable and popular for ships' provisions and for export to the former Dutch tropical territories. Leiden's coat of arms, two crossed keys (*sleutels*), is stamped into the rind.

Size: 6½–22lb wheels; Affinage: Minimum 13 days

Tasting notes: This firm, supple cheese has cumin seeds mixed through the yellow interior. The molds are lined with plain curd, witte bodems ("white bottoms"), so the seeds don't collect in the usually annatto-dyed rind. Granular and suitable for grating when aged.

Pasteurized: No; Country: Netherlands (Zuid-Holland)

▬ 🐄 Kugelkäse

Literally "cheeseballs" (*kugel* means "balls"), this Austrian cheese is made by rolling quark (see page 47) into small balls. They're often flavored with pepper, caraway seeds, or paprika, then eaten immediately or salted, dried, and aged for months.

Pasteurized: Either; Country: Austria

▬ 🐄 Kanterkaas PDO

This traditional semi-hard cheese from the northern Netherlands, produced plain (*friesekaas*), with cloves (Kanternagelkaas), or cumin (Kanteromijnekaas), is named for its straight sides (*kant* means "sharp edge") as opposed to the typical bulging-wheel shape of gouda and edam (see page 202).

Pasteurized: Yes; Country: Netherlands (Friesland, Groningen)

▦ 🐄 Danbo

These popular, 19–31lb blocks of semi-hard Danish cheese are produced in both plain and caraway-flavored versions. The hard, yellow rind is sometimes waxed and the pale, supple, mild, buttery interior is similar to samsø (see page 213).

Pasteurized: Yes; Country: Denmark

▧ 🐄 Nøkkelost

Modeled on Dutch Boeren-Leidse met Sleutels, Norwegian nøkkelost ("key cheese") was developed in the 1860s. The yellow interior of these supple, 11–22lb wheels and blocks is studded with cumin or cloves. Sometimes called kuminost or nøkkelost, but not in Norway.

Pasteurized: Yes; Country: Norway

cheeses flavored with herbs & spices

Herbs and spices have been used since ancient times for their medicinal and preservative properties. The fact that many of them taste good and enliven otherwise mild-tasting foods was really just a happy bonus. All sorts of flavorings, from sun-dried tomatoes to exotic fruits, are added to mass-produced industrial cheeses today to provide a point of difference. Most of these are best avoided. Some traditional cheeses, however, have local herbs or spices (including pepper, chile, paprika, chives, and garlic) added to them, and these are often worth seeking out. See also flavored cheeses (pages 70, 196, 264, and 268).

Serve: with slices of crusty bread and nothing else; there's enough flavor in these cheeses.
Drink: a rich red wine, such as Cahors from southwestern France.

Crusty bread is the ideal accompaniment to these flavorful cheeses.

Afuega'l Pitu PDO

There are four variations of this ancient cheese produced along the Narcea and Nalón Rivers in northwestern Spain: truncated cones (*atroncau*) or squash-shaped spheres (*trapu*), either plain (*blancu*) or dyed red (*roxu*) with paprika. The name, meaning "choke the chicken" in dialect, has many possible explanations, including tying off the neck of the bag used to drain the cheese.

Size: 7oz–1½lb truncated cone or log; Affinage: 5–60 days

Tasting notes: Either white, turning pale yellow as it matures, or reddish-orange if paprika is added, these cheeses have a creamy, slightly tangy and salty flavor, and a fairly firm, dry texture. The paprika gives a stronger, spicier, sometimes slightly smoky flavor.

Pasteurized: Either; Country: Spain (Asturias)

Gaperon

The name of these small (9–12oz) flat-bottomed domes from Auvergne may come from a dialect word for buttermilk, which was traditionally used to curdle milk to make them. The pale, supple interior is flecked with garlic and ground black pepper.

Pasteurized: Either; Country: France (Auvergne)

Schabziger

These very hard, small, truncated cones with a tart, salty flavor and very pungent aroma are pale green from the Swiss Alpine herb, blue fenugreek, mixed through the curds. Served grated over salads or mixed with butter. Called Sap Sago in the USA.

Pasteurized: Either; Country: Switzerland (Glarus)

Tomino di Talucco

These small, 2oz–1lb, traditionally goat's milk cheeses from Piedmont are now sometimes made with cow's milk and eaten fresh or dried, sprinkled with black pepper or thyme, and packed in terra-cotta jars. Soft, creamy, and mild, they become tangy with age.

Pasteurized: Yes; Country: Italy (Piedmont)

Grimbister Farm Cheese

This semi-soft, crumbly, wensleydale-like cheese (see page 195) is made by Eddie and Hilda Seator in Scotland's remote northeast Orkney Islands. Eaten young (1 week), it's light and lemony, developing honey notes with age. Flavored versions include caraway, chive, whisky, and smoked.

Pasteurized: No; Country: UK (Scotland—Orkney)

truffle-flavored cheeses

Truffles, fungi that grow underground on the roots of trees (typically oak and hazel), are among the world's most highly prized foods. White truffles (*Tuber magnatum*), mostly from northern Italy, are the rarest and most expensive. Black truffles (*Tuber melanosporum*), mainly from southeastern France, can still fetch $1,000 or more per pound, while white spring truffles (*Tuber albidum*) are more affordable but still have some of the penetrating truffle aroma variously described as earthy, woody, and musty. The aroma is enhanced in combination with high-fat foods, such as cheese, especially if it's mixed with hot food. See also robiola d'Alba (page 147).

Serve: on top of risotto or tagliatelle or shaved over carpaccio.
Drink: Alsatian pinot gris; its rich fruitiness will balance the earthy truffles.

Brie aux Truffes is made by sandwiching black truffle slices inside a split wheel of brie.

▮▮🐄🐑 Boschetto al Tartufo

Produced by Tuscany's Il Forteto cooperative, this young semi-soft cheese is made from blended cow's and sheep's milk and mixed with flecks of white spring truffles (*tartufo bianchetto* in Italian). The word *boschetto* means "small forest," referring to the woodlands where these aromatic tubers are found. They were originally designed as Christmas gifts in their small woven baskets, but are now available year-round.

Size: 1⅓lb flat-bottomed domes; Affinage: Typically 3–4 weeks

Tasting notes: Wrapped in plastic, these rindless cream-colored cheeses have a semi-soft interior flecked with pale brown pieces of white truffle. The creamy cheese has a mild, slightly sweet taste with the rich aroma and flavor of the truffles.

Pasteurized: Yes; Country: Italy (Tuscany)

▮▮🐄 Brie aux Truffes

Created in 2002 by Marc Rouzaire, young French brie (see page 92) is halved horizontally; black truffle slices, crème fraîche, and mascarpone (see page 53) are sandwiched between the halves; then it's matured for a month, producing a soft texture and rich, earthy flavor.

Pasteurized: Either; Country: France

▮▮🐄🐑 Crutin Tartufo

These 2lb drums with a rough, mottled, white and ocher rind, from Beppino Ocelli in northern Italy, are made from a blend of cow's and sheep's milk. The pale, semi-hard interior has pieces of black Piedmont truffles scattered through it.

Pasteurized: Yes; Country: Italy (Piedmont)

▮▮🐑 Cacio di Bosco Pecorino al Tartufo

This 4-month-old pecorino (see page 246) combines the sweet nuttiness of sheep's milk with the earthiness of white spring truffles mixed through it. Cacio di Bosco ("forest cheese") refers to the Tuscan woodlands where truffles are found.

Pasteurized: No (thermized); Country: Italy (Tuscany)

▮▮🐄 Sottocenere

Sotto-cenere means "under-ash" and these 12lb wheels of semi-soft cheese, from northeastern Italy, are coated in spice-flavored ash. The smooth, creamy interior is sometimes flecked with pieces of black truffle. Also called Perla Grigia ("gray pearl").

Pasteurized: No; Country: Italy (Veneto)

appellation systems

Most European countries have a long, proud history of cheesemaking. Some have developed appellation systems to protect products traditional to specific regions from imitation, as well as to give buyers a guarantee that cheeses bearing a specific name are true to type. Following is a brief guide to the major appellation systems within Europe and a list of accredited cheeses by country.

Traditional cheeses are often seen as an important part of local history and culture.

european appellation systems

Five of the major traditional cheese-producing nations—France, Italy, Spain, Portugal, and Switzerland—have developed appellation systems similar to those used for their wines. Appellations typically define a number of parameters that describe a cheese.

they may include some or all of the following:

- the area within which the milk is sourced
- the area where the cheese is produced
- the area where the cheese is aged
- what type of animal(s) the milk comes from (cow, goat, sheep, buffalo...)
- the breeds of those animals (e.g., only Simmental cattle or Merino sheep)
- the animals' feeding regime (e.g., only pasture-fed)
- whether or not the milk is pasteurized, thermized, or raw
- the shape(s) of the cheese, the minimum and maximum weight, and dimensions (height, diameter, width...)
- the minimum and/or maximum aging period
- the techniques employed in making the cheese
- whether it may be smoked or flavored

The purpose of these systems is to protect traditional cheese names from being used for substandard or nontraditional products or on cheeses produced outside the traditional area. The names of these systems all basically mean "controlled appellation [or designation] of origin."

france's appellation system

France's system, AOC (*Appellation d'Origine Contrôlée*), established in 1919, was the first, and in 1925 the blue cheese Roquefort (see page 168), was the first cheese granted AOC status. In 1951 the concept was introduced into international law with the signing of the International Convention on the Use of Appellations of Origin and Denominations of Cheeses, in the northern Italian city of Stresa (referred to as "The Stresa Convention," not to be confused with the pre-World War II meeting between the French, British, and Mussolini also held in Stresa).

The participating countries (Austria, Denmark, France, Italy, Netherlands, Norway, Sweden, and Switzerland) committed to prohibiting the use of "false designations of origin." Gorgonzola (see page 172), Parmigiano Reggiano (see page 250), Pecorino Romano (see page 247), and Roquefort achieved protection under this convention, limiting their production to the specified place of origin. It was further agreed that other cheeses, considered quasi-generic and already widely produced outside their traditional area, including Asiago (see page 208), camembert (see page 96), Danablu (see page 261), edam (see page 202), emmental (see page 210), Esrom (see page 261), Fontina (see page 229), Gruyère (page see 214), samsø (see page 213), and Svecia (see page 261), could be made in any country that was a party to the agreement as long as they met certain requirements (mainly shape, weight, size, type and color of curd/rind, and fat content).

later appellation systems

Italy's system, DOC (*Denominazione di Origine Controllata*), was developed in 1954, while Spain introduced its system, DO (*Denominación de Origen*), much later in the 1980s as did Portugal with its *Denominação de Origem Controlada* (DOC) system. Switzerland, which is geographically part of Europe, but because of its longstanding neutrality has chosen not to join the EU, adopted an AOC system (*Appellation d'Origine Contrôlée*) in 1997, so that it could negotiate with the EU for a bilateral agreement whereby Swiss AOC cheeses will be recognized within EU countries and the EU system will be recognized within Switzerland.

Each country's appellation system is largely only enforceable within that country's borders, though the Stresa Convention provided some mutual recognition within participating countries. So in 1992, just before the European Economic Community became the European Union (EU), a standardized system was introduced across all member countries, generally recognizing those cheeses already accredited within the above four member countries as well as registering appropriate cheeses produced in other member countries. In early 2010, Switzerland and the EU were close to finalising a bilateral agreement.

the european union grants three different appellations

- Protected Designation of Origin (PDO) is the strictest, covering products produced, processed, and prepared in a defined geographical area using specific techniques

- Protected Geographical Indication (PGI) covers products closely linked to a defined geographical area; at least one of the stages of production, processing, or preparation must occur within the defined area

- Traditional Specialty Guaranteed (TSG) covers products with a traditional character either in their composition or means of production

The PDO system has helped reinvigorate traditional cheeses, no doubt protecting some from dying out, but it has also occasionally created confusion. In 1994 when the Lancashire Cheese Makers' Association applied for registration of traditional Lancashire cheese made in the county of Lancashire (see page 189), it seemed unlikely to be accepted because producers all over the UK were selling cheese labeled as "traditional Lancashire cheese." So it was decided that a more specific geographical indicator was required and the name of a local hill (which most people outside Lancashire have never heard of), Beacon Fell, was chosen and the name "Beacon Fell Traditional Lancashire Cheese" was registered. This leaves the name "traditional Lancashire cheese" unprotected, and only one of the seven Lancashire Cheese Makers' Association members (Singletons) uses the confusing Beacon Fell appellation, even though they all follow the PDO guidelines and truly produce

Lancashire cheese (left) has been difficult to protect under appellations.

"traditional Lancashire cheese." In 2010 negotiations were underway to have "Beacon Fell" removed from the title and to tighten the use of the "Lancashire" name.

There is hope that they will succeed, as Greece did with its much bigger fight over Feta. In 2005 Greece was granted PDO accreditation for "Feta," which had previously been produced in countries all over Europe and further afield. The granting of a PDO appellation to Greek "Feta" means that other members of the EU can no longer label a cheese they produce as "Feta" and that it can only be produced, from sheep's and goat's milk, within a designated area of Greece.

While non-EU countries, such as the USA and Australia, are not obliged to comply with EU rulings (meaning they can continue to call their products "Feta" or any of the other protected names), such products cannot be exported to Europe and there is increasing pressure on non-EU countries to respect these designations.

Below is a list of all cheeses with PDO, PGI, or TSG appellations at the time of printing. Other cheeses currently have applications before the European Union and no doubt many more will apply in the future. Swiss cheeses with AOC appellation are also listed below.

country	cheese	appellation
Austria	Gailtaler Almkäse	PDO
Austria	Tiroler Almkäse; Tiroler Alpkäse	PDO
Austria	Tiroler Bergkäse	PDO
Austria	Tiroler Graukäse	PDO
Austria	Vorarlberger Alpkäse	PDO
Austria	Vorarlberger Bergkäse	PDO
Belgium	Fromage de Herve	PDO
Belgium	Remoudou (covered by Fromage de Herve PDO)	PDO
Denmark	Danablu	PGI
Denmark	Esrom	PGI
France	Abondance	PDO

country	cheese	appellation
France	Banon	PDO
France	Beaufort	PDO
France	Bleu d'Auvergne	PDO
France	Bleu de Gex Haut-Jura; Bleu de Septmoncel	PDO
France	Bleu des Causses	PDO
France	Bleu du Vercors-Sassenage	PDO
France	Brie de Meaux	PDO
France	Brie de Melun	PDO
France	Brocciu Corse; Brocciu	PDO
France	Camembert de Normandie	PDO

country	cheese	appellation	country	cheese	appellation
France	Cantal; Fourme de Cantal; Cantalet	PDO	France	Ossau-Iraty	PDO
			France	Pélardon	PDO
France	Chabichou du Poitou	PDO	France	Picodon de l'Ardeche; Picodon de la Drôme	PDO
France	Chaource	PDO			
France	Chevrotin	PDO	France	Pont-l'Évêque	PDO
France	Comté	PDO	France	Pouligny-Saint-Pierre	PDO
France	Crottin de Chavignol; Chavignol	PDO	France	Reblochon; Reblochon de Savoie	PDO
			France	Rocamadour	PDO
France	Emmental de Savoie	PGI	France	Roquefort	PDO
France	Emmental Français Est-Central	PGI	France	Sainte-Maure de Touraine	PDO
France	Époisses	PDO	France	Saint-Nectaire	PDO
France	Fourme d'Ambert	PDO	France	Salers	PDO
France	Fourme de Montbrison	PDO	France	Selles-sur-Cher	PDO
France	Géromé (covered in Munster-Géromé PDO)	PDO	France	Tome des Bauges	PDO
			France	Tomme de Savoie	PGI
France	Laguiole	PDO	France	Tomme des Pyrénées	PGI
France	Langres	PDO	France	Valençay	PDO
France	Livarot	PDO	Germany	Allgäuer Bergkäse	PDO
France	Maroilles; Marolles	PDO	Germany	Allgäuer Emmentaler	PDO
France	Mont d'Or; Vacherin du Haut-Doubs	PDO	Germany	Altenburger Ziegenkäse	PDO
			Germany	Odenwälder Frühstückskäse	PDO
France	Morbier	PDO			
France	Munster; Munster-Géromé	PDO	Greece	Anevato	PDO
France	Neufchâtel	PDO	Greece	Batzos	PDO

country	cheese	appellation	country	cheese	appellation
Greece	Feta	PDO	Italy	Casatella Trevigiana	PDO
Greece	Formaella Arachovas Parnassou	PDO	Italy	Casciotta d'Urbino	PDO
			Italy	Castelmagno	PDO
Greece	Galotyri	PDO	Italy	Fiore Sardo	PDO
Greece	Graviera Agrafon	PDO	Italy	Fontina	PDO
Greece	Graviera Kritis	PDO	Italy	Formai de Mut dell'Alta Valle Brembana	PDO
Greece	Graviera Naxou	PDO			
Greece	Kalathaki Limnou	PDO	Italy	Gorgonzola	PDO
Greece	Kasseri	PDO	Italy	Grana Padano	PDO
Greece	Katiki Domokou	PDO	Italy	Montasio	PDO
Greece	Kefalograviera	PDO	Italy	Monte Veronese	PDO
Greece	Kopanisti	PDO	Italy	Mozzarella	TSG
Greece	Ladotyri Mytilinis	PDO	Italy	Mozzarella di Bufala Campana	PDO
Greece	Manouri	PDO			
Greece	Metsovone	PDO	Italy	Murazzano	PDO
Greece	Pichtogalo Chanion	PDO	Italy	Parmigiano Reggiano	PDO
Greece	San Michali	PDO	Italy	Pecorino di Filiano	PDO
Greece	Sfela	PDO	Italy	Pecorino Romano	PDO
Greece	Xynomyzithra Kritis	PDO	Italy	Pecorino Sardo	PDO
Ireland	Imokilly Regato	PDO	Italy	Pecorino Siciliano	PDO
Italy	Asiago	PDO	Italy	Pecorino Toscano	PDO
Italy	Bitto	PDO	Italy	Provolone Valpadana	PDO
Italy	Bra	PDO	Italy	Quartirolo Lombardo	PDO
Italy	Caciocavallo Silano	PDO	Italy	Ragusano	PDO
Italy	Canestrato Pugliese	PDO	Italy	Raschera	PDO

country	cheese	appellation	country	cheese	appellation
Italy	Ricotta Romana	PDO	Portugal	Queijo de Cabra Transmontano	PDO
Italy	Robiola di Roccaverano	PDO			
Italy	Spressa delle Guidicarie	PDO	Portugal	Queijo de Castelo Branco (covered in Queijo da Beira Baixa PDO)	PDO
Italy	Stelvio; Stilfser	PDO			
Italy	Taleggio	PDO			
Italy	Toma Piemontese	PDO	Portugal	Queijo de Évora	PDO
Italy	Valle d'Aosta Fromadzo	PDO	Portugal	Queijo de Nisa	PDO
Italy	Valtellina Casera	PDO	Portugal	Queijo do Pico	PDO
Netherlands	Boerenkaas	TSG	Portugal	Queijo Mestiço de Tolosa	PGI
Netherlands	Boeren-Leidse met Sleutels	PDO	Portugal	Queijo Picante da Beira Baixa (covered in Queijo da Beira Baixa PDO)	PDO
Netherlands	Kanterkaas; Kanterkomijnekaas; Kanternagelkaas	PDO			
			Portugal	Queijo Rabaçal	PDO
Netherlands	Noord-Hollandse Edammer	PDO	Portugal	Queijo São Jorge	PDO
			Portugal	Queijo Serpa	PDO
Netherlands	Noord-Hollandse Gouda	PDO	Portugal	Queijo Serra da Estrela	PDO
Poland	Bryndza Podhalanska	PDO	Portugal	Queijo Terrincho	PDO
Poland	Oscypek	PDO	Slovakia	Slovenská Bryndza	PDO
Poland	Wielkopolski ser Smażony	PGI	Slovakia	Slovenská Parenica	PGI
			Slovakia	Slovenský Oštiepok	PGI
Portugal	Queijo Amarelo da Beira Baixa (covered in Queijo da Beira Baixa PDO)	PDO	Spain	Afuega'l Pitu	PDO
			Spain	Cabrales	PDO
			Spain	Cebreiro	PDO
			Spain	Gamoneu; Gamonedo	PDO
Portugal	Queijo de Azeitão	PDO	Spain	Idiazábal	PDO

country	cheese	appellation
Spain	Máhon-Menorca	PDO
Spain	Picón Bejes-Tresviso	PDO
Spain	Queso de la Serena	PDO
Spain	Queso de l'Alt Urgell y la Cerdanya	PDO
Spain	Queso de Murcia	PDO
Spain	Queso de Murcia al Vino	PDO
Spain	Queso de Valdeón	PGI
Spain	Queso Ibores	PDO
Spain	Queso Majorero	PDO
Spain	Queso Manchego	PDO
Spain	Queso Nata de Cantabria	PDO
Spain	Queso Palmero (Queso de la Palma)	PDO
Spain	Queso Tetilla	PDO
Spain	Queso Zamorano	PDO
Spain	Quesucos de Liébana	PDO
Spain	Roncal	PDO
Spain	San Simón da Costa	PDO
Spain	Torta del Casar	PDO
Sweden	Hushållsost	TSG
Sweden	Svecia	PGI
UK	Beacon Fell Traditional Lancashire Cheese	PDO
UK	Blue Stilton Cheese	PDO

country	cheese	appellation
UK	Bonchester	PDO
UK	Buxton Blue	PDO
UK	Dorset Blue Cheese	PGI
UK	Dovedale Cheese	PDO
UK	Exmoor Blue Cheese	PGI
UK	Single Gloucester	PDO
UK	Staffordshire Cheese	PDO
UK	Swaledale Cheese	PDO
UK	Swaledale Ewes Cheese	PDO
UK	Teviotdale Cheese	PGI
UK	West Country Farmhouse Cheddar	PDO
UK	White Stilton Cheese	PDO
Switzerland	Berner Alpkäse, Berner Hobelkäse	AOC
Switzerland	Emmentaler	AOC
Switzerland	Formaggio d'Alpe Ticinese	AOC
Switzerland	Gruyère	AOC
Switzerland	L'Étivaz	AOC
Switzerland	Raclette du Valais	AOC
Switzerland	Sbrinz	AOC
Switzerland	Tête de Moine	AOC
Switzerland	Vacherin Fribourgeois	AOC
Switzerland	Vacherin Mont d'Or	AOC

Cheese wheels for sale in an open market in Italy.

index

acknowledgments

This book could not have been written without the help of hundreds of cheese producers and provedores who were generous with their time and knowledge—often working across challenging language barriers. There were some people, however, on whom I relied more heavily and so I would like to especially thank:

Australian cheese guru Will Studd and provedore Simon Johnson, who inspired me and offered their support, as well as the staff at Simon Johnson's Castlecrag store for access to their wonderful cheese room; Barry Keegan from the European Commission for answering so many questions about the EU's accreditation system and for introducing me to the amazing DOOR database (a repository of information on all PDO, PGI, and TSG products); Sid Cook from Carr Valley Cheese for setting me straight on all things Colby and Jack; Greta Cooper and Bruce Smith from Kraft Foods Limited for helping me untangle the history of American-style cream cheese; Manuela Sonderegger from Switzerland Cheese Marketing for many detailed emails regarding Swiss Cheese; Frère Bernard Marie from Abbaye Mont des Cats and Frère Matthieu from Abbaye de Belloc for clarifying the Monastic trademark; Giovanni & Davide Fiori from Luigi Guffanti Formaggi 1876, and Eleonora, Carmine and all at Italian stagionata Casa Madaio for help with all things Italian; from the Spanish Commercial Office in New York, Ana Garcia, and in Sydney Mónica Brun and María Gorriti, for help with Spanish Cheeses; the staff at Consorcio de los Quesos Tradicionales de España, for their assistance and their support of small Spanish producers; and the Spanish Ministry of Economy for its invaluable publication, *Spain GourmeTour*; Nick Christodoulidis from the Consulate General of Greece in Australia for helping me better understand Greek cheeses; and the Hellenic Foreign Trade Board for their wonderful publication *Greek GourmetTraveller*; Kirsten Spangenberg and her colleagues at Mejeriforeningen, the Danish Dairy Board, for help with Danish Cheeses; Mary Quicke of Quicke's Traditional for her hospitality and for making one of the most abused cheeses, cheddar, the traditional way; Tom Biggins of Westry Roberts & Co. for his detailed explanation on the origin of Shropshire Blue; Google translate without which communication with so many cheese producers would have been impossible.

Also my husband Franz Scheurer, mother Joan Muir and dear friend Janni Kyritsis who told me I had to write this book; as well as authors and editors: Alan Davidson, Sarah Freeman, David Gibbons, Juliet Harbutt, Ron Herbst, Evan Jones, Kazuko Masui, Max McCalman, Gigi Piumatti, Patrick Rance, Jeffrey P. Roberts, Roberto Rubino, Piero Sardo, Will Studd, Sharon Tyler Herbst, and Tomoko Yamada, whose works inspired and informed me.

picture credits

The photographs in this book are used with the permission of the copyright holders stated below. Images are listed by page number. All other illustrations and pictures are © Quintet Publishing Limited. While every effort has been made to credit contributors, Quintet would like to apologize should there have been any omissions or errors, and would be pleased to make the appropriate correction for future editions of this book.

Key: a = above; b = below; c = center; l = left; r = right

2 Stockfood; 5a Stockfood, 5c Stockfood, 5b Shutterstock; 7 Shutterstock; 8 Stockfood; 10b Stockfood; 13 Stockfood; 18 Shutterstock; 19 Shutterstock; 21 Shutterstock; 23 Stockfood; 25 Stockfood; 26 Stockfood; 29 Stockfood; 31 Switzerland Cheese Marketing AG; 35 Stockfood; 36 Stockfood; 39 Shutterstock; 40 Shutterstock; 43 Stockfood; 45 Malta Dairy Products Ltd.; 46a Shutterstock, 46b Shutterstock; 48a Shutterstock, 48b Shutterstock; 50a Shutterstock, 50b Becky Stayner/Vermont Butter & Cheese Creamery; 54b Shutterstock; 56a MEVGAL S.A., 56b Shutterstock; 58a Shutterstock, 58b Stockfood; 60a Shutterstock, 60b Shutterstock; 62a Tirol Milch, 62b Stockfood; 64a Tatrzan'ska Agencja Rozwoju, Promocji i Kultury, 64b © calimero – Fotolia.com; 66a Shutterstock, 66b Stockfood; 69b Shutterstock; 70a Stockfood, 70b Stockfood; 73 Shutterstock; 75 Shutterstock; 76b Stockfood; 78a Mozzarella Company, Dallas, Texas; 80a © CuboImages srl / Alamy, 80b © John Ferro Sims / Alamy; 82a CONSORZIO TUTELA PROVOLONE VALPADANA - ITALIA, 82b Shutterstock; 84b Stockfood; 86a Shutterstock, 86b © Jon Arnold Images Ltd / Alamy; 89 Shutterstock; 91 Stockfood; 92b © Hemis / Alamy; 94a Shutterstock, 94b Stockfood; 96b Shutterstock; 98a Shutterstock, 98b © imagebroker / Alamy; 100a Shutterstock, 100b Shutterstock; 102b Shutterstock; 104a Fromagerie Guilloteau, 104b Shutterstock; 106b Shutterstock; 108b Shutterstock; 110a © MARKA / Alamy, 110b Shutterstock; 112a Rogue Creamery, 112b Ben Rowe ;115 FROMART; 117 J.Musial; 118a Chimay Fromages S.C., Belgium ,118b Bronwen Smith; 120a Shutterstock, 120b © Ray Roberts / Alamy; 122b © Objectif MC – Fotolia.com; 124b Joseph Widmer; 126a Stockfood, 126b Shutterstock; 128b Stockfood; 130b Stockfood; 132a Stockfood, 132b © FORGET Patrick/SAGAPHOTO.COM / Alamy; 134a Switzerland Cheese Marketing AG, 134b Switzerland Cheese Marketing AG; 136b © Funky Travel - Paul Williams / Alamy; 138b Shutterstock; 140b Cypress Grove Chevre; 143 Stockfood; 145 © contrastwerkstatt – Fotolia.com; 146a Stockfood, 146b © CuboImages srl / Alamy; 148a © Comugnero Silvana – Fotolia.com, 148b © CuboImages srl / Alamy; 150a icex0010661-Antonio de Benito / Copyright ICEX, 150b Shutterstock; 152b © Cro Magnon / Alamy; 154a Shutterstock, 154b © Sebastien Eich – Fotoloa.com; 156a Emmi International Ltd., P.O. Box 545, CH-3422 Kirchberg, Switzerland, 156b Shutterstock; 158b © Fabian Gonzales Editorial / Alamy; 160 Shutterstock; 163 Stockfood; 164b © JAUBERT BERNARD / Alamy; 166b Stockfood; 168 Stockfood; 170b © Hemis / Alamy; 172a Shutterstock, 172b Stockfood; 174a icex0010668-Antonio de Benito / Copyright ICEX, 174b © Alberto Paredes / Alamy; 176b © Daniel Jones / Alamy; 178b Stockfood; 180a shutterstock, 180b Shutterstock; 183 istock; 185 istock; 186b Stockfood; 188a Shutterstock; 188b Stockfood; 190a Shutterstock, 190b Shutterstock; 192a Lincolnshire Poacher Cheese, 192b Stockfood; 194a Caws Cenarth, 194b Shutterstock; 196a AH Marketing, 196b Stockfood; 198a istock, 198b Orb Weaver Farm; 200a istock, 200b istock; 202b © Arco Images GmbH / Alamy; 204a Shutterstock, 204b Shutterstock; 206a © Emmanuelle Guillou – Fotolia.com, 206b istock; 208b Shutterstock; 210a Switzerland Cheese Marketing AG, 210b Stockfood; 212a Jarlsberg, TINE BA, Norway, 212b Shutterstock; 214a Switzerland Cheese Marketing AG, 214b Shutterstock; 216a Shutterstock, 216b Stockfood; 218b Stockfood; 220a Switzerland Cheese Marketing AG, 220b Shutterstock; 222a Switzerland Cheese Marketing AG, 222b Switzerland Cheese Marketing AG; 224b Stockfood; 226a Stockfood, 226b Shutterstock; 228b Switzerland Cheese Marketing AG; 230a Stockfood, 230b Stockfood; 232a Shutterstock, 232b Shutterstock; 234a icex0010651-Antonio de Benito / Copyright ICEX, 234b Shutterstock; 236a Shutterstock, 236b Shutterstock; 238a Shutterstock, 238b Stockfood; 240a icex0010682-Antonio de Benito / Copyright ICEX, 240b Shutterstock; 242b Stockfood; 244b Syndicat AOC Ossau–Iraty; 246b Stockfood; 248a Stephen Fletcher, 248b Stephen Fletcher; 250b Stockfood; 252a Shutterstock, 252b Stockfood; 254a Stockfood, 254b Malta Dairy Products Ltd; 256a Humus alias Helmut Pöschel, 256b Humus alias Helmut Pöschel; 258a MADETA a.s., 258b Shutterstock; 260a Olomoucké tvaru°z°, 260b Stockfood; 262a Tatrzan'ska Agencja Rozwoju, Promocji i Kultury, 262b Shutterstock; 264b Voorlichtingsbureau Boerderijzuivel; 266a icex0010659-Antonio de Benito / Copyright ICEX, 266b © Clive Sawyer / Alamy; 268a, Stockfood, 268b © Bon Appetit / Alamy; 270 Stockfood; 273 Stockfood; 279 Shutterstock.